Dream on It

Dream on It

Unlock Your Dreams, Change Your Life

Lauri Quinn Loewenberg

ST. MARTIN'S GRIFFIN 🐾 NEW YORK

DREAM ON IT. Copyright © 2011 by Loewenberg Inc.
d/b/a The Dream Zone. All rights reserved. Printed in the
United States of America. For information, address St. Martin's Press,
175 Fifth Avenue, New York, N.Y. 10010.

www.stmartins.com

Book design by Ellen Cipriano

LIBRARY OF CONGRESS CATALOGING-IN-PUBLICATION DATA

Loewenberg, Lauri Quinn.
    Dream on it : unlock your dreams, change your life / Lauri Quinn
Loewenberg.
        p. cm.
    ISBN 978-0-312-64432-1 (pbk.)
    1. Dreams.   2. Dream interpretation.   I. Title.
    BF1091.L564 2011
    154.6'3—dc22

                                                      2010043577

First Edition: April 2011

10 9 8 7 6 5 4 3 2 1

To all the dreamers who have shared their dreams with me.
Only with your trust in me would my research
and this book be possible.

And to my grandfather, Miles Quinn, who came to me in a
dream and changed the course of my life.

Thank you.

Contents

Acknowledgments   *xi*

1. INTRODUCTION   1

2. PEOPLE DREAMS: 8
    Your Many Roles in Life

3. LOCATION DREAMS: 39
    The Different Areas of Your Life

4. VEHICLE AND TRAVEL DREAMS: 62
    Navigating Your Chosen Paths

5. ANIMAL DREAMS: 85
    Your Instincts and Behavior

6. BODY DREAMS: 106
    Your Emotional and Psychological Abilities

7. HOUSE AND HOME DREAMS: 128
   Your Self-image and Your State of Mind

8. WEATHER DREAMS: 148
   Your Emotional Forecast

9. SEX DREAMS: 165
   The Urge to Merge

10. NIGHTMARES: 192
    Ignored, Mishandled, and Difficult Issues

11. FINAL CHECKLIST: 221
    Rules to Remember

    Dream Glossary   229

    Index   297

Acknowledgments

First and foremost I would like to thank God for creating us all with these built-in nighttime theaters. It's a rather cool design feature, I think, that not only allows us to view our lives and our behaviors from a wiser perspective, but also makes us all a bit more interesting. I am eternally grateful to my strikingly handsome husband who is and always has been my biggest supporter and cheerleader. I want to thank my son for putting up with and complying with my constant requests . . . er, demands to, "Turn the TV down! Mommy's writing!" Katia Romanoff, PhD, I cannot thank you enough for mentoring me and for being a lifelong friend. I am full of gratitude to the wise individuals who paved the road before me in bringing the practical common sense of dreams into the main stream: Carl Gustav Jung, Patricia Garfield, PhD, and Gayle Delaney, PhD, just to name a few. I am thankful to my agent Meredith Dawson for believing in me and working hard for me and to my editor Hilary Teeman who gave birth to her first child at the same time she helped me give birth to this book. I want to be sure to let all the dreamers who contributed a piece of their psyches and their lives to this book, know how much I appreciate you. And finally, I want to thank Facebook who provided a format that allowed me to easily network with dreamers, which expedited the process of putting this book together. Who would have dreamed of such a thing only a few years ago?

Dream on It

1

Introduction

Twilight . . . Avatar . . . Google . . . the Sewing Machine . . . the Theory of Relativity . . .

These were all inspired by a dream . . . an actual REM kind of dream that you have when you sleep. Throughout history, artists, writers, inventors, and scientists have solved problems and drawn great inspiration from their dreams. You'd be surprised how many great ideas and personal solutions you are literally "dreaming up" each and every night, too.

You see, we *all* dream every night, whether we remember them or not. In fact, we enter the dream state (also known as REM, Rapid Eye Movement) every ninety minutes throughout the night. Every cycle of dreaming grows in duration throughout the night. The first dream of the night may only be three minutes or so and the last dream you have before waking in the morning, provided you had a good seven to eight hours of sleep, can be forty-five minutes to an hour long. On average, you will dream about five times every night, and if you're lucky enough to live to

Can't remember your dreams or want to remember more of them? It's easier than you think. Whenever you wake up, whether it is in the middle of the night to go to the bathroom or you're waking up for good in the morning, stay put! It is essential that you remain in the same position you wake up in because that is the position you were dreaming in. If you move your body you disconnect yourself from the dream you were in *just seconds ago*. If you have to wake up with an alarm, go ahead and turn it off then get right back into that position you woke up in and give yourself just a few minutes to let the dream come back to you. Don't think about what you have to do that day. Quiet your mind. Stay put. You'll be surprised what is there, waiting for you to capture it.

If nothing comes to you then start asking yourself questions such as, how am I feeling? Who was with me? What was I doing? These questions will help jog your memory because we always experience some form of emotion in our dreams, we are usually with someone, and we are certainly doing something. Whatever it is you remember, even if it's just a tiny piece, please be sure to write it down or at the very least, tell it to somebody or *it will be gone* after breakfast. Make this a habit and you'll start remembering more and more. It's like a muscle, the more you do this simple exercise the stronger your dream muscle will get. I promise, those floodgates will open and you will be amazed at how much of a life you have been living at night, a ripe old age, you will have had well over 100,000 dreams throughout your lifetime!

That's a lot of great ideas, advice, and solutions that unfortunately will go unnoticed, unremembered, or simply dismissed as "just a dream." Let me assure you, after reading this book, you'll never dismiss your dreams again.

So, what are these strange movies that play in our heads at night when we sleep? Where do they come from? What purpose do they serve? Does my dream last night about purchasing a baby crib full of spaghetti mean I need to seek professional help? WTF?

Since prehistoric times mankind has wondered about dreams. In 2001, an expedition into the Chauvet Cave in the valley of the Ardèche River in France discovered cave drawings that are believed to be depicting a dream. The ancient Romans thought dreams were messages from the gods and many would take long pilgrimages to dream temples where they would spend the night in hopes of receiving a dream of wisdom or healing. There are over 700 references to dreams and visions within the pages of the Bible, all suggesting that dreams are messages from God or His angels. The ancient Chinese believed that a dream is when the soul leaves the body to travel the world. However, if they should be suddenly awakened, their soul may fail to return to the body. Even today some Chinese aren't too keen about having an alarm clock! Essentially, the time-tested consensus is that dreaming is a powerful experience and is connected to something greater than ourselves.

The Greek philosopher Plato was one of the first to get it right that dreams don't come from some outside source but rather from the self . . . although the part of the self he believed they originated from was the liver. Two thousand years later, Sigmund Freud, the father of modern psychoanalysis, affirmed that dreams indeed come from the self, the subconscious part of the self. He even brought us a step closer by teaching us that dreams not only *come from* the self but are *about* the self . . . the sexually suppressed self. According to Freud, just about everything in our dream can somehow be connected to our genitals and our wanton, misguided, and lustful desires. Sigh. I guess living in the prudish Victorian Era will do that to you. Thankfully, Freud's protégé, Carl Gustav Jung, came along and taught us that yes, dreams do come from the self, dreams are indeed about the self, and what's more, understanding dreams helps us to improve the self, not just the sexual self but the entire self. In fact, I subscribe to Jung's dream philosophy. I believe that everything in our dreams is connected to some part of the self or to something or someone that directly affects the self. I believe there are many common archetypes (symbols, images, and themes) that appear in all of our dreams that hold a collective or shared meaning for almost all of us. I believe that dream analysis, or onei- roscopy, which is the medical term for it, is the most insightful form of self discovery available.

I believe that dreams are so insightful and powerful because I believe that *dreams are thoughts*. You see, when you are dreaming, you are thinking, but on a much deeper and focused level than when you're awake. Think about it, when you go to sleep the lights are off, your eyes are closed, and the world around you is shut out. There are no distractions. The mind doesn't stop working at this point. Whatever your stream of thought is as you drift off contin- ues and begins to go inward, and as your conscious, waking, literal mind slips into a state of rest, your deep inner subconscious mind takes over. Once you enter the REM phase of sleep, which is when dreaming takes place, a structure located on the brain stem called the pons, sends signals to the cerebral cortex (the region of the brain responsible for most of our thought processes) that dream- ing has begun, which means some very serious and deep thinking is now happening. So, that waking stream of thought that was using words and that your conscious mind had control of is now controlled by your inner subconscious mind and is no longer using just words but is also using images, experiences, and emotions. Your thoughts have turned into dreams.

If dreams are thoughts, then why are they so bizarre? The best way that I can explain it is that when you are dreaming you are thinking with metaphors.

"He's as healthy as a horse"; "It's raining cats and dogs out there"; "She is such a big baby." Metaphors compare two things in order to create a picture that helps us make our point. The next time you have a conversation, try to take a mental note of how many metaphors are used between you and the other person. You'd probably be surprised how quickly the tally will go up. We naturally communicate this way. Dreams work in the same way. But rather than speaking the metaphor, they bring it to life.

For example, if you dream of drowning, it's no fun, but when you wake up and catch your breath, you need to ask yourself what part of your life could be compared to drowning. Where in your life are you having a hard time staying afloat? What's bringing you down? Like a metaphor, your dreams illustrate what's going on in your life and how you truly feel about it . . . and even what you need to do about it!

Believe it or not, there are many times in which our dreams will show us how to handle specific problems, especially when we dream about people we see in everyday life, like our children, our spouses, or our bosses. In this book, using real life examples, I will show you how—through our dreams—we speak to ourselves about what is going on in our lives, how we guide ourselves through difficult situations, and how we point ourselves toward what we really, truly, and deeply need to live the life we are meant to live.

This book is divided into the most common dream themes we

all get such as animals, vehicles, nightmares, etc. I will show you how these various themes are connected to a specific area of your life or your personality. Rather than flipping through to the particular theme you are most interested in, I encourage you to read straight through because the skills, tips, and interpretations you'll learn in each themed chapter tend to build on the previous chapter and I don't want you to miss out on any important and valuable lessons. But of course, once you've read the book all the way through, I recommend you keep it handy so you can continue to use it as a reference. If you have a crazy dream about a lion, for instance, you can flip straight to the section about predatory cats and get the answer you are looking for.

As I mentioned before, I will be illustrating these themes with real life dream examples from real people. The examples I've chosen do not in any way imply that these are the only dreams that can be had containing these themes and symbols. I chose them because they are good examples of how these common themes and symbols work within the context of a dream in order to convey a message to the dreamer about his or her waking life situation. Odds are you're going to relate to a lot of the dreams and real life stories that are in this book. Even if you have never had any of the dreams found in this book, the process by which I examine the dream can still be applied to your own dreams so that you can get those powerful made-for-you messages yourself. There is a method to the madness of our dreams and there is also a method to the madness of figuring them out.

When you can understand your dreams, you'll find that they are the best glimpse of reality available. They are the way you are brutally honest with yourself when your conscious waking mind refuses to be. They are the way you nag yourself over a recurring behavior you need to correct or an issue you aren't giving enough attention to, hence the persistent recurring dream. They are also your very best friend and adviser when you need to make a tough decision or solve a difficult problem. No one truly knows what is best for you . . . than *you*! The truth is, your best thinking isn't done in the shower, it's done while you dream. In fact, when we say, "Let me sleep on it," what we're really saying is, "Let me *dream* on it."

....

FASCINATING DREAM FACT: Ever wonder why your eyes are moving back and forth under your lids during REM? It's because you are watching what's going on in the dream!

2

People Dreams

YOUR MANY ROLES IN LIFE

Mother, Father, Unknown Men and Women,
Baby, Child, Celebrities, Boss, Doctor, Police, Classmate

The human experience allows us to be multidimensional creatures. We have many sides to our personality, as well as many roles that we play in life. There are the natural, constant roles such as parent, spouse, and friend, for example. And then there are the roles we have to take on from time to time in order to accomplish something, such as the role of judge when we have a decision to make, the role of therapist when a friend has a tough issue to sort out, or even the role of banker when a relative needs a loan. Because there are many parts to the self and countless roles to play in waking life, a variety of characters take to the

When you dream of someone who lives under the same roof with you or whom you deal with closely on a daily basis, such as your spouse, child, or business partner, these people are not symbolic but are more likely to be playing themselves and are appearing in your dream because there is a current issue or concern in which that person is also involved. The way they behave in the dream as well as the way you are behaving toward them can often give you great insight as to how helpful or harmful, positive or negative, this person is, or your relationship currently is, in waking life.

stage in dream life, and it's important to keep in mind that each of those characters is actually the self in disguise!

In other words, everyone in your dream represents a part of you. You play all the characters in your dream productions because your dreams are messages from you, to you, and about you. So when you, seemingly out of the blue, dream about the head cheerleader from high school, it's not about her . . . it's about *you* and how you took on that role the previous day or how you need to take on that role right now. Maybe you were able to cheer someone up or encourage them, or your dream may be telling you that *you* need to cheer up, that things aren't so bad. Do you see how it works? Remember, every *person* in your dream, whether they actually exist or not, is a part of your *person*ality and is there to show you how you are currently performing a particular role in your life.

In this chapter we will explore the most common people who visit our dreams, and how they not only mirror us but also teach us about the many roles we play while awake.

MOTHER

According to my research, our mothers show up in our dreams an average of once a week, which is why I wanted to start with Mom. The mother figure is the central most important figure to just about every human on this planet. Mother nurtures and cares for us, comforts us, disciplines us, loves us unconditionally, forgives us, and knows what is best. Mother teaches us how to wash behind our ears, how to eat right, how to treat a cold, and how to nurse a wound. Once we leave the nest, we take this nurturing know-how with us and continue to apply it to ourselves and to the ones we love. We also, from time to time, find ourselves in need of the comfort only a mother can provide. When we are sick, when we are faced with difficulties, when life brings us to our knees, we—if only on the inside—want our mommies. This nurturing know-how and this need for comfort then shows up in our dreams in the form of our very own mother or mother figure! Basically, Mom in a dream is the manifestation of all that you would typically associate with the word mother: comfort, nurturing know-how, paternal discipline, even fertility.

> *I always have this dream of me and my mother fighting, but it's not just verbal fighting it's physical fighting. We get along pretty well and fight sometimes, but when I have this dream it seems to be when we are on good terms.—Carol, 28*

LAURI: Most likely, these dreams aren't about your mother at all but rather about *your* role as Mom. Is there anything you are beating yourself up about? Anything you are feeling guilty about as far as the way you are mothering your child or children? You may

There are occasions when our mother will be playing herself. This is when there is a current issue with her in waking life. If she is ill, for example, and is constantly on your mind, if there is some situation that you and she are actively involved in that is causing you to deal with each other on a daily basis then yes, Mom is most likely not symbolic of your own nurturing energy but is herself. In these instances, you want to pay attention to how she is behaving or what condition she is in as this will be an honest portrayal of how ineffective, ineffective, helpful, or harmful you feel she is in your waking life situation.

find you get this dream whenever you have an inner conflict about how to discipline your child or when you feel you aren't being the best Mom that you can be. Your dream is showing you what you are doing to yourself. Stop beating yourself up.

CAROL REPLIES: *As far as my being a mother I do feel like I don't do enough. The thing is that I hardly spend any time with my kids due to work, and going to school to study nursing, so I leave early and get home late, and that is what I beat myself up about. This makes sense.*

Carol's dream was showing her herself in the form of her own mother in order to help her realize that she was being too hard on herself. She would never be so harsh with her own mother, so why is she being so harsh with her children's mother?

If you are a mom, like Carol, then your mother dreams are most likely commenting on your role as Mom. Any negative element to

If your mother, or mother figures, were absent, neglect-ful, or abusive in waking life, she may then show up in a dream and behave menacingly, negatively, or be downright frightening. In this respect, especially if the dreams are re-petitive, Mother would represent your own sense of disap-proval, anger, and dissatisfaction with yourself or that you are projecting onto others at the time of the dream, If the negative mother dreams are repetitive it is a good indica-tion you have not been able to move past the negativity that was instilled in you as a child through your mother or mother figure and it may be a good idea to seek help in over-coming this.

the dream is likely a reflection of your own frustrations with motherhood. If you are not yet a mom but are trying or hoping to be, you're going to be dreaming of your own mother . . . well, a mother load! If you are a man, Mom most likely represents your ability to take good care of yourself or those around you.

The message of mother dreams: Take a good look at the nurturing side of your personality and compare it to the mother figure in your dream. Have you been taking good enough care of yourself? Have you been "mothering" others too much? Are you at a loss with your kids? Do you feel your maternal nurturing instincts have died off? When Mom is ill, injured, angry, or threatening, then your own ability to nurture and comfort yourself or others needs attention and redirection. This may be a call to take better care of yourself or someone around you or reevaluate how you are mothering your children. Less often, this could point to a fertility issue that needs your focus. When Mom is a happy, healthy, and helpful character in your dreams it shows that your inner nurturer is working well in your life. We all need our Mommies after all, even our inner one.

FATHER

Traditionally, the father is the bread winner, the one that makes the decisions and wears the pants, as well as the one that tends to dole out the tougher discipline. Therefore, Dad in a dream often represents these roles within you. When you are having financial trouble, when you are faced with a tough decision, when you are having a job or career issue, or you need to assert yourself in some way during the day, don't be surprised if dear old Dad makes an appearance in your dreams at night.

I dreamed that my father passed away, but when I visited his home he was there and helped me make his funeral arrangements.—Jamie, 28

LAURI: Unless you are concerned for your father's health in real life, this dream is not about him at all. Your father is standing in for your own "inner father," meaning the part of you that makes decisions and that brings home the bacon. For your father to die in a dream suggests that you feel your ability to make a good firm decision or your ability to bring home the bacon and manage said bacon is no longer available to you. So what's the story? The way he helps you make the funeral arrangements leads me to believe this is about finances. Even though you may feel your financial savvy is dead in the water, your dreaming mind is reassuring you—through the form of your dad—that this part of you is alive and well. Your dream is also showing you that financial—rather than funeral—planning and arranging is the key. You can do it. Don't be so quick to bury this part of you.

JAMIE REPLIES: *I was feeling very "stuck" in my financial situation. I am a full-time student, have a full-time job, and two little ones at home. It makes complete sense that I was trying to tell myself that I could find ways to lessen my burden through financial planning and arranging. And sure enough, when I started looking for alternative ways to earn a bit of extra cash, I stopped having the dream!*

Keep in mind, the father symbol is not meant to be sexist. Whether or not it's true in an individual's family, it's true as a universal archetype. Even if one doesn't perceive men as money makers and decision makers, it is the cultural norm, and the subconscious often subscribes to norms. I've found that men and women tend to dream of their father equally when facing financial issues. This archetype may change in time as more and more women take on the role of financial provider in the home. But for now, as far as the dreaming mind is concerned, Dad is the money man.

For men who are fathers, Dad in a dream often refers to his own role as a father, just as a woman's mother in a dream can refer to her role as Mom. So Dads, the same rule applies to you. Any negative element to the dream is likely a reflection of your own frustrations with fatherhood. If you are not yet a father but are trying or hoping to be, you're going to be dreaming of your own father quite a bit.

The message of father dreams: Father knows best, as they say, so pay close attention to Dad in the dream because he reflects your inner knower, decider, disciplinarian, and financier. A sick or dying father most likely points to financial trouble, or an inability to lay

If your father or father figure was absent, neglectful, or abusive in waking life, then he may represent your own sense of disapproval, anger, or dissatisfaction with yourself or that you are projecting onto others at the time of the dream. The best way to know if this is the case for you is to look at what happened the day before you dreamed of your father. Did your thoughts or behavior remind you of your father and his ways? If so, and this is a repetitive theme in your life, then it is a good indication you have not been able to move past the negativity that was instilled in you as a child from your father's behavior or lack of presence, and it may be a good idea to seek help in overcoming this.

down the law. A threatening or harmful father is connected to your own fear or anger toward your finances or decisions and a healthy, helpful father is most likely your own reasonable and healthy financial savvy or paternal know-how.

UNKNOWN MEN AND WOMEN

You've probably heard of the Chinese concept of yin and yang. According to the philosophy, yin and yang are complementary opposites within a greater whole . . . the negative and the positive, the dark and the light or the most popular of these opposites, the male and the female. Male, or yang energy, is that which makes you assertive, in charge, and even aggressive. Female, or yin energy, is sensitivity, creativity, nurturing, and passivity. These male and female energies within each of us are often in conflict with each other, one often overpowering the other. Those who have lots of male assertive energy often struggle with backing down, giving up, or admitting to feeling uncertain or vulnerable. And those with lots of female sensitive, nurturing energy often struggle with standing his or her ground, pushing through setbacks or taking on a leadership role. The idea of yin and yang is that these opposite energies, when balanced, will complement rather than conflict with each other. When there is an equal balance of both, an individual is considered complete, which is why the yin yang symbol, also known as the Taiji, is a perfect circle with an equal amount of black (yin) and white (yang).

Your dreaming mind will present your own male and female energies to you in the form of a man or woman in order to show you how well or how poorly you are utilizing your yin and your yang. No matter what your gender, unknown men in your dreams are reflective of the side of you that, when needed, can "man up," "grow a pair," and handle the situation. Unknown women are reflective of your passive, sensitive, nurturing, and creative side.

Remember, every *person* in your dream is connected to a part of your own *person*ality.

> *Ever since my separation, I keep dreaming of men I don't know in real life. We end up sitting and talking and they are always gently holding or caressing my hands.—Brenda, 48*

LAURI: You are realizing that you may have to provide for yourself and run your own household alone for a while, and you may be feeling a little concerned about this. So your dreaming mind is stepping in and reminding you that everything you really need is already inside of you. You are already fully equipped to handle things on your own, if need be. Your dreams are trying to get you in touch with your male side, the part of you that is assertive, makes decisions and brings home the bacon. Believe it or not, we sometimes discover our whole self once we go through a separation or divorce because we are forced to. Certain built-in qualities and skills become idle when "our other half" is handling some of the work. That seems to be what is happening to you, you probably have to take care of more things than you used to, especially the "man things" like taking out the trash and tightening the leaky faucets. Notice how the men are always caressing your hands? Your hands symbolize your capability. Your dreams are focusing on your hands because this is how you are reassuring yourself that you are fully capable of handling all the things that now rest on your shoulders. These dreams are good for you and are coming to you to empower you, sister!

BRENDA REPLIES: *Makes perfect sense. I have been a bit concerned about my capabilities of handling things on my own. There's been a lot of stress for quite some time.*

Brenda's dream is a perfect example of how male energy will manifest itself in our dreams in the form of an unknown man. In Brenda's case, her male self is reassuring to her. But many times, the unknown men in women's dreams can be threatening. This is often due to fear of utilizing our own assertive energy; as women we don't want to be labeled the B word, so we tend to be more pleasant than firm and forceful.

This same rule applies when a man dreams of an unknown male. The unknown male is his own assertive, "ballsy" self. In the dreams of either gender, the condition and behavior of the unknown male is a portrayal of his or her own current waking life male energy. A small, sick, or injured male indicates a need to strengthen your male assertive energy. A helpful, even attractive male (yes, both genders included) points to a desire to and often success at being assertive, and a large, angry, or hostile male often denotes overaggressiveness or, particularly in women's dreams, fear of her ability to be aggressive.

But when our yin or yang is being ignored, rather than feared, it will act out, like a child that wants attention, and show up in our dreams as an unknown man or woman doing odd things.

> I'm talking to my coworker in our ink room and I notice this practically naked girl rolling around in the powder on the floor (we have been working with a lot of white clay powder and it is covering everything right now). This girl is wearing the signature Daisy Duke shorts and a middriff shirt. Not wanting to know why this girl that I don't know is rolling around in my production area, I tell my coworker that I'm going to go check on something else.—Ryan, 30

LAURI: The unknown girl in this dream is the yin to your yang, she is your female energy, that which is creative, sensitive, and perhaps even passive. The way she is rolling around in the powder leads me to believe that she is most likely your creativity . . . your muse! Is there a creative project you want to dive into and get your hands dirty with? This may be why she is rolling around and getting dirty in the powder. But rather than doing so, did you cut the project *short*, hence the Daisy Dukes? Did you pass on some project or idea in waking life as the same way you left the room after seeing the girl in the dream?

RYAN REPLIES: *If she is my yin to my yang, then my other half looks pretty damn good! I have been working on creating a snow village for a popular gift-store chain. I had started to move forward on the project, sculpting out foam to make hills and levels to my village, making chan-*

nels in the foam to hide all the power cables and the like. Then I got in a relationship and was never home other than to sleep and get ready for work, so it all stopped. I was really hoping to have it finished for the holiday season but I think I am too far behind at this point. Once you put meanings to all the symbols it really does make sense. It sounds like basically she (my other half) is saying, "Hey, I want to come out and play!"

While Ryan's unknown female is representative of his creative energy, remember that no matter what your gender, unknown females can also be linked to sensitivity and compassion. Most often, unknown women in men's dreams are the typical "damsel in distress" and are in some form of weakened state or jeopardy in order to show him that he needs to strengthen his female side. This is due to the fact that many men do not feel comfortable with their yin energy because exhibiting sensitivity can be perceived as a sign of weakness. But the wiser inner mind wants that yin energy to be utilized because the truth is that knowing when to be a good listener and knowing when to be sensitive to others only makes you a more powerful and well-rounded individual.

We all have male and female energy within us. Generally, men have more yang and women have more yin. The key in life is to create the perfect balance of both of these energies. No matter what your gender, we all need to be able to be sensitive and nurturing without being overly emotional, firm, and determined without being too aggressive.

The message of unknown men and women dreams: Time to balance out the male and female parts of your personality. Pay attention to what the male or female is doing in the dream as that will show you how well you are utilizing your assertive male energy or nurturing female energy. Like a tightrope walker, without the right balance you are sure to tumble.

BABY

Humorist Don Herold once wrote, "Babies are such a nice way to start people." How true! Babies are brand new, untainted, and precious new beginnings. Babies are the start of a whole new life and that is precisely what a baby is in a dream, the start of a whole new part of you or your personality.

> *I have a recurring dream that involves an Asian baby that is left on my doorstep. I get ready for school and am about to walk out my door, and there sits this adorable baby! It has only happened since I started nursing school last August.—Katrina, 23*

LAURI: Babies symbolize something new in our life, mostly a new part of our self that needs *lots* of care and attention in order to grow and reach its full potential. That would certainly apply to nursing school because once you graduate a whole new life as a nurse will begin. But you didn't give birth to the baby; it was placed on your doorstep. In waking life, was nursing school a sudden decision? Did you not have time to incubate the idea? The doorstep also shows us that you know this is an open door of opportunity for you. The fact that the baby was Asian indicates that nursing school may be something that is "foreign" to you, something hard for you to understand at the moment but that with diligence you can learn to understand.

KATRINA REPLIES: *I am forever saying how nursing is a "foreign" language and they are teaching us to walk, talk, think, and act like a nurse as if joining another culture or breed of people. The whole situation with getting accepted into the program happened so quickly and it has been a huge adjustment in my life. So yes, it was sudden. Thank you!*

Like the baby on Katrina's doorstep, she has a *brand-new life* waiting for her should she continue to nurture it and focus on it. It also is significant if, in the dream, the baby belongs to you or someone else. As in Katrina's dream, she did not give birth to the baby; it suddenly showed up, which is connected to the fact that she didn't carry the idea or prepare for nursing school like most do. It was very sudden. When you know the baby in the dream belongs to you and if you even give birth in the dream, it suggests that the new element in your life or within you is due to your own hard work, your *labor,* and the fruits of that labor are now here and ready for further nurturing and attention from you.

If you find a baby or are given a baby that is not yours, that is a good indication that in waking life you have taken on something, a project or idea, that did not originate from you but still has the potential to create a new life for you.

Sometimes, a baby can be connected to the part of the self that acts like a baby and needs to be babied or to someone around you whom you feel is being a baby.

If the baby in the dream is your actual waking life baby, then the dream is most likely about your baby and not yourself. But if your children are now grown and you are dreaming that they are babies then you need to ask yourself if you are still babying them rather than treating them as the adults that they are.

The message of baby dreams: So, what's new? There must be a new element in your life or within you that is in need of your care and attention; something that may seem small now but is likely to grow and improve. How you feel toward the baby in your dream is directly connected to how you feel about the new aspect of your life. The condition of the baby in the dream reflects the condition of this new part of your life or your self. And like a baby, this new element—if given the proper care—has endless possibilities.

CHILD

While a baby is a brand-new beginning, a child is in progress and is still growing, learning, developing, and still needs focus and attention. We often describe a brand-new idea, project, skill, etc., as "being in its infancy." Well, the dreaming mind looks at an idea, project, skill, etc., that is in progress and still growing and developing as "being in its childhood" by presenting it to us in the form of a child.

> I've had a dream for about seven years now where I have a little boy with me who is lost. I'm searching all over with him in a crowd trying to help him find his family. Everyone keeps trying to stop me, telling me that he's my child. The boy is just as confused as I am. I never do find his family in the dream. I used to think it was telling me I would have another child some day, but I have finished having children and have no desire to adopt.—Treena, 33

LAURI: This dream isn't about some child that's out there somewhere. This dream is about you. The child in the dream is lost so he represents something in your life you have lost touch with and need to find again. It could be an idea or project or relationship or even a part of yourself that you abandoned for one reason or another and that your inner mind wants you to reclaim. Male children in dreams often represent male energy that is not yet fully developed. Did becoming a mom soften you up to a degree? Has something been going on for the last seven years that re-

quires you to recognize and nurture and develop that male assertive energy?

TREENA REPLIES: *I guess seven years ago is when I had decided I
wanted to parent alone because my kids' "father" clearly had better things
to do. Maybe that male assertive energy needs to come out more in ways
of disciplining my kids and getting them to listen to me. I am definitely
soft with my kids. With only a mom and no father they don't have that
male assertiveness in their lives.*

Remember when we discussed the yin and the yang, the male
assertive energy and the female nurturing energy that often show
up in our dreams as an unknown male or female? These energies
can, and do, show up in our dreams as male or female children as
well. This happens when our male or female energy is not fully
developed, like we see in Treena's dream, and needs our attention
so it—and we—can reach full potential. As soon as Treena decided
she needed to parent her children by herself, her wise dreaming
mind stepped in and began giving her these lost little boy dreams
to let her know that, in order to parent effectively by herself, she's
going to have to get back in touch with that assertiveness she left
by the wayside once her children were born.

Notice how people in Treena's dream are telling her that the
child is hers. What you are told in a dream is important to pay attention to because it is what your inner mind is telling you. "This
child is yours," means this undeveloped, male energy belongs to
Treena. It is time for her to take it on, nurture it, and grow it, so
she can be the complete parent she needs to be: a soft, nurturing
mom as well as a firm disciplinarian.

While a child in a dream can point to a part of your personality or a part of your life that has more growing to do, I've found

that, most often, dream children reflect the "inner child," the childlike or childish part of you. On the positive side, it is that part of you that doesn't want to grow up, that still likes to have fun and be carefree, on the negative side, it is the part of you that acts childishly, is selfish, and throws tantrums. Our child dreams often show us how positively or how negatively our own child self is performing in our life. Usually, the best way to know if the child in your dream is representing your "inner child" is if the child is the same gender as you.

I am a police officer and every night for the past two weeks I have dreamed that I respond to a person who wants to commit suicide but when I get there it's a ten-year-old boy. He jumps in front of me. I see him falling and landing on the ground and I try as hard as I can to bring him back but I can't. I call it in and I wake up crying. Please help me. I hate going to sleep now.—Guillermo, 29

LAURI: Don't worry. You are not seeing a glimpse of a future incident you are called to respond to. That little boy is more likely your inner child, the fun-loving part of you. Has something been going on lately that has sucked the fun right out of your life? It is also possible this child represents some sort of project or idea or even relationship that is still growing and developing but on the verge of coming to a tragic end. Whatever it is, it is something that is ending by your own doing, just as suicide is a self-afflicted ending. The child also falls, which may be connected to you feeling like you are failing in some area of your life. What in your life is so close to its demise that you no longer feel you can save it and is causing you to no longer have joy?

GUILLERMO REPLIES: *My marriage is falling apart and I do sometimes feel that it is too late and can't be saved. I've been on the force for one year but with my previous job I was very successful and made a lot of money. The last two years with that company is when everything went downhill. I was forced to take a lower-paying job and that is when my marriage started falling apart. No, there is no joy lately.*

Poor Guillermo. The troubles in his life have caused him to lose touch with his inner child. But when career and marriage is at stake, it's hard to think about how to have fun. What I find most interesting about Guillermo's dream is that the child was taking his own life, which reflects guilt Guillermo is harboring that all these endings in his life are self-afflicted. He may even feel his own immature behavior (the child) is the cause. Guillermo's dream is also interesting in that the child has two layers of meaning as it is pointing to two childlike elements of his life that seem to be ending: a marriage still in its child phase and his own fun-loving inner child.

These recurring dreams are a recurring reminder Guillermo is sending himself that he has to find a way to lighten up, despite what he is going through. As the Chinese philosopher Mencius once said, "The great man is he who does not lose his childlike-heart."

The message of child dreams: Do you need to reconnect with your inner child and let loose and have some fun? Or have you or has someone around you been acting childish lately and needs some scolding or discipline? The child dream is often a reminder that there is something within you or something in your life that has more growing and developing to do and, like a child, needs your attention right now so it can become what it is meant to be.

CELEBRITIES
We call them celebrities because we celebrate them. They shine, stand out, and are awarded and applauded for their performance.

If you dream about your own child, he or she will likely be playing his or herself if they are still under your care, in which case they are a part of your dream because there is a current waking concern or issue with the child and your dream is trying to help you with it. As always, you want to look at what happened the day before the dream and see if you can connect the details, emotions, and behavior surrounding your child that day to the imagery, emotions, and context of the dream. This should help you pinpoint the issue the dream is commenting on as well as give you insight as to how serious or how minor the situation is, also how well or how poorly you are processing or handling the situation.

In that same vein, we all have a part of our personality that wants to stand out, shine, and gain recognition for our performance in some area of our life.

Just the other night I dreamed I was tickling Ellen DeGeneres on her chin. Upon awakening, it seemed awfully random but I knew better than that. So I told myself to play the word association game and see what is the first thing that comes to mind when I think of Ellen. The first thing I thought of was that she's just really, really funny. What a great sense of humor she has! She's definitely one of my favorite comics. So then I asked myself what I may need to have a good sense of humor about right now . . . oh yeah. I remembered. The day before I did a radio interview and it went horribly. The audio was really low on the host and I couldn't hear her very well. I kept talking over her and it just didn't go well. I was very upset the rest of the day about that. Sigh. Okay, I get it now! My dream was telling me to laugh it off, find my sense of humor (find my inner Ellen), and "take it on the chin," hence me tickling Ellen's chin. I love it when a dream uses a celebrity to convey its message.

Whether it's Oprah Winfrey, Madonna, or Donald Trump, the best way to figure out why a celebrity is making a guest appearance in your dream is to do what I did and ask yourself what it is that celebrity is best known for. Is it a character they have played on TV or in the movies? Can you relate that character or show to your life right now? Is it a song? If so, do the title or the lyrics speak to you right now? Whether you are a fan or not, there is something about that celebrity that your inner mind connects with and it uses that celebrity to convey a message to you, about you, so that you can continue to shine.

> *Last night I dreamed I was standing in the kitchen with Gordon Ramsay from the TV show* Hell's Kitchen, *and a big alligator came in! I jumped on top of the island and started smacking it with a spatula. Gordon Ramsay then asked me to marry him and I told him I couldn't wait to tell my husband because he thought he was such a cool guy! Ha, ha!!—Tracy, 30*

LAURI: Anything with large sharp teeth in a dream refers to someone in waking life who has sharp, biting remarks . . . and Gordon Ramsay is certainly known for his sharp criticism of the contestants on his show. Have you had a verbal conflict with someone recently? Any sharp criticism aimed at you or that you fired off at someone else? As evidenced by your dream, it seems you handled the criticism just fine . . . and apparently gave someone the smack down as well!

TRACY REPLIES: Yes!! *Last night in fact! I was sitting down to write my Christmas cards and my husband loves to give me a hard time about it. He thinks it's a big waste of time in this day and age of e-mailing. We go through this every single year. I shot back at him that I enjoyed sending the cards and he needs to leave me alone about it. He also grumbled about the photo I picked for the front of the card and it irritated me to pieces! I definitely felt criticism about the photo.*

Through this dream, Tracy identified with her inner Gordon Ramsay, the part of her personality that takes no BS. This is also why he proposed to her in the dream. During her dispute with hubby, Tracy professed her *commitment* to her *ritual* of sending Christmas cards. And it went so well that she committed to taking on that attitude for good, till death does she part. *Plus,* this all took place in the *kitchen*. It must have really felt like *Hell's Kitchen* in Tracy's house that night!

It's fun to dream of celebrities because when you wake up, it feels like you actually had an encounter with them. In my research, one of the most dreamed-about celebrities for over a decade now is Brad Pitt. While it is interesting that he has remained one of the top most dreamed-of male celebrities for so long, it is even more interesting that the meaning behind Brad Pitt has changed.

Brad used to stand in for what we perceive as the ideal man. For a woman, he represented everything she wanted in her intimate relationships and would find herself dreaming of Brad when her relationship wasn't going so well *or* when she was pleased with her own male or yang energy in her life. For a guy, Brad often stood in for what he wanted to be. When a guy was feeling really good about himself and his accomplishments, Brad would be a common symbol in his dreams. But in the last three years or so, Brad's meaning has changed.

I dreamed I was grocery shopping with Brad Pitt. He was buying some chicken. I said to him, "Brad, I got to get some chicken too.

*What do you say we just go in on a big bag of it?" What does that
mean?—Atom, 33*

LAURI: When you're shopping in a dream it means you're "in
the market" for something you want, something you need. The
chicken may be a reference to the fact that you are a little fearful,
a little chicken to do what it is you gotta do to get what you want.
What about family? Brad's a big family man now. Has there been
talk of having children?

ATOM REPLIES: *Yes. That's what it is! My wife wants children, another one. I say no . . . because I'm chicken. Everything makes sense now.*

Atom's dream is equating Brad to Dad because Brad not only
has a brood of many but also happens to be a rather attractive individual. Atom's inner mind wants him to be attracted to the idea
of having more than one child.

I have spoken to Atom since this exchange, and it just so happens that he and his wife are in fact expecting their second child.
Looks like Atom's inner Brad won.

The message of celebrity dreams: Remember, celebrities are known,
seen, recognized, and applauded; the celebrity in your dream is
portraying a part of you that wants recognition and approval, and
it is most likely connected to what that celebrity is best known
for. So give yourself a critique of your performance in life lately. Do
you deserve two thumbs-up and applause, or boos and hisses?

BOSS

A boss makes the decisions, manages the business and tells you
what to do. Unless you are currently working closely with your

boss, the boss in your dream—even if it is a former boss—
symbolizes the part of your personality that is large and in charge.

> *I had a dream last week that my boss died. I was at work and we*
> *were all dressed up for the funeral. I was crying in my dream and*
> *woke up really crying. It was weird.—Laura, 33*

LAURI: Death in dreams rarely points to an actual physical death
but rather the end of something in your life. Your boss is standing
in for your own inner boss, the part of you that makes decisions,
that is authoritative, and that manages your life and your issues.
Are you facing a tough decision and have no idea how to handle
it? This would certainly make your dreaming mind feel that your
inner boss, your ability to manage and decide, has died.

LAURA REPLIES: *I believe this has to do with ending a relationship*
I have been in for four years that was not healthy. When I was dreaming
this, things were only getting worse. Since then the relationship has ended
and I have closure.

Like Laura, when we wake up crying from a dream it is always connected to a waking life issue that makes us feel the same
way. In Laura's case, her crying wasn't actually about the death of
her boss but rather her relationship and her lack of power in it.
Luckily, Laura got the message and her power back and made like
a boss and terminated an unhealthy situation.

The message of boss dreams: Are you having a hard time asserting
your authority at work or at home? Or perhaps you are dealing
with a lot of issues or responsibilities, and are having a hard time
prioritizing them. Maybe you are realizing you are being too

bossy. Your boss, even if it is a former boss or an unknown dream boss, is the part of you that can take charge of and manage your life. Your dream will show you just how in charge you really are right now. Author Napoleon Hill once wrote, "Your real boss is the one who walks around under your hat."

DOCTOR

We go to the doctor when we are sick, when something is broken or when we just want to make sure everything is okay physically. But when something is wrong emotionally, that's when we visit our dream doctor, who is actually the part of the self who knows how to heal and care for an emotional wound.

> *In this dream, a doctor was trying to remove something he believed was cancer from inside my rear end! To me, this dream is so disgusting I at first did not want to share it, but I need to know what it could mean.—Sharon, 44*

LAURI: Is there anything or anyone that has been a real "pain in the ass" lately? Whomever or whatever it is shows up in your dream in the form of cancer to let you know that if you do not remove this issue or person from your life then it will continue to grow and eat away at you. The doctor is the part of you that knows what is emotionally healthy for you as well as your ability to remove the cancerous issue or relationship.

SHARON REPLIES: *How did I miss that connection? There are three cancerous relationships in my life: my boss, my daughter-in-law who hates me, and my biological daughter who won't speak to me because her boyfriend hits her and I finally went to the police.*

Like Sharon, our dreaming mind will place a doctor in our dreams to show us that we do have the skills to make an unhealthy situation better. After this dream, Sharon was able to better understand how unhealthy these relationships had become and, in fact, channeled her inner doctor and began working on healing her relationships. She switched jobs and has improved communication with her daughter and daughter-in-law and, last I heard, things were going well.

Similar to Sharon's metaphoric cancer, the medical issue the doctor is treating you for in your dream will give you a good idea of the waking life issue that needs healing. Look at the qualities of the ailment. What are its symptoms? What does it do to the body? How does it typically affect the patient? Then compare it to the negative and unhealthy issues and relationships in your life. For example, laryngitis causes the patient to lose his or her voice. Where in your life do you feel you have no say? What do you need to speak up about? It's surprising how precisely this will point out the waking life area of concern.

While a doctor is most often a symbolic representation of the part of you that can make a bad situation better, a doctor in a dream can sometimes refer to an actual medical issue. If you have a concern about your health and you think your doctor dreams may be connected to that, it never hurts to get checked out.

The message of doctor dreams: When you get the doctor dream, pay close attention to what the doctor says or does to you, as this will likely help you diagnose what the unhealthy waking life problem is, as well as the treatment. Just as you trust your waking life doctor with your physical health, it's time to trust your inner doctor with your emotional health.

POLICE

The motto of our fine men and women in blue is "to protect and serve." The police patrol our streets to keep us safe, nab the bad guys to reduce crime, and enforce our laws to keep the peace. But they can also be viewed as the enemy if you've done something wrong. Depending on your perspective, they are honorable heroes or evil oppressors. When the police patrol your dreamscape they most often represent the part of you that can "arrest" or put a stop to a negative behavior or issue as well as the part of you that guards and protects your best interest. They can also represent the guilt you are running from for doing something wrong, in which case the police serve as your conscience.

I dreamed I was running from the cops, as fast as I could. As I ran through town, I was worried I would miss my doctor's appointment.—Chris, 45

LAURI: Running from something or someone in a dream is a telltale sign that there is something you are avoiding in waking life. Often whatever or whoever is hot on your heels is a clue as to what it is you're avoiding. In your case, it's the cops. That's a good indication that there is something that you should be policing better but are avoiding it such as a diet, an activity, or a behavior. Running from the cops can also suggest there is guilt you are harboring in waking life, in which case the cops are your ability to do the right thing about it and "arrest" or put a stop to the guilt. And finally, the doctor's appointment . . . Is there a real-life health concern playing a role here? Otherwise, the doctor may be in reference to your need to make a certain issue in your life better. I believe your dream is telling you that, no matter what the case, your continued avoidance of doing what is right will only prolong the problem.

CHRIS REPLIES: *I am supposed to be following a special diet for medical reasons, but I've been really, really bad about eating sweets lately! It's making my symptoms a lot worse than they need to be. I've been feeling like a failure over neglecting this part of my life, and feel that it's in the way of my success, since I feel like crap most of the time. And yes, I definitely harbor guilt over this, not to mention the guilt I feel every day when I see how hard my husband works and me unable to get a job or pull in enough clients from my struggling business. I think the overeating of the sweets has a direct correlation.*

When we don't play by our own personal rules and guidelines during the day, the dream police are likely to come after us at night, just as they came after Chris. She broke the law that she and her doctor had agreed she would follow . . . and then guilt ensued! Her dream is letting her know, under no uncertain terms, she must follow her own personal laws, or else.

> *I dreamed I had become a cop and had to wear these ridiculously enormous fake breast bullet protectors as well as this really heavy chest vest. And then I had to wear enormously high heels as extra protection, which I could use as daggers against bad guys. The setting all took place in a grocery store.—Kristen, 37*

LAURI: You must need to police or protect yourself in some way in waking life. The breast protectors and heavy chest vest are most likely connected to your need to protect yourself from heartbreak since the chest is where the heart is. That is, unless there are any health issues you need to protect against. Let's talk about the heels. I think it may be a play on words and is actually about healing. The big heels mean a large amount of healing is taking place. The bad guys are the negative issues in your life right now. And the grocery store is where the biggest message is. Your dream may be telling you that the best way to continue your healing and protect yourself from the proverbial bad guys, is to police your food. Watch what you eat, etc.

KRISTEN REPLIES: *Your analysis makes sooo much sense! I recently had a double mastectomy due to breast cancer and I definitely worry about it coming back. It is always in the back of my mind. Plus, my husband just had a heart-related issue brought on by extreme anxiety which probably had a little to do with my recent health issues. The grocery store makes sense because the doctor said my husband must change his lifestyle such as eating much better and lots of exercise and antioxidants. Powerful stuff, these dreams we dream! Thank you for helping me understand what my mind was telling me.*

Kristen's dream was empowering her by placing her in the role of cop rather than having her run from them or calling on them to help. The difference in being the cop rather than needing one is that Kristen has played that role before. Because of her cancer, she already knew what foods harm health and what foods protect health. Playing food police was second nature to her at this point.

The message of police dreams: Ask yourself if restraint in some area is in order or if some new laws need to be laid down for yourself or for someone around you. If the flashing blue lights are hot on your heels then ask yourself what you need to surrender or own up to in waking life. Whatever the case, it is time to put some law and order into your life.

CLASSMATE

According to my research, former classmates are in the top ten of the most common people we dream about. The classmate dream can especially be a head-scratcher when it's a classmate we haven't seen, spoken to, or thought of since our old school days. As out of the blue as these dreams can seem, there is a method to their madness. As you know by now, the dream is not about the classmate but about you. There is something about that classmate, even the classmate from long ago, that is a part of you or that you would do well to make a part of you.

There's a certain old classmate I regularly dream of and I haven't seen nor spoken to him since the seventh grade. His name was Bill and he was the class clown, always cutting up, cracking jokes, and disrupting class. Apparently, he made quite an impression on my psyche because my inner mind keeps using him to let me know I'm not taking something seriously enough in my waking world. Bill has come to represent my inner clown that, ironically, comes with a serious message! When an old classmate comes to visit you in your dreams, ask yourself what role they played in the social structure of your class because, odds are, that is the role they represent in the structure of your life.

> Last night I dreamed that I was in the house I grew up in. A young man I went to college with and have not seen since was keeping me trapped in my old bedroom unbeknownst to all who lived there. I finally managed to escape, went downstairs, shocked the new residents, found my father and said, "Get me out of here now, Dad!" and that's when I woke up.—Lisa, 40

LAURI: You are trapped in your old bedroom because part of you has not been able to grow and evolve from a certain mind-set you had when you lived there. Your old college classmate may be a clue as to which part. He either represents that point in time *or* he represents a part of *you* that is like him, that is holding you back and keeping you in the past. The good news is that you were released and there were new residents in the home, which means you can finally move on in waking life. You call for your dad at the end of the dream because it is your inner father, your inner decision maker that will move you past that imprisoning behavior.

LISA REPLIES: *When I lived at home I felt very stifled and that has held me back in life, but I am finally getting past it. The college classmate was very kind and helpful and good to everyone. So you're right—I'm that way, too. In fact, I'm that way in all parts of my life, and it is holding me back. I get taken advantage of. Honestly, I've been getting fed up with going the extra mile for people just to get dumped on. You're so right—my dreams are pushing me to get past that mind set, and no longer be a doormat.*

Because of this dream, Lisa is now able to put a form and face to her "door mat" persona. Giving an identity to that part of herself makes it tangible and easier to manage, especially now that she sees that it is a part of her own self that imprisons her.

Like Lisa's dream, classmates stand in for a part of the self that is like the classmate or that needs to be like the classmate. Whether it is the head cheerleader, the bully, or the quiet kid, there will always be something about that classmate, their appearance, their behavior, or even their reputation, that has left an impression on you that you remember about them to this day. When you can recognize that classmate as being a part of you, and their behavior in the dream being connected to your own waking behavior or perhaps that you need to take on as your own waking behavior, then you've got yourself a pretty clear picture of what is wrong or what is right with your current situation and conduct.

The message of classmate dreams: What do you remember most about the classmate you dreamed of? There is something about that classmate that either needs to be implemented into your personality, that is already a part of you that you need to reunite with, or that needs to be expelled for good. Back then you learned alongside them, now it's time to learn from them.

By now you should have a good understanding of how to figure out what the people who accompany you in your dreams mean, as well as how to determine those times when the person is not a symbol but actually playing himself or herself. Once you recognize the people in your dreams as being a part of you, you will understand yourself like never before. In your dreams, people give you a very clear picture of how well or how poorly you are playing your different roles, when you need to take on a certain role or when it is time to ditch it. Think of the people in your dreams as your reflection in the mirror. Do you like what you see?

FASCINATING DREAM FACT: It is a myth that we dream in black and white. This myth was born in the era of black-and-white television. That's not to say that there has never been a dream that was void of color. If your dream is full of gray tones, then it may be an indication of depression.

3

Location Dreams

THE DIFFERENT AREAS OF YOUR LIFE

School, Public Bathroom, Parking Lot, Prison, Hospital,
Hotel, Battlefield, Wedding, Restaurant, Amusement Park

You never know where you will find yourself after your head hits the pillow and the warm blanket of sleep envelops you. The next thing you know, you could be at an amusement park trying to fit yourself into a tiny roller coaster, or in your old biology class trying to figure out why you had no clue about the exam the teacher is handing out, or even in a medieval castle trying to get to the top of an endless staircase.

No matter where your dreaming mind places you, the setting of your dream not only sets the stage for the storyline, but is also a major clue as to what real life issue the dream is about. You see, where you are in your dream is either directly connected to *where you are* in life, or it is directly connected to a certain *area* of your life. We all compartmentalize our life. We have our social life, our home life, and our work life for example. We also have different places or points in our life for which our dreams will create a backdrop. For instance, you may be in a place in your life right now where you are ready to start a family, in which case you may dream you are in a garden planting seeds. Or perhaps you are at a place in your career where you are no longer fulfilled and are no longer feeling productive; therefore, your dream places you in a desert to illustrate the lack of growth.

Location, location, location is the real-estate mantra, because where a home is located is a vital selling point. I think that same mantra would work quite well in dream analysis because even though the location may not always be the main focus of your dream, it is still a vital clue that will help unlock its meaning. In fact, the location or setting is one of the first symbols I look at when analyzing a dream because it pinpoints the area of concern for the dreamer. After that, evaluating all the other components of the dream fills in the blanks and reveals the entire message.

SCHOOL

Unfortunately, the most popular dream location is not a sunny beach in Maui or even the Champs-Élysées in Paris! Nay, t'is the cinder blocked halls of our old alma mater. Even if you graduated ten, twenty, even fifty years ago, your dreaming mind keeps pulling you back into chemistry class wearing nothing but your Nikes or roaming the halls trying to find your locker. It's a very aggravating dream.

The reason school is such a popular dream locale is because the dynamics of the school setting continue on into your job or career and also into your social life. School is where you first learn the importance of being on time and meeting deadlines, it is where you learn how to prepare and "do your homework," it is where you learn how to deal with scrutiny, how to move on up the ladder, and also how to fit in. Basically, it's where you learn all your basic job skills and social skills. School dreams are most often connected to your work life and slightly less often connected to your social life.

I often dream of being in high school again and I can't remember my locker combination. Also, I've lost my class schedule and have no idea where I'm supposed to be. Sometimes I dream of being in college and the semester is almost over and I've forgotten to go, all semester long, to a class I hate! I meant to just avoid it a little but ended up forgetting about it completely. Sometimes I'm faced with taking the final exam, knowing I haven't been to even one lecture.—Heidi, 38

LAURI: Your locker is your place at school. It is the only thing that is designated to you, therefore it most likely represents where you feel you belong in life, or more specifically, in career. When you can't find your locker or get into your locker in a dream it's a good indication you are feeling uncertain of yourself in some way in waking life . . . you haven't "unlocked" your potential. The same goes for dreams where you can't find your class, which is another popular "back at school" dream. Are you uncertain of your place at work or even uncertain of your career choice? The forgotten class is most likely connected to a sense of missing out, as well as a feeling of being unprepared and not up to par, or good enough, or experienced enough. But notice how you hate the class in the dream. That's a telltale sign you aren't too happy with your job in real life.

HEIDI REPLIES: *I'm often uncertain of my career choice because I've never been in a job I just loved and couldn't live without. Working has*

always been something I've had to do for income. I have always wanted
to be a sign-language interpreter and have taken many classes toward
that goal. But I'm always derailed by having to move, not being able to
find appropriate classes, etc. Currently, I work three jobs just to be able
to share duties with my husband and not have the kids in childcare. I
know I'm not working at my potential in any of the jobs, but I am grate-
ful to have them so I can be at home with the kids.

The key to Heidi's dream is when she says, "I have no idea
where I am supposed to be." Heidi has a dream job in mind for
herself, a sign-language interpreter, but she holds all these other
less fulfilling jobs, which leads her inner mind to pose the question, "Hey, exactly where are we on this job thing anyway?"

And that's where the final exam comes in to play. It is most
likely connected to waking life pressure Heidi puts on herself
that, *this is it,* we gotta finally make this happen now or it never
will . . . final being the operative word here. Heidi will keep getting this dream until she gets to the place in her career where she
finally feels like she belongs.

Another common school dream is the dream where you are
back at school, and you know you have already graduated but find
out you have to do a class or your senior year all over again. The
main thought in these frustrating dreams is that you've already
done this, why do you have to do it again? Grrrr! This dream
thought is connected to the waking reality that you are in a situation where you have to prove yourself. You know you've got what
it takes, but someone else needs to be shown you've got the goods.

I dreamed I was back in high school because I had to take my senior
year all over again. As I was walking the halls I was trying to figure
out how I could fit school into my current life of work and raising a
child. I also wondered what all the students would think of me. I

figured that, since I'm older and wiser now, perhaps the students would really like me and that I should also be able to breeze through all my classes.—Dina, 41

LAURI: Sounds like you must be in a waking life situation where you are feeling the need to prove yourself to others. Look at work first as most back at school dreams are triggered by work issues. Are you having to relearn something? Do you have a new boss or coworker you need to impress? If work doesn't seem to fit, then look at your social life. You are very concerned in the dream of what others will think of you. Is there someone in waking life with whom you'd like to make a good impression? The good news is that your confidence at the end of the dream will certainly penetrate into your waking life situation so I wouldn't sweat it.

DINA REPLIES: *This absolutely fits what is going on in my life. My family just moved to a new state two months ago. I don't know a soul here. My next door neighbor invited me to a coffee social at her house. I am very nervous about meeting new people and worry how I may come across to them. I was a social butterfly in my previous town so deep down I know I'll get along just fine. I like how my dream is reassuring me. That's cool.*

Dreams can indeed be reassuring. What we are unsure of in waking life, our inner self is certain of in dream life. Dina's dream was reassuring her about the social area of her life by comparing this new social pressure to the social pressures of high school: wanting to be liked and wanting to fit in. Unlike her time in high school, she has learned her social graces and is a seasoned pro. Nothing to worry about.

Yes, the majority of school dreams can be connected to your job because school was, essentially, your first job. And like school, your job is a place you have to get up every morning and go to do what is expected of you and deal with the people there, some you like and some you don't, and try to improve your skills so you can eventually move up to the next level. But sometimes it is the social or learning aspect of school that plays a role in its meaning. When you have to deal with a social issue, when you have to learn a new skill, or even when life throws a lesson at you during the day, you may find yourself in the hallowed halls of learning at night.

The message of school dreams: You are either dealing with job-related stress right now or perhaps pressure from your social circle. Compare the thoughts and emotions you had in your school dream to the thoughts and emotions you have about your job or social situation. See the similarities? There is probably some unpreparedness, uncertainty, or even vulnerability that needs to be addressed. There is a lesson to be learned here, so sit up straight and pay attention!

PUBLIC BATHROOM

When you gotta go, you gotta go, even if you have to brave the dreaded public bathroom. In waking life, public bathrooms often smell, don't always have enough toilet paper, and sometimes are even out of order. But the public bathrooms in our dreams are far worse . . . and you would probably prefer I not go into detail on this. The reason our dreams will sometimes place us in a smelly, backed-up, less than desirable public loo is because we have come to a place within ourselves where we can no longer "hold in" our frustrations, yet we fear how we may appear in others' eyes should we let it out, hence the bathroom being public rather than private.

I have a recurring dream that I have had since I was a young girl. In these dreams I have to go to the bathroom in a public place. The stall doors are always gone, the toilet is disgusting, and is covered with you-know-what! The floor is never level so I always lose my balance and fall into the disgusting toilet!—Dolly, 43

LAURI: Your dreaming mind keeps placing you in a public bathroom in order to let you know you have come to a place where you need to "relieve yourself" of all that frustration you have been "holding in." And the "you-know-what" in your dream is the "crap" you are dealing with at that time. The slanted floor is telling you that that there is an imbalance within your personality. No, girlfriend, I'm *not* telling you that you have a chemical imbalance or need medication . . . nay, nay! This dream is showing you a behavior weakness. You—like me—probably have a hard time letting it be known when you are really upset. Rather than letting others know, you "hold it in," and this recurring behavior certainly does not lean in your favor.

DOLLY REPLIES: *All I can say is* wow! *I do take a lot of "crap" in my life, from my childhood, to my job as a flight attendant, to my somewhat controlling (okay, very controlling) husband. I am going to start looking for some books to read to learn how to get my point across to people and stop caring what they think of me.*

The most common element to the public bathroom dream is the inability to use it because of its condition. This can be directly linked to the inability to express to others what is really bothering you. But sometimes we can complete our business in the bathroom successfully in our dreams. And that is always a good sign that you have let it out, expressed your frustrations, and relieved yourself of the angst.

The message of public bathroom dreams: There is something you need to get off your chest. You have reached a place within your psyche where you need to unload it and flush it away no matter what others may think, which is why your wise dreaming mind placed you in a bathroom. This dream is warning you that your emotional plumbing is backed up. The more you allow your frustrations—and what you view as crap—to build up, the bigger "mess" you'll have to deal with in the end.

PARKING LOT

A parking lot is a place we park our car, temporarily, until we need it again. It is also a place where, compared to a freeway where there is constant movement, there is none. It is a place of inactivity and stillness, a waiting place, if you will. So when your dream places you in a parking lot, you need to ask yourself what area of your life is parked? What area of your life was once in motion, like the car, but now is on hold? In what way are you, or some area of your life, in wait-and-see mode?

> *I dreamed I was in a multistory parking lot and I couldn't find my car. There was dirty slushy snow all over and I was circling every floor, yelling. I ran into my mom who was sitting on someone's bumper drunk and smoking a cigarette. She doesn't smoke and I've never seen her drunk. I cried.—Blaire, 29*

LAURI: Losing your car is a classic dream symbol for feeling directionless. Dirty water or even dirty snow points to depression. Are you depressed about someone around you growing cold toward you? The way you circle every floor indicates that you are going in circles in some area of your waking life, exhausting your energy and going nowhere. Your mom may not be playing herself but rather standing in for your ability to nurture yourself or "mother" those around you, or perhaps this is about your own role as a mother. Are you a mom or wanting to become a mom? Do you drink and smoke? If so, is this something that will interfere with motherhood and is something you need to "bump" off, hence the car's bumper. This dream is equating your life to being lost in a parking lot. It's telling you it's time to make a decision that will get you going in the right direction and in a better place.

BLAIRE REPLIES: *That seems entirely relevant to my world right now. I recently moved in with my boss. We planned to get married and have a baby. Things got complicated at work and at home. Suddenly, he decided that he did not want to have kids. All of my married friends started getting pregnant; I knew I would be missing something I always wanted. I was so depressed I turned to vodka more than I should have. You are very much right on with your unraveling. I will try to listen to what my subconscious is telling me.*

The area of Blaire's life that is now on hold is her family life. As painful as it has been for Blaire to have put that on hold after she thought that area was moving forward, she can find comfort in the fact that it's not by any means final. It's just parked for the time being.

The message of parking lot dreams: Some area of your life is parked and going nowhere or perhaps needs to be put on hold. The good news is that parking lots are temporary places so this lack of movement in your life will not last. You will be able to move full speed ahead soon enough if you take the right precautions.

PRISON

It is human nature to freely express ourselves, make our own choices, and follow any path we please. We are blessed with free will, after all. But sometimes things stop moving or something or someone forces us back and holds us down. This is when a prison dream may emerge in order to show us how we really feel about our circumstances or to show us that we are allowing ourselves to be imprisoned by someone or something.

Prison dreams are similar to parking lot dreams in that they indicate a certain area of the dreamer's life is stuck, but the difference is that with a prison dream, the lack of movement or progress is usually caused by an outside source—or perceived to be an outside source—rather than the dreamer's own doing.

> I dreamed I was in prison. I was with a black man whom I trusted and we get out of the facility by sneaking through a closet. Once outside, I began to squeeze through a hole in the fence and that's when I woke up.—Ken, 40

LAURI: In what area of your life are you feeling trapped or restricted? The unknown black man is your ability to get out of this tough situation in a way that you may not be comfortable with. People of different races in our dreams often stand in for parts of our personality we do not recognize or that we suppress. He is an unknown part of your personality that you need to utilize right now and that you may need to call upon again in the future. You escape through a closet. Closets symbolize secrecy. What are you secretly thinking or doing right now? Do tell! The fence suggests you have been "on the fence" about a decision and the squeezing through not only suggests you may be feeling squeezed out of something, but also that you are making it through this situation just fine. In fact, your dream may be showing you that a decision does not even need to be made and the imprisoning situation must be about over.

KEN REPLIES: *At the time of my dream, my boss had left the company. She always kept me informed on things and depended on me to research and gather important data that would help her make more informed decisions. The man who stepped in to help out squeezed me out of all these areas and viewed me as a gofer and nothing more. I did feel trapped. I have secretly begun looking for other employment but this dream has helped me to realize that I can make it through this because we should have a new boss in less than a month. Thank you.*

The area of Blaire's life that was unmoving, symbolized by the parking lot, was caused by her choices, whereas the area of Ken's life that left him feeling stuck, symbolized by the prison, was caused by something beyond his control, his boss leaving. But while Ken's dream was triggered by a situation that was indeed beyond his doing, sometimes the root of prison dreams is a restrictive circumstance in some area of our life that really is of our own doing, but we do not see it that way. Sometimes we are imprisoned by our own actions or by our own recurring behavior patterns, and rather than recognize our own role in our lack of progress we feel that we continually have bad luck. We simply don't see the fact that often we are our own warden.

The message of prison dreams: You are beginning to realize that somewhere in your life you are stuck, there is no progression, and you feel it is unfair. Your dream is challenging you to discover where in your life you are confined, and what you can do to break out and be free.

HOSPITAL

When our dreams take place in a hospital, it often raises our eyebrows and makes us wonder if something is wrong physically. This is usually not the case. While the hospital setting isn't necessarily alerting you to a physical ailment that needs healing, it is letting you know that healing is needed in some other area of your life. The best way to figure that out is to ask yourself what area of your life has become unhealthy.

> In my dream I am in a hospital waiting to have surgery. Apparently, the place had just been sprayed for cockroaches. The orderlies begin to lob gas pellets at me that are supposed to make me go to sleep, but it doesn't work and I am afraid that they will do surgery on me while I'm awake. I notice a large, dead, bloody dog and then I wake up!—Carol, 57

LAURI: The hospital setting suggests some area of your life is not doing well. The surgery indicates that some situation needs to be repaired or removed. Cockroaches are known for being able to survive a nuclear war, so this may be about something that's been "bugging" you lately and has been difficult for you to "exterminate." The ineffective gas pellets mean you are fully aware of what needs to be done. Unfortunately, the "procedure" of "removing" this situation from your life is probably going to be painful. The dead, bloody dog is a very significant symbol. Dogs symbolize loyalty, companionship, and friendship. Is there a particular relationship that has been bleeding you dry emotionally? Your dream is telling you it's time to remove this unhealthy issue so you can move on.

CAROL REPLIES: *There is a friend in my life that I am in the process of having to pull away from. She is very manipulative. The relationship is nearly over but still breathing slightly. This really pulls it all together for me. It's absolute confirmation that I* have *to end this relationship! I can't tell you how much I appreciate your insight.*

While the cockroaches and bloody dog seem to be the stronger symbols in this dream, because they are somewhat disturbing imagery, it is the hospital setting that is letting Carol know that this dream is about an area of her life that needs healing. This dream is showing Carol that the friendship area of her life has taken on the form of a hospital because it was in an unhealthy state, and either needed to be healed or removed for her own well being.

The message of hospital dreams: Your dreaming mind has placed you in a hospital because something somewhere in your life is unhealthy. An emergency room means you need to stop wasting time because the situation is urgent. Time to take on the role of doctor and mend what is broken.

HOTEL

Hotels are a surprisingly common dream location. This is because in waking life, a hotel stay is a temporary one. So the dreaming mind will borrow that sense of impermanence and apply it to our dreams when some area of our life doesn't seem like it is going to last.

I dreamed I was with my boyfriend at a convention in a hotel. We had a good time, but when we tried to leave through the parking

*garage we encountered a mob on the street that prevented us from
leaving. There were fires and chaos, and the police were murdering
people. We tried to go back up the elevators through the parking
garage, but two corrupt cops stopped us and tried to beat us up.
That's when I woke up.—Melanie, 29*

LAURI: When our dreams take place in a hotel it means we are
in a temporary place in our life or in a temporary mind-set. Sounds
like your inner mind is concerned that your relationship with your
beau is what is temporary. The parking garage suggests your relationship is "parked" and not moving forward. All that chaos
surrounding you in the dream reflects your anxiety about the relationship coming to a nasty end if things don't change and the corrupt police are a definite sign of confusion as to what is the right
thing to do. Step outside the situation and try to see if one of you
is rushing things or if one of you is holding the relationship back.
Hopefully you can find a way to be on the same page, if not then
just like in your dream, doomsday may be near. Good luck.

MELANIE RESPONDS: *Before even reading your response today I
broke up with my beau yesterday. I guess my mind was telling me that it
was doomed from the start. Fortunately, we are still really close friends.*

This dream has two locations, the parking lot and the hotel,
so you may be wondering—if this were your dream—which location to start with. The truth is, either location would lead you
to the meaning but I chose to start with the hotel because the
parking lot in the dream belonged to the hotel, so the hotel is the
dominant setting as well as the dominant message. This relationship is not going to last. Notice how Melanie and her boyfriend—
throughout the entire dream—were trying to get out. That's a
pretty clear message that she needed out of the relationship. Her

dream shows us that she had already reached a place in her mind where she knew the relationship was a fun but temporary stay. Getting out of the relationship was the problem . . . or so she feared. Thankfully, it went smoothly.

The type of the hotel, the condition of the hotel, the reasons for being at the hotel and what happens at the hotel all give hints as to which area of your life is temporary or transitional and how well or how poorly you are dealing with it. Remember, the hotel can also refer to a temporary mind-set. A grand hotel may be linked to a temporary emotional high, for example, and a run-down hotel would suggest a temporary slump.

The message of hotel dreams: Some area of your life is in a transient state. Depending on the context of the dream, you either need to check out and move on or appreciate it and enjoy it while it lasts. But when it is all said and done, make sure you take the lesson with you . . . not the towels!

BATTLEFIELD

Remember that Pat Benatar song from the eighties, "Love Is a Battlefield"? It's all about the power struggle and the tug-of-war of emotions within a relationship. Basically, whether it is two countries or two people, all wars are a struggle for power. When there is a power struggle somewhere in your life, your dreams are likely to take place in a war zone in order to drive home the message that the situation has reached a volatile level.

Many of my dreams are in the past, like in the Civil War or World War II. I can see the gunfire and death, and I am always running and running. I don't know why I run or who or what is chasing me. I always wake up exhausted from the running.—Mary Ann, 44

LAURI: Dreaming of the past doesn't necessarily mean you are seeing a past life, but rather your dream is commenting on something from *your* past. The settings of your dreams are always a war, which means there is a battle from your past that you are still fighting to this day. It is something you are continually "running from" or avoiding dealing with in waking life . . . and that is why you keep dreaming the same thing over and over again. Your dreams cannot move forward until you move forward. Clearly, there is something from your past you are avoiding rather than confronting and working through. When you get help with this, when you finally face it and stop running, your dreams will stop.

MARY ANN REPLIES: *I think this goes back to my first health issues. I have had twenty surgeries, ten on my lower back, seven for an artificial hip, and the rest for different things. I believe my war dreams started when I had one of my many hip surgeries; I freaked out and literally ran out of the hospital. Whenever I need another surgery, I freak and want to run. I had back surgery in January but called and canceled the surgery. That same day I got a calming phone call from my surgeon and we rebooked the surgery. I am tired of running. I will now face my health issues straight on.*

Mary Ann's health is a war zone. She's not only battling physical ailments but she is battling herself over getting the proper care she needs. She is having a power struggle between what she knows is the right thing to do and not wanting to do it. But now that she finally understands her dreams, she can see that she has waged a war on herself! That is surely no way to go through life.

The message of battlefield dreams: There is a war going on in some area of your life. What or whom are you in conflict with? Is it an inner battle, such as battling an addiction? Or is there a war of words you are in with someone else? Where is the power struggle? It is time to decide if you should go into soldier mode and fight the good fight or raise the white flag and sign the peace treaty. While there may never be world peace, t'is a good thing to have inner peace.

WEDDING

A wedding is a celebration of two people who are ready to commit to each other until death do they part. Commit is the operative word here. A wedding marks the ultimate commitment, which is why when someone is really committed to their work, for example, we say "he is married to his job." When we have come to a place within ourselves where we are ready to make some form of commitment in waking life, whether it be a commitment to ourselves to eat better and exercise or to someone or something, we will often find ourselves at or in a wedding in our dreams.

> *I had a dream last night that I was at a wedding at the Playboy Mansion but the groom never showed up so we partied. I said to someone who I had to share a really big room with that I could live this life as long as I didn't have to sleep with Hef. I asked if he had a son, then I woke up.—Julie, 30*

LAURI: The wedding setting may mean that you need to make a commitment to someone or something or perhaps even to yourself, but you must not be taking it seriously enough. You would rather "play," hence the Playboy Mansion, perhaps than meet that obligation. This is why the groom doesn't show up. He is your male half, the assertive take-action part of you and as of right now, that part is MIA!

JULIE REPLIES: *My doctor made me commit to run a 5km in March. I currently am only an occasional walker. But my word means everything*

*to me so I will follow through with the commitment . . . I just don't want
to get started training yet.* Wow!

In Julie's dream she is attending a wedding rather than being
in the wedding because someone else made the commitment, her
doctor, rather than the commitment coming from Julie. She hasn't
fully accepted ownership of this commitment yet. When she does,
she is likely to dream of being the bride rather than the guest.

The message of wedding dreams: You are in a place in your life
where you are ready to make a commitment. Is it to you? Is it to
something? Or is it to someone? If the wedding dream is pleasant, then you are ready and willing to commit and stick to it, till
death do you part. If the dream is disturbing, then you are likely
uncomfortable with the commitment and view it more as an obligation, in which case you need to examine your recent commitments and obligations and make sure you're down for the count!

RESTAURANT

When sitting in a restaurant, the enticing smells wafting from the
kitchen and the mouthwatering dishes on the patrons' tables only
intensifies the hunger you came in with. Because of this, the dreaming mind associates a restaurant setting with hunger; not with physical hunger but rather with emotional hunger. As you've learned by
now, dreams don't often comment on the physical side of life, instead they comment on the emotional and psychological side of life.
So when there is a psychological need or an emotional hunger in
some area of your life, your dreams will place you in a restaurant, a
kitchen, or even a grocery store. What happens within that dream
setting will reflect if that need or hunger is being fed.

I had a dream that my ex-boyfriend was living in the back of a sushi restaurant. I went there to talk to him and we started fighting and he told me he had been seeing his previous ex the entire time we were together. He was also really tall in the dream.—PJ, 22

LAURI: Your dream takes place in a restaurant because you must still be emotionally hungry for him, and he is living in the back because he is always in the back of your mind. That is why he is so tall in your dream: you have allowed him to be a bigger issue in your life than he ought to be. Just remember, sushi restaurants serve fish and this is why your dream took place in one: your dream is telling you that there are plenty of other fish in the sea.

PJ REPLIES: *Thank you so much! This makes perfect sense. I guess I have some moving on to do.*

PJ's hunger for her ex is not being fed, so her wiser dreaming mind is trying to show her that pining for him is a conflict of interest for her, hence the conflict she has with him in the dream. There is the restaurant setting but yet no food in this dream, which is a good indication that her hunger will not be fed. Eating in a dream usually means some area of your life is being fulfilled and nourished.

The message of restaurant dreams: You are craving something right now. Is it emotional, intellectual, spiritual, or career nourishment? For what or whom do you hunger? The type of restaurant, and what happens in the restaurant as well as the food in the restaurant, are all hints as to whether your hunger is being fed, as well as whether it is healthy and fulfilling to you or leaving you feeling empty.

If you work in a restaurant and your dream takes place in that restaurant, odds are the dream is simply about your work and the dynamics at your work, but if your dream takes place in a different or unfamiliar restaurant, then it is more likely about a need or hunger you have somewhere in your life.

AMUSEMENT PARK

Who doesn't love going to the amusement park? That's where we go, even as adults, to have fun, let loose, forget our troubles, and just simply enjoy ourselves. They don't call Disney World the happiest place on earth for nothing. The amusement park setting of a dream can refer to the recreational area of our life. But I've found that, most often, when we patron an amusement or theme park in our dreams, it unfortunately is not always a happy experience. The rides are often wrought with weird design flaws or malfunctions. The people are sometimes menacing and the food can be just plain bizarre. If the amusement park in your dream is less than amusing, then you need to figure out which area of your life, that ought to be enjoyable, has instead become rather dreadful.

I dreamed I went into a slightly sinister amusement park. It was dark. The entire place was deserted. Whatever ride I climbed on to just started on its own. In each case I was having to overcome my fear to get on and then try not to show my fear while the ride was in motion. As I was turning upside down on that last ride, I fell out of the seat . . . and woke up.—Joseph, 46

LAURI: What area of your life ought to be fun and enjoyable, but is causing you anxiety instead? The sinister feeling of the park suggests you have a sinister feeling about the situation. The amusement park is deserted. Are you dealing with this issue all on your own? Or perhaps you are feeling left out or abandoned in some way. At the end you fall out of the ride. Is there something going on where you fear you may suffer a big letdown? You keep having to overcome your fear in the dream. I think this is the way you are preparing yourself to step outside of your comfort zone in waking life.

JOSEPH REPLIES: *I am a public sector worker in the UK and about 500,000–600,000 of us are about to be made redundant. The fear in the dream certainly could be the fear of what happens if I lose my job. If I am made redundant, then it will be a struggle to get another job as we will all be looking. I do still enjoy my work—that's why I don't want to lose it. I've been there twenty years and I would feel left out in the cold without it.*

The work area of Joseph's life used to be fun and enjoyable, but now is full of fear and the darkness in his dream is connected to his inability to see what is around the corner for him. And notice how he falls out of the ride when it is upside down. Typically, upside-down rides are fun because we have the security of the seat belt and the safety bar. Joseph's ride in the dream did not have that because his job security is gone so his dream is warning him to prepare for an emotional, even financial fall. A scary situation to be in indeed, but I love the way Joseph's dream self keeps facing his fears in the dream. That's a very strong indication he'll be up for facing his fears in waking life.

When your dream takes place in an amusement park it is also important to pay attention to any rides you may get on as a lot of information can be gleaned from them. A roller coaster may refer to something in your life that is full of ups and downs, highs and lows, or possibly even point to emotional instability (if the roller-coaster ride is somewhat precarious). A Tilt-A-Whirl may indicate something is beginning to spin out of control, and a fun house could either point to something that has become loads of fun for you or something you or someone around you is not taking seriously anymore, depending on the context of the dream.

Like I always say, if you can find the figure of speech or metaphor in your dream, you've found a good chunk of the message. "Is someone taking you for a ride?" Are you on an emotional roller coaster? "Sometimes life isn't *fair*."

The message of amusement park dreams: What area of your life is full of fun and excitement? What area of your life do you enjoy the most? Right now you need to look at what is going on in this area of your waking life and compare it to the context of your dream. This will give you a better understanding as to how productive or problematic this area is. Life is short and shouldn't be spent dwelling on the ups and downs, what's spinning out of control, or what lays ahead, but rather just enjoying the moment.

Remember, where your dream takes place is just as important as what happens in the dream because it reflects *where you are* in your mind in regard to a particular issue or it is a commentary on some *area* of your life.

Take a good look at the location in your dream and see if you can connect it to a certain area of your life. Does the setting remind you of any part of your life? Also look at what the setting of your dream is used for in waking life. An airport, for example, is a place where we take off in a plane and go places. Is there an area of your life that feels like this? Or have you come to a place within your mind where you are ready for this?

We are all trying to get to a place in our life and within ourselves where we are happy, fulfilled, healthy, and at peace. Paying attention to your dream locations will show you how far or how near you are to being where you want to be.

....

FASCINATING DREAM FACT: Prince Charles, Pamela Anderson, and David Bowie have all reported that they keep dream journals.

4

Vehicle and Travel Dreams

✾

NAVIGATING YOUR CHOSEN PATHS

Car, Plane, Truck, Train, Ships and Boats, Bus, Motorcycle, Bicycle, Space Travel

Life is a journey. We all seem to naturally view it as such. Just think of all the journey-infused metaphors we use when talking about our lives: "We'll cross that bridge when we get to it," "I'm really at a crossroads right now," "Our relationship has hit a road block," and "I'm ready to take my life in a different direction," just to name a few. With this collective perspective of traveling through life, it is only fitting that our dreams would place us in a myriad of travel-related adventures.

In the literal world, there are many physical paths on which to travel, such as road, sea, air, and track. In the figurative world, there are many life paths to travel: career paths, relationship paths and spiritual paths, for example. And in the dream world, each type of path you may find yourself on, as well as each type of vehicle you may find yourself in, is not only related to your various life paths but will also give great insight into how successfully or how poorly you are navigating these paths. In other words, the path, whether it be the road, air, or water, is the particular path you have chosen; the vehicle is your ability to travel that path.

CAR

Without a doubt, the car is the most common mode of transportation we dream of because it is the most common vehicle used. Therefore its meaning is broader than say, a boat or a plane. The car dream can be a commentary on how you are maneuvering through a specific life path, such as career, but most often it is about the direction of your life as a whole. It can also be reflective of your "drive" or motivation to continue on down a certain road. It is always important to pay attention to whether you are the one behind the wheel or not as that points to who—or even what part of you—is in control of the direction your life is taking.

The specifics of the dream, such as the type or condition of the car as well as the condition of the road and how well you are driving will help you to zero in on which life path it is connected to.

Crashing is the most common element to the car dream that I've discovered in my research. It often means that some direction your life has taken has come to a sudden and messy stop.

I have been having recurring dreams where I am driving on a dark road and I don't know where I am. Suddenly I jerk the wheel, always to the left, spin, and then crash. I've been having it at least once a week for the last two months.—Jaime, 29

LAURI: The darkness in this dream is either connected to the fact that you are in a dark time in your life (have you been depressed?) or it is connected to being uncertain or "in the dark" about the direction your life is taking. You always jerk the wheel to the left. Going left is the wrong direction, had you turned right, that would indicate doing the right thing. The left also points to the past, that which you have *left* behind. Are you dwelling on a mistake or accident you believe you made? That may be why you continue to crash in the dream. When you stop dwelling on the past and start looking forward, the dreams will stop.

JAIME REPLIES: *I think you hit the nail on the head. I am dwelling on the past a lot because I am in a custody battle with my ex-husband. I have not received child support since June. I am also angry at him because he has not seen our daughter since the beginning of August, which is causing me to think a lot about the time we were married and how excited he was when we found out I was pregnant. I don't know where all of this is taking me, and I don't like not knowing.*

Jaime's dream car keeps crashing because she hasn't been able to move her life forward since her marriage crashed and burned. Even though there is another direction her road of life could take, she continues to allow herself to be stuck in the aftermath of a wrecked marriage. Her dream is trying to show her, again and again, that it is time to change the direction of her life and her thoughts, and it's as easy as *turning the wheels* of her mind the other way for once. She needs to start looking forward instead of backward at the man that *left* her and her daughter. Jaime is the one behind the wheel in the dream, which means she is the one that can steer herself in the *right* direction.

Having your car stolen or not being able to find your car is another very common dream occurrence and it points to an inability to move forward down a path you have chosen, most often due to unforeseen or uncontrollable circumstances or a lack of "drive" to continue on.

> *I constantly dream my car is stolen and I try all night long to get it back. Sometimes I know the person that took it and I go get it back and then, in the dream, I wake up in the morning and it is gone again. It stresses me out!—Jesse, 35*

LAURI: Your car is constantly stolen in your dreams because you may constantly feel directionless or feel you were robbed of an opportunity to reach a goal you had for yourself. Your dreaming mind wants you to find a new path, and get your drive or mojo back, which is why it keeps taking your car away from you in your dream. The path you are on now isn't going to get you anywhere.

JESSE REPLIES: *I have been trying to complete law school now for three years. I have not been able to finish because I had a baby. I am struggling with how to make graduation happen. Since becoming a mother, I am second-guessing what I should be doing for a career. This makes total sense!*

Even though Jesse's dreams are frustrating for her they are also motivating, now that she understands them. Her own deeper self is comparing her inability to complete law school to being robbed of her ability to follow a path she has chosen. This visual really put it in perspective for her. Jesse's dream is showing her that it is time to get her drive back and get back on the road to becoming a lawyer.

There are subtle yet significant differences between car-crash dreams and stolen-car dreams. Both dreams are linked to an inability to continue down the dreamer's current path, but the car-crash dream alone is linked to sudden, disastrous, or messy endings that the dreamer needs to rid themselves of, just as they would a totaled car (like Jamie's dream). Alternatively, the stolen-car dream is usually linked to a path that has ended because of the dreamer's perceived unfair or unforeseen circumstances (like Jesse's dream), but this path could be resumed, just as a stolen car can sometimes be recovered.

Retirees and senior citizens often get the stolen-car dream. We spend the majority of our adult life with the purpose of getting up and going to work every day in hopes of furthering our career path. But when that path comes to an end we find ourselves wondering where to go next with our lives. When there is no more *drive* to do anything in particular, the dreaming mind gets upset, feels robbed, and sends us the stolen-car dream to show us what we have allowed to happen to our lives.

So many things happen to our cars in dreams because there are so many things that can steer us off course in waking life. When the breaks on your dream car fail, odds are you are letting something get out of control, and you need to slow down and regroup in waking life. When your car won't start you have probably lost your motivation to continue on or your dream is telling you that this particular path just isn't going to work out for you. Sometimes you may find yourself driving from the backseat, like I do so often in my dreams. This means a goal you have put on the back burner needs to be brought to the forefront so you can complete that journey. And driving backward in a dream suggests that you either need to back out of a particular situation or you are doing things in a way that are setting you back on your path rather than moving you forward.

The message of car dreams: The direction of your life may be at a critical point. Are you on the right path? Is there momentum? Or are you parked, out of gas, or broken down? Your car dreams are your inner GPS pointing you where to go or telling you when to stop. If you follow the signs in your car dreams, you will never be steered off course.

PLANE

The path of a plane is up high in the sky, therefore planes often represent a journey you have high hopes for. In my research, I've found that planes are most often connected to one's career path because like a plane, your career is something you hope will take off, reach new levels, and take you places.

> *I was in a plane. It felt like something my business partner and I had hired. It was very big, and very comfy with huge seats. The plane started moving, and it moved incredibly fast. It thrust me into my seat. It seemed like a special mission, like going to outer space. We were looking forward to it, that's for sure.—Mark, 29*

LAURI: Your career or some other area of life must be taking off and rapidly reaching new levels. The big comfy seats not only suggest that you are comfortable with the direction you are headed but that you also hope it will lead to a financially comfortable life. The higher the plane rises, the higher your hopes . . . outer space is pretty high.

MARK REPLIES: Yes, hopes are high. We have come across new knowledge that could have an enormous impact on the way our business could grow, and at a rapid pace at that, if executed correctly.

Mark's dream not only reflects his high hopes but is also show-ing him that his career path is headed in the right direction . . . up!

I dreamed I was stuck in a bathroom on a plane and we hit turbulence. The plane seemed like it was going to crash. The flight attendant let me out and then puked on me! Then a guy came at me with a knife!! Good one, huh?—Stacey, 38

LAURI: Are you worried about your job right now? Are things a bit turbulent? Like the flight attendant that puked on you, has someone dumped on you at work? Did someone criticize you or cut you down (the knife)? You were trapped in the bathroom be-cause you probably had to hold in your frustrations rather than *relieve yourself* of them for the sake of your job.

STACEY REPLIES: *Yeah, there is someone at work that is a huge drama queen and she is trying to make me feel insecure about my posi-tion. She loves to dump on people. She crapped on me last week and while I shouldn't fear her, I do.*

Stacey's plane dream indicates her career path is not going smoothly due to the way others are treating her. But it is also showing her how she is really being treated so that she can better arm herself in waking life. How many times is she going to let someone verbally vomit on her?

Like dream cars, we want our dream planes to travel smoothly, too. Also like dream cars, dream planes can crash, and often do. This is a powerful expression of dashed hopes, again, most often connected to career-related hopes but can certainly be connected to just about anything one has high hopes for. The difference between watching the plane crash and being on the crashing plane often has to do with how involved you are in the waking life situation. You are likely to find yourself *on* the plane when you have already been actively involved and your career or other issue is in motion but winds up falling through in waking life. Whereas you will find yourself *watching* the plane crash when something you were hoping for but had not yet taken action on falls through; when you aren't yet directly connected to it, when it is still a distant hope rather than one you already have your hands on.

The message of plane dreams: There is enormous potential for a path you have chosen. Now is the time to be proactive in assessing and evaluating where your career path (or any high hope you currently have) is and where it's headed. Don't let a little turbulence throw you off course. Even a crash can be survived. The sky is the limit as far as you're dreaming mind is concerned. Keep aiming high.

TRUCK
The purpose of a truck is to haul a heavy load from one place to another. Therefore, a truck in a dream suggests you are currently traveling through life carrying a heavy burden that is weighing you down and that you really ought to unload at some point.

> My dream took place at a campsite. A local DJ and I were in this truck and she was driving. She stopped to make sure I had my seat belt on and that it was secure. We then took off and flew over this huge lake.—Tiffany, 24

LAURI: The campsite is a good indication there is something you need to get "out in the open." The truck means you've been carrying around a heavy load or burden lately. Remember what we learned in the people chapter, when a person appears in your dream, in this case a DJ, it's important to think about what part of you the person is standing in for. A DJ is someone who speaks for a living, someone known for his or her voice, so a DJ in your dream symbolizes *your* voice. That being said, is there something you need to speak up about? Your dream is reassuring you that it is safe to do so by buckling you in nice and tight. How cool that the truck flew over the lake! Again, your dreaming mind is reassuring you and even encouraging you to "rise above" your fears and not let them weigh you down or hold you back. Flying in dreams is also a sign of release, freedom and light-heartedness, which will come once you speak up.

TIFFANY REPLIES: *For some time now I've been interested in dating the same sex. I believe that's the issue I need to speak up about. Nobody knows about my sexual orientation except for me. I have been very lonely and wanting to find that special someone. So this made a lot of sense.*

Tiffany's got herself quite a heavy load and her dream is showing her that it is time she stop hauling it around. And notice how Tiffany is not the one behind the wheel. This shows us that she is ready to let her voice (the DJ) take control and steer her down a path that will lift her up and not weigh her down with this burdensome secret.

The message of truck dreams: Your current life's journey is weighed down with a heavy burden. The bigger the truck is in the dream, the bigger the burden in waking life. Why continue to burden yourself? No load is meant to be carried forever.

TRAIN

Trains travel on a track and follow a predetermined schedule. This is why trains in dreams often point to a planned route you have for yourself in life.

> *I was trying to catch a train and was running beside it. While I was running I got into a patch of bugs that bit me. Then someone gave me a hand and helped me get on.—Rachelle, 33*

LAURI: Trying to catch a plane, train, or bus in a dream means you fear some opportunity in waking life might be passing you by. Are you up against any sort of deadline? You were able to get on the train, which is a good indication that you are "on track" as far as this opportunity or deadline goes *but* there does seem to be a certain issue or person that has been "bugging" you lately. Has something happened recently that really "bites"? Your dream may be warning you not to let that pesky little issue keep you from embarking on this planned journey.

RACHELLE REPLIES: *This dream makes sense now. I have been wanting to go to college, but I have two young children at home and a husband that is not supportive about it, which does "bite." But I have to keep going for my kids.*

Rachelle has a predetermined path she wants to follow. It is showing up in her dream in the form of a train that is leaving the station so that she can better understand the urgency and will hopefully "get on board" with what she really wants for her life and get going down that path before it's too late.

The dreaming mind loves to play with words in order to get a message across, and trains come fully stocked with figures of speech that you should consider when figuring out your train dream: On the right track, a train of thought, on the job training, railroading someone, etc. I've said it before and I'll say it again, find the figure of speech hidden in your dream and you've found the message!

The message of train dreams: Are you on schedule for a route you planned for yourself? Or has something derailed your journey? Whether your plans have stalled, been thrown off track, or are right on schedule, remember the rhythmic mantra of the little engine that could, *"I think I can, I think I can, I think I can . . ."*

SHIPS AND BOATS

Ships and boats travel on water, and water—to the dreaming mind—is connected to your emotions. Like water, emotions are fluid, ever-changing and often run deep. So when you find yourself on a boat or a ship in a dream, it is because you are embarking on an emotional journey in waking life.

Most often, boats and ships in dreams are related to the emotional relationship path. Again, if you look at the figures of speech we use involving these vessels, you'll see why: the love boat, two ships passing in the night, he's a dream boat, etc.

> *I was in a boat speeding across the ocean toward the rocky cliffs. My ex was in the boat, driving. We were going straight toward the cliff, sure to collide with no slowing down. I woke up before the impact.—Darcey, 47*

LAURI: Your relationship with your ex must be rocky, hence the rocky cliffs. What once was a love boat has become a vessel of doom. Is he the driving force behind the turmoil? Your dream is warning you that you two are on the verge of disaster and close to the point of no return if one of you doesn't "trim your sails."

DARCEY REPLIES: *That makes total sense. We are like fire and ice. We have shared custody of the children, who are four and six years old. It is extremely difficult for us to even converse without tension and verbal fighting. Whenever we do have an exchange, there is guaranteed fighting. We fight about their clothes and who has them, about finances, school needs, etc. Sometimes he even throws in going to court and making me pay child support or getting full custody.*

Darcey's boat dream has a pretty clear message for her. She has allowed her ex to take control of the helm of their relationship path and he is steering it rapidly to the point of no return.

Whether the ship or boat in your dream is connected to a relationship path or not, you can bet it will always be related to a path that is highly emotional.

It was very stormy and I was walking through an eerie gray city on the banks of a raging ocean. I knew there was a large wave headed my way. Then I saw a rusted iron troller. It looked to be unseaworthy, but I knew in my heart that it was my only chance for survival. As I ran toward the deck of the freighter I could see the giant wave spreading through the rocky harbor. I made my way onto the boat just as the giant wave hit the shore and broke right over the boat completely swamping the city. As I saw the cityscape disappear under the raging water, I also felt the rusted old freighter rise up. The ties to the dock tightened and then broke as the boat heaved up in a gush of power. I held on as the boat turned and then broke away out to sea. The city was gone,

with only a torrent of white water left where the city once
was.—Scott, 51

LAURI: You're clearly in a stormy, rocky, uncertain time in waking life. The eerie gray is connected to the fact that you feel the
color has left your life. You may even be depressed about current
circumstances. The city is what you have built in your life and you
feel it is on the verge of destruction, and you want out.

The boat is your ability to navigate a path through this stormy
time. It seems unseaworthy because you may not have much
confidence in yourself. It is rusted because you have weathered
many a storm before and surely can weather this one.

You hang on to the boat just as you need to hang on in real
life . . . hang on to your self and your instincts and your confidence, ride out this stormy time, and know that even though you
have to let go of what you have built (the city being destroyed),
you are a survivor and this is not the end. In other words, if you
don't free yourself from what appears to be certain doom, you
will surely go under.

SCOTT REPLIES: *As is the case with many in this turbulent economic
time, I, too, am facing the fact that my business may not make it through.
And yes, at times it seems the color has gone out of my life as well. In fact,
I was just talking to a friend about this very subject last week.*

*I have built up a substantial business over the last fifteen years;
yearly gross sales in 2008 were over twelve million. So you can imagine
that I have a lot of emotions invested. The city, if it is what I have created in my life, is certainly sinking as I struggle to save it.*

*The boat, being my ability to navigate through this stormy time, is
me. Yes this makes sense. I have been knocked down many times and
have gotten back up. And though I may be just barely hanging on right
now, my vessel it seems, is still seaworthy.*

Finally, to let go of the city. This is hard to accept, for I believe I can survive. Reality, though, may have a different vision of what happens than I do. As the boat broke free of its moorings I could feel a freedom, an excitement of where I would find myself next.

Notice how Scott says, *"Reality, though, may have a different vision of what happens than I do."* Your dreams, when you can understand them, are the best glimpse of reality available. They are the way you are brutally honest with yourself when your conscious waking mind refuses to be.

Scott's dream is being brutally honest with him by demonstrating to him that he needs to let go of the business he has built, because the reality is that it is going under. But it is also comforting and reassuring him through the excitement he felt in the end of the dream. His wise dreaming mind is reminding him that this freedom could lead to countless potentialities. The feeling, thought, or action that is experienced at the end of the dream is often the message your dreaming mind wants to leave you with. Remember that. When all else fails, the ending of your dream often holds the most powerful part of the message.

The message of ship and boat dreams: You have embarked on an emotional journey, whether it be a relationship, a business venture, or something else of equal significance. Remember that the state of the water, the condition of the vessel, and how well it is traveling will clue you in to whether you should stay aboard or abandon ship.

BUS

A bus is a mass transit vehicle as well as being one of the slower forms of travel, so when you find yourself on a bus in your dreams, odds are a path you have chosen in waking life is either unfolding rather slowly or you are depending on others to help you along that journey.

> *The other night I dreamed that I was on a bus, and enjoying the ride, when suddenly I noticed people getting off, little by little, and then the driver, who I think was a woman, also got off. I was on the bus alone! People seemed angry at me; meanwhile, I was scared!—Donna, 57*

LAURI: A bus is a vehicle you are a passenger on rather than driving it yourself, therefore it suggests you are not currently in complete control of the direction your life is going. Are you dependent, to a degree, on others? You are enjoying the ride in the dream because you may be finding comfort in not having to be behind the wheel right now in your own life, but your wiser dreaming self is giving you a heads-up that you ought not get too comfortable. The people leaving the bus, and even the *driver* leaving, are a good indication that deep down you know you are going to have to take the reins in your life pretty soon. The people in the dream are angry at you because they represent the parts of yourself that are angry at you for being too dependent on others. Your life and the road you go down are ultimately entirely up to you, no one else.

DONNA REPLIES: *Everything you said in this analysis is totally accurate! Yes, I am indeed way too dependent on others and have been for a few years. I am on disability due to an anxiety disorder that was very severe. I am slowly recovering. So I collect disability and earn no money of my own. My sister is letting me rent a room in her home. Only a few years ago I was very independent and happily divorced. Then I foolishly remarried and he turned out to be an alcoholic and ruined my life. I would very much like to be back on my own two feet. I am very angry* at myself, *as you say, for letting me get into the comfort zone of no responsibilities.*

Donna's self contempt is showing up in her dream in the form of angry *people* because there are *many* reasons she is mad at herself. All the different angry people are all the different personalities that Donna is and has been (remember, most people in your dreams are actually some part of you): the wife, the sister, the independent woman, etc. They are none too pleased with the direction that she has allowed her life to take. The main reason is the fact that she has let others take the wheel in her life and because of that, her journey has taken on a much slower pace. Once she takes control and owns her life, just as one owns their own vehicle, she's likely to find herself behind the wheel of a hot red Mustang in her dreams rather than a city bus.

The main aspect of the bus dream is that the bus is designed to accommodate many as opposed to just one or a few. There is a lack of personal connection to a bus, unlike the personal connection and control we have with a car. As a result, the bus dream will almost always imply that the dreamer is not standing on his or her own in some way in waking life. Like Donna, your bus dreams may suggest you are conforming to a crowd or are going along with someone else's wishes rather than following your own road.

A school bus is slightly different in that the path you have chosen leads to new knowledge, for example, going back to school is an obvious one. But also, choosing a job that has on-the-job training is another. Starting a relationship where you are learning your mate's customs, language, or traditions is yet another.

Whatever the case, the direction your life is currently taking is providing you with many lessons and in most cases, indicates others are on this journey with you.

The message of bus dreams: You are on a path that is not solely your own. And you may not be reaching your goals as quickly as you like. Time to ask yourself if you're ready to get behind your own wheel or continue along your life's journey as a passenger.

MOTORCYCLE

The motorcycle is the opposite end of the spectrum in meaning as the bus. A motorcycle is primarily built for one; therefore, it often represents a need to go solo down a chosen path. Another element to a motorcycle is the fact that there are no walls holding you in and no belts holding you down, which creates a sense of freedom for the rider. So when you are in the process of breaking free from a previously constricting path during the day, you may find yourself riding a Hog during the night.

> I rode up to an abandoned building on a motorcycle. I was going to be working with others to restore the building into an alternative therapy building for a hospital. My job was to clean and to restore the windows, and to install solar panels. A woman told me I should not live there anymore because I made too much money (as if). Anyway, in real life, I do not own or seek to own one. Nonetheless, in the dream I took the motorcycle across town to get some parts for the solar panels and I had to pull over to fix my bike, which was a stunning masterpiece of a bike, let me tell you. A car pulled over and asked me what I was doing. When I told him, he said I didn't belong there, that I could do much better for others if I worked on my own.—Sean, 37

LAURI: It seems you are in the midst of trying to rebuild something, to heal it. A relationship? Your self-esteem? Your career? The motorcycle is your need for freedom, no restrictions, and no passengers on your journey. But again, it also needs repair. Has your confidence in yourself broken down? That may be where the reinstallation of the windows comes in. Your dreaming mind wants you to reinstall your outlook (the windows) and make it a bit sunnier, hence the solar panels.

What you are told in a dream—no matter who is saying it—is coming from your own intuition, that voice in the back of your head that speaks to you daily but that you may ignore. You must be in a waking life situation that is beneath your value (being told you are making too much money). Perhaps you are, in fact, good enough to stand on your own without others diluting your abilities. Look at career first, if not there then look at relationships, etc. Whatever it is, your intuition thinks you are better off going solo and moving on rather than rebuilding.

SEAN REPLIES: *I left my wife. No matter how much I made she would spend all of it. She is the former passenger. My esteem is low because I am working for less money than before.*

Notice how Sean describes his dream motorcycle as a stunning masterpiece. That right there is his own self-confidence taking on the form of a motorcycle. Despite the difficult decision he made and that he is now sporting an outer lack of confidence, his inner dreaming mind is stepping in and saying, "Look! You are quite a fine piece of machinery and you need to recognize this and know that you are fully equipped to go down this path alone." The truth is, when you have confidence in yourself it shows. Others can't help but see it and as a result place a higher value on you.

Motorcycles in dreams can also be associated with raw (usually male) sexual energy! Oh yes. It is a powerful, purring motor between your legs that can cause you problems if you are unable to control it. So if you ever dream of losing control of your motorcycle or driving it into water, etc., take a good look at your sexual energy; your dream just might be showing you whether you have a good handle on it or not.

The message of motorcycle dreams: You are likely feeling a sense of freedom to go down any road you choose. In addition, you are probably not interested in any passengers joining you on this journey for now. Like the engine on a chopper, that is a powerful and fearless mind-set. Keep your focus on the road before you and the bugs out of your teeth.

BICYCLE

In order to ride a bicycle, you must first be able to balance yourself upon its two wheels, therefore your ability to balance or give equal attention to two life paths—such as career and family—is the most common meaning of a bicycle dream. But you must also look at all other elements in your life that need balance: emotional and psychological balance, a balanced check book, etc. These all could play a role in the meaning behind a bicycle.

> *I dreamed this guy was trying to kill me so I jumped on a bike to try and get away but the bike wouldn't go anywhere, which made me mad for wasting time that I could have spent running.—Nicole, 30*

LAURI: The bicycle is your ability to balance two things in your life, such as your ability to balance your time at work and your home life. But since the bike isn't moving in the dream, you must have an imbalance in your life that is holding you back, keeping you from moving towards a goal you have for yourself. That may be where this guy that's trying to kill you comes in. He's the male assertive, go-getter part of yourself that wants to put an end to some part of your life; he doesn't want to end your whole life, just a part of it, probably the part that is holding you back.

NICOLE REPLIES: *I am starting grad school tomorrow in hopes of changing careers because I hate my job! So I will be doing both at the same time. That must be what I need to balance, work and school. I very much feel stuck at my current job. I enrolled in grad school as a way to help me move forward with another career. Until I leave my current career, I fear I will continue to feel like a slave to my finances and not in control of my own path. I've always been a path-maker, and not necessarily a cubicle-sitter. This makes so much sense now.*

Nicole's inner self knows she's going to have to balance out her job path and learning path before she can move on to a career path that she loves, which is why it presented her with a bicycle as a means of escape. Unfortunately, the bike wouldn't move. This is because, deep down, she is coming to terms with the stagnation she will have to deal with until she completes school. Even though her impatience is showing up in this dream in that she feels she is wasting time on the bike instead of running, she knows she needs to stay put for now and learn to balance these two elements of her life before there can be any movement.

The message of bicycle dreams: Like a bicycle, life is a balancing act. Whether it is career, family, relationships, finances, or even your emotions or decisions, be careful not to overdo one thing because that will cause you to neglect another. When there is an imbalance, you will lose your power and fall. How well you are riding the bike in your dream will show you how balanced or imbalanced your current journey is.

SPACE TRAVEL

Spaceships, UFOs, rockets, space shuttles, all these vehicles are capable of traveling not only high into the sky but beyond this world, so when they travel into our dreams they represent our extreme high hopes of being able to travel above and beyond our current personal world.

> *I was in what looked like the body of a plane and we were being towed by the Space Shuttle. And we were going very fast but when the Space Shuttle takes off, you know how the booster rockets will fall off? We then fell off, into the ocean, unharmed. That was my dream.—Mike, 38*

LAURI: Is there anything going on right now where you feel you're being elevated in some way, in your career, in your relationships in any other area of your life? Anything going on that could be taking you above and beyond where you are now? Falling off the shuttle indicates you have suffered a letdown. Perhaps something you thought was going to take off, in fact, fell through.

MIKE REPLIES: *Yes! I am a rising superstar in the radio world. Ha ha! My company keeps saying, "We're going to syndicate your show. We're going to syndicate your show." And just when it starts to happen it falls off, just like when the damn Space Shuttle chucks me off in the dream. Well, I'll be damned!*

A syndication deal would certainly transport Mike to another world as far as his career path goes. But unfortunately, as his dream suggests, he's had to suffer letdown after letdown. What the dream is also showing him is that the letdowns and setbacks are not of his own doing but of his company, because he was being towed by the Space Shuttle (his company); he wasn't piloting it. The good news is that, since this dream, Mike did pick up another market and he also has his own local TV show as well.

I've found in my research that vehicles capable of space travel are also common in dreams we have of loved ones that have passed on. These dreams reflect our built-in understanding or belief that there is another world and a higher intelligence after this one.

UFOs in particular tend to be connected to a path in life that is "alien" to the dreamer, something never encountered before. In a positive context, it is a journey capable of changing the dreamer's world; in a negative context, it is a path that threatens to pull or "abduct" the dreamer out of his or her comfort zone or daily routine.

The message of space travel dreams: The sky is not the limit for you! You have hopes and plans that can utterly change your world. Whether the space vehicle is operating correctly or not, intriguing or threatening, it is *your* ability to transport yourself to a life beyond the world you now know.

Like a vehicle, your life is in motion, and like a vehicle the motion of your life can sometimes feel like it is flying or crashing, speeding along or breaking down, smooth sailing or sinking. So whenever you awaken from a vehicle or travel dream, try to figure out which of your life paths the dream seems to be connected to. As you've learned, the ease or difficulty at which you are traveling is a big clue. The type of vehicle is another. The control over the vehicle or the lack thereof is yet another. Ask yourself which of your life paths resembles the journey in the dream, and how does the action of the vehicle resemble the way you are currently handling that path.

Consider your travel dreams postcards sent to you from your dreaming mind giving you updates on your life's many ventures. Pay close attention to these updates as they are your road map to the destination we all are aiming for: fulfillment and peace of mind.

....

FASCINATING DREAM FACT: After the sinking of the *Titanic* in 1912, hundreds of people reported that they had dreams and premonitions of the ship's demise. Nineteen of those experiences were authenticated.

5

Animal Dreams

YOUR INSTINCTS AND BEHAVIOR

Dogs, Cats, Snakes, Predatory Cats, Wolves, Horses, Bears, Birds, Bugs, and Spiders

Sometimes our dreams are a menagerie of the most exotic and wondrous animals. No matter how fantastical and Dr. Seuss–like or how real and menacing, the animals our dreaming mind presents to us symbolize our primal instincts and behaviors, the way we naturally act or respond to situations without giving thought to it.

As humans we are capable of giving great thought to something before taking action. We weigh the pros and cons, we discuss with others to get their opinions, we research, we think, and then we do . . . well, most of the time. Animals primarily act on instinct.

Of course, there is a certain level of thought process to the animal mind, but for the most part, animals just do what they do. And each specific animal has their own specific behavior they are known for: dogs are loyal, cats are independent, elephants never forget. We also use animalistic behavior in our speech: *I ate like a pig; my sister is very catty; you're as stubborn as a mule; etc.*

These characteristics that we project onto animals often appear in our dreams in the form of that animal in order to show us our own current actions and behavior, or to show us how the actions and behavior of someone else is directly affecting us. By understanding our own behavior in this way, or the behavior of someone around us, we can determine if we are currently behaving correctly in a current situation, or if someone we know is behaving in a healthy or harmful manner toward us.

DOGS

Dogs are the most dreamed-of animal, according to my research, because of the characteristics they possess and because those characteristics are a basic, fundamental human need. I am talking about loyalty and friendship. Dogs are known to be loyal to their masters and are also known as man's best friend. It is their instinct to befriend humans and the relationship between man and dog throughout history has proven to be beneficial to both. Because of this, dogs in dreams have come to represent our own instinctive loyalty toward someone as well as someone's loyalty toward us. When you get a dog dream it is always best to look at your relationships first as well as the behavior you and the other person are exhibiting within the relationship. Do that and, odds are, you'll find that the condition and behavior of the dog(s) in the dream are eerily similar to the condition and behavior of the people in the relationship.

This dream was a while ago but it still bothers me. I was in my room, but it was very open, like it could be connected to the world outside. I was with Max, the dog I grew up with (who has passed away). He was very sweet, completely loyal and protective. Suddenly, a very mean German shepherd, crazy with rabies, came in and jumped on me. I fell backward and Max jumped in to fight it off. The fight was very loud, I remember seeing fire in the background, and a lot of growling, barking, etc. I felt frightened to death, and I woke up screaming.—Leslie, 32

LAURI: Your room being open to the outside world suggests you left yourself vulnerable in some way and because of that a major threat entered your life. Most likely this threat was a relationship, someone you thought was a loyal friend, like Max was, but instead turned out to be aggressive toward you. I believe the fight between Max and the German shepherd is reflective of your inner conflict over this relationship. Did you struggle with wanting to keep the relationship because of the friendly elements of it (Max), but also wanting to rid yourself of it because of the harmful elements (the shepherd)? The breed of dog is important in dreams. German shepherds are best known for being police and guard dogs. Your dreaming mind may have been telling you that you should have been more guarded as far as this relationship was concerned.

LESLIE REPLIES: *I had a very bad relationship in college, and though it didn't last too long, it really marked me, because until that relationship, I didn't understand people who were in abusive relationships of any kind (mental, physical, sexual), and stayed with their partner. My boyfriend started hitting me after a couple of months of us dating seriously and I did become guarded after that. I guess I've really softened up since then because I recently got married and just before the wedding I dreamed I was playing with and stroking a very friendly German shepherd.*

Another part of Leslie's dream that I now find interesting after learning of her waking life situation with the abusive ex is the fire in the background while the dogs were fighting. That suggests that Leslie's inner mind was trying to figure out her boyfriend's abusive, angry behavior and surmised that it is likely caused by anger and rage (the fire) from his own background. Most people who are abusive are this way because they were victims of abuse as well. None the less, Leslie's dreams beautifully illustrate how dogs in dreams can teach us how to better manage our relationships and monitor our behavior in them.

Even if you dream of your own dog, it's not necessarily about him but about the friendship and companionship you have with someone else that your dog has come to represent. When a dog attacks in a dream, like in Leslie's, it is a good indication a once trusted relationship has turned on you or that you fear commitment. If a dog runs away from you in a dream, as another example, then you or someone else in the relationship is being elusive or may be showing signs they want out in real life. Even the type of dog you dream about plays a role in its meaning. Chihuahuas, for example, tend to be nervous and timid, in which case they would suggest someone else in the relationship may be feeling uncertain or nervous. And a puppy would indicate a new relationship that requires your loyalty.

The message of dog dreams: Time to look at your relationships and your behavior in them. Which relationship reminds you of the behavior of the dog in your dream? Are you or is someone around you being as loyal as a Labrador or as vicious as a pit bull? Your dog dreams will clue you in to the degree of loyalty within you or around you and whether it needs some obedience training or needs to be let loose.

CATS

Cats come in as the second most common dreamed-of animal, not only because they are a popular pet but also, like dogs, because of the characteristics they possess. Cats are known to be aloof and independent, not needing the constant attention and approval that dogs require. They also slink and purr and have a certain sexiness to them, which is why, when they slink into your dreams, they symbolize your own independent behavior or your feminine sexuality. Think about it, ladies, when you're feeling particularly sexy or when you are turning the flirtation up a notch, you instinctively slink and sway like a cat . . . perhaps you even put a bit of a purr in your voice. And men, you instinctively are drawn to this catlike behavior. And by the way, men, when you dream of a cat, it can stand in for the sexual energy or catlike behavior of a woman around you.

> I dreamed I found a sack of kittens in my house. They were alive but needed care. It scared me and saddened me at the same time. I woke up before I found out what happened to the cats.—Brenda, 64

LAURI: When we find something in a dream it means we have recently discovered something new in waking life. What recent real-life discovery have you made? Kittens, in a woman's dream, often symbolize her sexuality, her inner "sex kitten"! Are there any new developments in the ol' intimacy department? Or do you need to rediscover this part of you? Have you "sacked" this part of your life? Whatever the case, just as the kittens were alive and needed some TLC, so does your sexuality. Your dream is telling you it's time to nurture it.

BRENDA REPLIES: *I think you hit the nail on the head. We just found out my husband can't have sex anymore and I think it has bothered me more than I thought. I am going to work on building up my feelings about myself and know that I am okay. Amazing how dreams help us have better lives.*

Notice the emotions Brenda experienced in this dream, scared and sad. These are directly connected to her waking life emotions concerning her husband's condition; it scared and saddened her. Her waking mind decided to bag her sexuality, but her wiser dreaming mind said, "Whoa, hold on there!" This dream helped Brenda realize that her sexuality still needs attention. There is no reason her husband still can't pet her and make her purr. There is no reason she can't do it independently as well . . . ahem. It is also important that Brenda woke up before she let the cats out; this is because she had not opened up yet to her husband in waking life. Her dream is showing her, through a popular figure of speech, to "let the cat out of the bag," and to tell hubby what she needs.

While cats usually point to female sexual energy and behavior, as with any dream symbol, there could be a figure of speech hidden in your cat dream, like we saw in Brenda's. I say this many times throughout this book because it is so very true: If you can find a figure of speech in your dream then you have found the message!

The message of cat dreams: Your catlike behavior needs your attention. Have you or has someone around you been curious, aloof, exerting independence or cattiness? Or is there sexual energy that needs to be petted and rubbed, or collared and declawed? The condition and behavior of the cat in your dream will help you to better understand and manage your own catlike prowess to purrfection!

SNAKES

When I first began studying and researching dreams, I was surprised how often snakes slither into the collective dreamscape. All these years later it still amazes me how many snake dreams are reported to me daily, and the majority of them are rather frightening . . . with good reason. Snakes evoke fear in most of us, even to the point of phobia! They have sharp teeth, a demonic forked tongue. They can strike at lightning speed and inject you with their poison. Shudder.

Because of these widely feared characteristics, the dreaming mind often uses a snake to represent the dangerous, venomous behavior of yourself, or more often of someone close to you who is typically male. Yes, the phallic shape of the snake plays a big role in its meaning.

Interestingly enough, snakes in a dream can also signify the onset of emotional or physical healing. The connection can be found in the caduceus, the symbol for medicine, which is two snakes wrapped around a winged staff. We've grown accustomed to seeing this symbol on the side of ambulances, in pharmacies, and in hospitals, and therefore it is embedded in our subconscious that snakes equal healing. Shelley's dream below is a great example of the duality of the snake symbol.

I've had several dreams about snakes in the past few weeks. In the first dream I was trying to get away from a multicolored poisonous snake. It kept striking at me, but never bit me. A few nights ago, I dreamed I was riding my bike and was being pursued by a snake that kept trying to strike at my ankles.—Shelley, 42

LAURI: Is there a man in your life that is causing you problems? Or is there a physical or emotional issue you are trying to heal from? The bicycle in your second dream leads me to believe you are trying to balance both of these issues. The fact that the snake never bites is an indication that there is no resolution to either.

SHELLEY REPLIES: *Yes and yes! There are issues with my spouse and I am also trying to heal from health and emotional issues: narcolepsy, depression, arthritis, and a variety of other things that give me low energy. My husband would go out of his way to help a stranger. He seemed to have a kind, caring heart. However, things changed once we were married. I feel like he punishes me for being ill. He also uses my mother as a weapon against me. He will purposely aggravate and needle her until she is furious. Then, she takes her anger out on me. He finds this to be extremely entertaining. He walks away from me when I'm grieving the recent loss of my father. He threatens to get rid of our pets just to get a reaction out of me. He seems to enjoy upsetting me. I could continue on and on, but I think you get the idea.*

Wow. Shelley's dream is showing her the big picture of her husband's behavior. He is like "a snake in the grass" that repeatedly strikes at her with venomous words and actions. Shelley's dream is showing her his true colors, hence the colors on the snake in the first dream.

Believe it or not, despite the fearful element of a snake in a dream, a snake bite is a good sign that healing, whether it be emotional or physical, is underway. Think of a snake bite in a dream as an injection of healing serum. However, Shelley's healing has yet to begin because her husband's behavior only aggravates her illness and her illness only aggravates her husband. She is in a vicious, poisonous cycle, and her wise inner mind will continue to nag her with snake dreams until she puts a stop to it, one way or the other.

While Shelley's dreams contain both the vicious and healing elements of the snake archetype, many of our snake dreams are likely to contain only one or the other. The best way to determine which meaning applies to your snake dream is to look at the day before the dream, remember dreams are always connected to the previous day, and ask yourself if someone around you (particularly a male) was causing you to feel threatened in any way. If that doesn't seem to fit then ask yourself if there are any physical issues that need better attention. For example, last night I had a snake dream. Two cobras were fighting. They wound themselves around each other and then died. So I looked at yesterday. No men in my life—or even women in my life—were exhibiting venomous or low-down behavior, so then I looked to my health. Oh yes . . . I did talk to my health insurance company and found out that blood tests I need done will not be covered by my plan. Bingo! There's the health issue. Of course, the snakes wrapped around each other, resembling the caduceus, was also a big clue.

The message of snake dreams: Beware of your own or someone else's low-down, poisonous behavior. In order to improve your situation, you may want to work on your snake charming skills. In other words, it may be time to shed your own venomous behavior or the way you react to someone else's. You can't change others, only yourself. Alternately, it may be that you are telling yourself, through the dream, that it is time to heal an emotional wound or physical ailment. If the snake bites, healing is underway.

PREDATORY CATS

Tigers, lions, panthers, any sort of predatory animal that prowls into our dreams will symbolize our own predatory behavior, our ability to "hunt down" and catch what we want in life, whether it be a job, a relationship, a promotion, etc. Predatory cats are particularly popular in women's dreams because we gals identify with their feminine, feline nature.

> For the past few years, I have recurring dreams that tigers are chasing and hunting me down. I'm either finding ways to hide, run or just stay still, hoping they'll leave and won't hurt me.—Melissa, 24

LAURI: These tigers that have been appearing in your dreams are symbolic of your feminine prowess, your aggressive female energy, your inner huntress . . . your girl power! They are chasing you because you are afraid to acknowledge or use these qualities. Have you been running from a relationship? Have you been avoiding being more aggressive at work or in other areas of your life? You keep getting these dreams because you are running from your inner tigress instead of welcoming it. Your dream tigers don't want to harm you, they want to get your attention. They are a part of who you are. You are telling yourself, through these dreams, that it is time for you to be fierce and assertive. From time to time you may find your instincts telling you to go out there and hunt down what you want but instead you do what we see you doing in the dream, avoid the situation or do absolutely nothing. It's in you! Don't be afraid of it.

MELISSA REPLIES: *This has really helped. I'm constantly struggling with being more assertive. I've always been a quiet and shy person, but I think if I can imagine myself as a "tigress," I can be more assertive.*

This is one of the things I love about the dreaming mind. It gives us tailor-made visuals to work with so that we can improve ourselves and our lives. We don't always give ourselves enough credit or trust that we can actually accomplish just about any goal we set. But if we imagine ourselves as someone or something else, if we role-play, that often gives us just the right mind-set to "get 'er done"!

Aside from the hunter/stalker behavior that predatory cats point to, you also want to pay close attention to each cat's particular characteristics, as that can certainly play a role in the meaning. A lion, for example, is known for his courage and bravery, as well as his roar. Do you need to find your own courage in order to deal with a current situation? Or do you need to roar and make your voice heard? A cheetah is known for its speed. Are you moving too fast in some area or do you need to speed up?

And finally, like many dream symbols, certain predatory cats can also serve as a play on words. A lion can refer to "lying" and a cheetah can mean "cheater." "A leopard can't change his spots." Are you, or someone around you, unwilling to make changes right now?

The message of predatory cat dreams: You must have your sights set on something or someone. Time to channel your primal predatory instincts, rather than fear them. This will allow you to hunt, tackle, and capture what you hunger for in real life with agility and skill.

WOLVES

Remember the big bad wolf in all of those fairy tales when you were a kid? His ravenous, greedy behavior left quite an impression on all of our tender young minds. He gobbled up Little Red Riding Hood's Grandma, he blew down two of the little pigs' houses and he feasted on Peter's flock of sheep . . . and even Peter! To this day our dreams will borrow his image in order to let us know that we, or someone around us, are behaving in a less than cordial manner. And just as predatory felines tend to point more to those of the assertive female persuasion, wild predatory canines tend to point to aggressive men.

> I was outside. Down the road wolves were everywhere, knocking over trash cans and raising hell. The largest wolf came toward me. I started to run as he was snapping at my heels. I decided to turn and face him, narrowly dodging a bite to the ribs. I caught him by the neck, forced him down onto his back, and choked him. He went limp and I thought he was dead. I released his neck, and he sprang up again, attacking! I was able to force him down again. I knew the only way to make him stop was to break his neck. Snap! I let go of his head, and he lay motionless on the ground.—Nick, 18

LAURI: Wolves in dreams symbolize greed and ravenous desires, and are quite common in young men's dreams. Just as you battled the wolf in your dream, have you been battling your raging hormones? All those wolves are your wild behaviors you are trying to keep under control, the parts of you that instinctively want to go on a wild, predatory rampage (hunting girls perhaps), your party "animal" ways, and so on. This urge is not something you ponder, it's just there. This dream shows that you were successful in overcoming a recent urge, but there are many more waiting down the road for you, you healthy young man you! Not to worry, this was a good dream, showing you have control over your desires and temptations.

NICK REPLIES: *As you can imagine, there are plenty of things I can get into as a high school senior and it has been tough to fight that tempta-*

ion.

tion. *Your interpretation is very uplifting and I'm extremely relieved to hear that it is a fairly normal dream.*

Wolves in men's dreams usually reflect his own brooding, lustful, or raging Wolverine-like behaviors, and in a woman's dream the wolf is often reflective of a hungry wolflike man around her. Of course, this isn't written in stone. In my research, while the wolf has been linked to male greed and lust more often than not, it has been linked to female greed from time to time as well.

I woke up in the woods in the middle of the night and sat up. And about five feet from me there was a black wolf with red eyes, and it ran to me and just before it bites me, I woke up.—Nicole, 21

LAURI: Is there someone around you that you would describe as greedy or ravenous or perhaps even predatory? Someone you feel may be out to get you? Or is there a part of you that you would describe this way and that you fear may be starting to overpower you? The wolf's eyes are red. When the color red stands out in a dream, it is often a warning or red flag you are sending yourself that there is currently something you need to be made aware of. I'm guessing your dream is telling you that you need to be aware that someone has their sites set on you in some negative way. The fact that you "woke up" in the dream means you have had a recent realization . . . perhaps about this wolflike person in your life.

NICOLE REPLIES: *Yes, my mother. My fiancé and I just moved in with her and she keeps trying to drain every penny out of us. It makes it hard to save money. We give her money for bills and rent and food, and every month she raises our rent more and more. She keeps asking for more money but there is never food after that so she can buy beer and cigs and booze. Basically, I'm a bank.*

Nicole's dream is showing her that her mother has become a predator and she is the prey. While Nicole did recently wake up to this unfortunate reality, seeing her mother's behavior in the way her dream presented it to her really resonated with her. She informed me that she and her fiancé are working extra hard to get out of there as soon as possible.

I've shown you examples of how wolves in dreams most often illustrate selfish, lustful behavior. It is also important to keep in mind that the wolf can also have a spiritual element to it and is dreamed of often by those who have a strong connection to the Native American culture, as well as those who are natural spiritual leaders, Alphas, leading others in the pack down their own spiritual path.

The message of the wolf dream: Who's the big bad wolf in your world right now? Is it you? Or is it a self-indulgent person around you? Your dream may be alerting you to someone that is "a wolf in sheep's clothing." Aggressive wolves indicate this behavior is getting out of control and is beginning to threaten your sense of well-being. Friendly wolves suggest that either this behavior is agreeable with you or it is time to acknowledge your Alpha self and be a pack leader.

HORSES

When looking at a horse, it's hard not to respect it as the mighty and noble beast that it is. And when riding a horse, it's hard not to feel somewhat powerful and "high on your horse" as you control the muscular steed with just a tug of the reins or a gentle kick to its sides. Sturdiness, reliability, strength, and nobility; these characteristics will show up in our dreams in the form of a horse when circumstances call upon us to behave this way in waking life.

> I am sitting in my backyard at the patio table when I see my childhood horse, Blaze, sauntering up to the table. I tried to give him a carrot from my salad but he snorted and nudged me until I grabbed the reins and walked with him. We went down to the river and he showed me a campfire which had burned out. In the ashes was a small, tin box. He kept nudging me with his head. I picked up the box. Inside was a shining key. I walked back with Blaze and just when we get to my house, he disappeared. I searched my pockets for the key to make sure this had happened. I put the key in my hand and I was flying.—Virgil, 56

LAURI: Like the campfire, have you been "burned out"? Or has something in your life died down or been extinguished? Your horse is most likely your ability to get back into the saddle. His name may even play a role "Blaze," like the campfire blaze that is out. Maybe there was a burning passion for someone or something that you need to reignite. Your inner strength (your horse) is urging and nudging you to do so. I think your dream may be showing you that "the key" is to realize your ability to "rise above" the situation, get back in the saddle and get this project, idea, or passion "off the ground again."

VIRGIL REPLIES: *I am burned out from working hard, recovering from a bad accident, as well as worrying about the economy, my business, etc. Luckily, I am basically fully recovered from the accident, but it is something that "burns one out." I loved that horse with all my heart and so the "passions" of my life and my inner strength are certainly marshalling together to go on in new directions, so the "key" is figuring out a way to open up the future. Understanding this dream really made me think about my possibilities, such as making my travel business international rather than just local.*

Virgil's dream not only shows us how a horse represents strong, noble, determined behavior, but can also represent ones health. Remember the old saying, "I'm as healthy as a horse"? Yep, it certainly applies here. Virgil's dream was letting him know that he was healthy as a horse again after his accident and that it's time to stop worrying, saddle up, and persevere.

The message of horse dreams: Has life knocked you down? Whether your dream horse is ill, wounded, starving, or wild, it is your inner strength. Your dream is telling you that it is time to get back in the saddle, take the reins, and behave as the strong, trusted steed you know you are so you can gallop off into your future with your head held high.

BEARS

Bears have an interesting duality, in many respects. There is the idea of the cute, cuddly teddy bear like Winnie the Pooh, and then there is the reality of the dangerous angry mother bear; God forbid you get in between her and her cubs! They also have a seemingly dual life, one part spent active and in the wild foraging berries and salmon, and the other hidden in a cave, hibernating away the winter. In addition, there is a duality in the meaning behind a bear in a dream. The meaning of a bear is often based on its characteristics, like all animals in dreams. But just as often the meaning can be derived from a play on words. Keely's dream below shows us the duality of meaning in a dream bear.

There was a bear in my house. I escaped to my room but it was
trying to break through the door. I was yelling for help but none of
my family was helping me. The dream ended with the door slowly
breaking open.—Keely, 24

LAURI: Are you dealing with something that seems to be too much to *bear*? Or are you or someone you know emotionally inconsistent, sometimes behaving like a sweet teddy bear and at other times behaving like an angry mother bear? Whatever it is, your dream is showing you that, just as the bear is breaking into your home, this issue has become an intrusion into your otherwise peaceful state of mind.

KEELY REPLIES: *I do have too much to* bear. *That is awesome that my dream would do a play on words. There are emotional inconsistencies in my family. My mom and sister have always been hot and cold, and you never really know what you are going to get from either of them. However, recent events have really increased their emotional inconsistencies. My sister was raped and it has been really hard on our family. She is certainly going through more mood swings than normal. Some days she is her usual self, and other days she cries over anything, is cranky, etc. I have been the "psychologist" for both my mom and my sister but I really can't* bear *it all myself.*

Something vicious has clawed its way into Keely's life, causing the members of her family to behave with a great deal of emotional inconsistency; no doubt Keely has her ups and downs, too. But she can't *bear* the role of psychologist forever. The whole family needs to behave as the angry mother bear and attack this intrusion head-on and not hibernate and hope it eventually goes away. Unfortunately, rape creates more than just one victim. And this is precisely why Keely is calling for help in the dream, because she needs help, too. That is the answer this dream is giving her.

The message of bear dreams: You or someone around you is behaving in an inconsistent manner. Comparing the context of your dream to your current waking life situation will help you determine who it is as well as which bear they are behaving like at the moment: the grumpy, angry, overprotective mother bear or the cuddly teddy bear. In addition, there may be a situation that is an awful lot to *bear* right now.

BIRDS

Birds are distinct in their ability to fly, to soar high in the sky and be free of gravity. This is why birds are such a common dream creature; they represent our innate free will, our need to make our own choices, to live our lives the way we choose, and be free of what weighs us down. When we have the need to exercise our freedom and behave in the way we desire—not the way someone else desires of us—we get birds in our dreams.

> *I was walking down the street when a flock of birds, carrying a nest, crossed my path. I pushed the nest to get past it. One of the birds flew to me and pecked my hand. I held the bird like you would a dove. I decided to let it go but it flew back into my hand. I release it again but it came right back.—Nicole, 31*

LAURI: The birds represent your desire to be free and behave freely. The bigger the bird or the more birds, the bigger the need. The nest represents your home. Just as you pushed the nest to get by, are there any domestic/family issues you are "trying to get past"? The bird that comes over and pecks your hands is the part of you that wants to liberate yourself from things that are bringing you down. And it is pecking your hands because your hands are your ability to "handle" your affairs. Have you been feeling incapable lately? The bird keeps coming back because your inner mind doesn't want you to give up.

NICOLE REPLIES: *This interpretation was just what I needed! I've been living miserably in my childhood home providing for my grandmother, sister, and niece since 2001. I've been planning to move since last year but I need to get past some financial and family issues. I was losing hope until I got this interpretation. I've had a headache for about four days now and it went away as I was reading your interpretation. Clarity is a wonderful thing!!!*

Indeed it is! And nothing provides more clarity for your life than being able to understand your dreams. Nicole now understands that her need to behave freely still needs her attention. When anything or anyone in a dream is persistent, like the bird in this dream, it means *you* are nagging yourself about something you aren't giving enough attention to.

While the broader meaning for birds in dreams is about the need to be free, the type of bird can certainly have a specific message as well that you can easily apply to your life. A swan may be telling you to be gracious, a crow or black bird suggests you have a bad feeling about something, and a dove might be letting you know it is time to make peace with someone or something, for example.

The message of bird dreams: Something that will give you more freedom in your life is about to—or needs to—take flight. If the bird in your dream is ill or wounded, then you must give more attention to this issue. If the bird or birds are threatening to you, then ask yourself what you are afraid of in waking life. No matter

what the case, the bird in your dream is urging you to spread your
wings and soar.

BUGS AND SPIDERS

There's nothing more annoying than a roach scurrying across
the floor, or an army of ants invading the pantry, or a swarm of mos-
quitoes chomping on everyone at your barbecue. That is why,
when we get annoyed over situations or people that pester and in-
fest our mental space, we say that something or someone is really
"bugging" us. This is also when these little suckers will creep and
crawl into our dreams.

> *I've been dreaming of bugs a lot lately. Last night I dreamed that a lot
> of little bugs were crawling all over the place. There was one spider in
> particular I kept trying to kill but it never would die!—Tim, 28*

LAURI: This dream reflects that someone is behaving in a way that
is really "bugging" you. The more bugs there are, the more annoying issues there are. The spider specifically points to someone who is
deceitful and spins a web of lies. Is there anyone around you that
behaves this way? Or are you the one not being truthful lately? You
are unable to kill the spider because you aren't taking enough action
in your waking life to make this bothersome issue go away.

TIM REPLIES: *I'm in a custody battle with my wife and I haven't
seen my son in a while. She keeps making lame excuses as to why I can't
see him and I keep accepting them. Looks like I need to try harder to break
through her web of lies. Thank you.*

Tim obviously knew his wife had been lying to him, but that
apparently wasn't enough for him to do anything about it. But now

that his dream has presented her behavior to him in the form of a spider that won't die, Tim is able to understand that his wife's behavior has infested his peace of mind and he will now do what is necessary to untangle her web so he can see his son again.

The message of bug and spider dreams: Someone or something's got you "bugging out." It's time to channel your inner Orkin Man and "exterminate" the situation for good . . . or, like a bug infestation, this dream might come back!

We all have a menagerie of beasts that inhabit our dreams. Many cultures believe that the animals in our dreams are actually our animal spirit guides. I think that's a fine way to look at them because they certainly are there to guide you, and they certainly are a part of you and your own behavior. When an animal or creature appears in your dream, ask yourself what characteristics that particular animal is known for. Then ask yourself if your own instincts lately match the animal in your dream. Also, ask yourself how channeling those characteristics or behaviors could be helpful to you right now. Is it the playfulness of the dolphin? Or the wisdom of the owl? Take note of the behavior and condition of the animal because it mirrors your own current behavior or the behavior of someone around you. Does it need to be revived or rescued? Or does it need to be tamed and controlled? When you put on your zoologist hat and study the animals in your dream, you will find that they are teaching you how to keep your instincts sharp and your behavior at its best!

FASCINATING DREAM FACT: Elephants sleep standing up, but lie down when they enter REM sleep.

6

Body Dreams

YOUR EMOTIONAL AND
PSYCHOLOGICAL ABILITIES

Teeth, Hair, Eyes, Chest, Hands, Stomach,
Butt, Legs, Feet, Genitals, Pregnancy, and Birth

Your body is your temple. It is a wondrously complex machine composed of hundreds upon hundreds of movable and systematic parts, each with different functions but all working together perfectly and harmoniously so that you can live, think, communicate, experience, move, and do.

When your body is healthy and everything is in working order, you have unlimited potential to do just about anything you put your mind to: play basketball, go for a run, paint the bedroom, weed the garden, etc. But when a part of your body is afflicted, such as a broken leg or loss of sight, you become limited and your ability to do becomes less.

Your dream body also represents your ability to perform, not your physical ability, but rather your mental and emotional ability, such as your ability to be compassionate, to be a good listener, to be stubborn, or to change your mind, etc. All the different parts of your dream body represent all your different mental and emotional parts. Your dreaming mind will give form to your mental and emotional abilities so you can better understand how well or how poorly you are using them. So when a part of your dream body is afflicted at night, odds are that you are suffering from an emotional or psychological limitation or flaw during the day.

TEETH

The most common affliction our dream bodies suffer is that of losing teeth or cracked and crumbly teeth. Were this a problem with your waking physical body, you'd probably want to get thyself to the dentist ASAP! But when your teeth are a problem in your dreams, you're better off seeing a communications expert. To the dreaming mind, your teeth, as well as any part of your mouth, are symbolic of your words. Paying attention to your teeth dreams helps you to monitor and improve the way you communicate.

> *I have a dream several times a year that deals with my teeth getting loose and falling out. I keep spitting them out, but I never seem to run out of teeth.—Anna-Marie, 46*

LAURI: Loose teeth in dreams are often connected to loose speech in waking life. Your teeth dreams are recurring so I'll bet the farm you have a recurring behavior pattern of speaking without thinking first, or gossiping or perhaps saying too much. Take heart! You are in good company with Halle Berry. She gets this dream, too. All those teeth that keep on coming out are the words that keep on coming out that should have remained in your mouth permanently, like your real-life teeth. Your dreams are trying to show you that you must be careful about what comes out of your mouth because once it is out, like a tooth, you can't put it back in.

ANNA-MARIE REPLIES: *As much as I hate to admit it, you are 100 percent correct. I tend to spread gossip and I give away too much information. For so long I was the quiet one in the group and never opened my mouth, until I met my husband. He is very outgoing so I have had to get used to being around lots of people when we are out. I have started to talk more and I guess my bad habits started because I felt like I had to have something to say.*

Now that Anna-Marie understands this dream, she can be more cautious of what she allows out of her mouth at future social gatherings. The more aware she is of this behavior, the more she will work to curtail it, and once she has mastered the fine art of polite conversation, the dreams will stop.

The opposite end of the spectrum of loose speech is weak or no speech. This is where the crumbly or cracked and broken teeth dreams come in to play, because when something cracks or crumbles it is a sign of weakness.

I have dreams of my teeth crumbling into pieces. I hold my hand to my mouth so my teeth don't fall out.—Pauline, 50

LAURI: Your recurring crumbly teeth dreams most likely reflect recurring concern over your inability to speak up about something or your inability to make your point. Not that you are unable to speak up, but more that you lack the confidence in your ability. You hold in what you would like or need to say, just as you hold in your teeth in the dreams. Do you find that when there is personal drama in your life you tend to hold back? Do you also avoid confrontations?

PAULINE REPLIES: *I had goose bumps when I was reading your analysis. Pretty much my whole life I wished I had the ability to speak out and let my voice be heard. I definitely lack confidence in myself and I have a hard time expressing my feelings. My whole adult life I avoided confrontation, especially with my ex-husband, probably because I wanted peace in my life. When I was growing up my parents argued all the time and I didn't want to repeat their mistakes.*

Pauline's dream is helping her by allowing her to see her words in the form of crumbly teeth. No one wants to possess something that is weak and falling apart because it is rendered useless. Keeping this image in mind should help Pauline to work on strengthening her confidence and her words, because words are very useful and powerful tools when they are strong.

Trying to pull an endless wad of gum, string, or hair out of your mouth is another common dream for folks who lack the confidence to speak up. Remember, lips, tongue, teeth, and the throat all give you the ability to use your voice and when they are afflicted in a dream, it is a good indication your ability to communicate is limited or flawed in waking life.

The message of teeth dreams: Your dreaming mind is alerting you to a problem with your ability to communicate. You've either recently misspoken, said more than you ought to have, or simply didn't speak up at all when you knew you should. The loss of teeth in waking life would make you worry about your looks the same way bad communication might make you worry about how you appear to others. Just as you polish those pearly whites for aesthetics, polishing up your communication skills will make you shine, too.

HAIR

Shining, gleaming, steaming, flaxen, waxen. It can be cut short, straightened out, tangled, wild, twisted, calm, colored, and even lost. Hair is the one part of your body that you can easily and continually change. The same can be said of your thoughts, which is why your hair, to your dreaming mind, is your ability to change and improve your thoughts, ideas, plans, and beliefs.

The state of your hair in your dreams reflects the current state of your thoughts. Having long, luxurious hair points to an abundance of ideas or an extended amount of thought you are giving to something or someone. Tangled hair means confusion. Having things stuck in your hair indicates an inability to get something off your mind. Getting a new hairdo is connected to changing your mind. Losing your hair suggests you are out of ideas as to what to do about something or someone or perhaps a lack of belief. But the most common hair dream of all is of getting it cut.

In real life I have long brown hair but lately I keep dreaming that I have cut my hair short and bleached it. I do not think I would ever really do that to my hair so why do I keep having this dream?—Kellie, 28

LAURI: Hair represents your thoughts and ideas because, like hair, they sprout from your head. Cutting your hair in a dream is a good indication that there is some idea or mind-set that has gone on for too long that you need to cut short. Have you been depressed or angry? I ask because the blonde suggests that you really oughta "lighten up"!

KELLIE REPLIES: *That is amazing how my dream is completely in step with what is going on in my life. I gave birth to a beautiful baby girl three months ago and have been suffering from postpartum depression. I had enough of the dark thoughts and have started seeking out a therapist.*

Cutting hair is such a commonly dreamed event because the deep inner mind does not like being stuck in a mind-set, even though we allow ourselves to do just that all too often. We hold grudges, we dwell on the past, we close our minds. Thoughts are meant to flow and change. When a negative or unhealthy thought goes on for too long, as in Kellie's case, the dreaming mind will chop off our locks to let us know; enough already!

The message of hair dreams: Time to closely examine the thoughts that are sprouting from your mind. The style and condition of the hair in your dream is connected to your current thoughts, ideas, and beliefs. Are your current thoughts helpful to you or are they harmful? Are they currently enhancing you as a new stylish do would or are they taking away from you and your quality of life like a bad hair day? As Willie Nelson, a famous crooner known for his hair once said, "When you replace negative thoughts with positive ones, you'll start having positive results."

EYES

While the eyes of your physical body give you the ability to see, the eyes of your dream body represent your ability to know, to understand: "I *see* what you mean." The eyes of your physical body allow you to physically focus on an object, while the eyes of your dream body represent your ability to mentally "focus" on a goal or task. The eyes of your physical body also give you the ability to view what surrounds you, while the eyes of your dream body represent your point of view, your opinion, and your ability to change it.

In dreams, your eyes can suffer an array of afflictions because, in waking life, we all have an array of issues or behaviors that keep us from our focus, that sway our opinion, or that keep us from opening our psychological eyes to see what is really going on. The most common affliction our dream eyes suffer is that of blurry vision.

I have a reoccurring dream that I am trying to drive down the road but everything is so blurry. I cannot focus on anything. What does this mean?—Lauren, 25

LAURI: This dream comes to you whenever you are not "focusing" enough on a particular issue in your life. Since you are always driving in these dreams, my guess is that it is your career path. Something is hindering your "drive" and motivation. These dreams are a constant reminder you are offering yourself that you need to give this the proper attention and focus it deserves so you can go as far as this road will take you.

LAUREN REPLIES: *That interpretation makes great sense! I am going through a divorce. My soon-to-be ex finally admitted he was an alcoholic. Having to deal with his problem daily has kept me from focusing on a career I love. I finally realize that I do not need him to hold me back, or try to hurt things that I have worked so hard for.*

Notice how Lauren says in her dream report, "I cannot focus on anything." That is the message her dreaming mind wanted to convey. Lauren's career path, if not her whole life, had been blurred by her husband's alcoholism. She was so focused on him that she could no longer see her career goals, or any goals, that she originally chose for herself.

Another common eye affliction dream that gets reported to me on a continual basis is the one where the dreamer cannot open his or her eyes.

> *I used to have this recurring dream that I could not open my eyes. In most of the dreams I am in bed waking up but can't get my eyes open to save my life! Other times I'll be driving and can't get my eyes open, or I'll be at the dog park with my husband and our dog and I'll hear Lucky, our dog, growling at another dog and I can't open my eyes to see what's going on or stop it.—Becka, 36*

LAURI: When this dream was going on, can you think of anything that you were "turning a blind eye" toward? Was there something you knew was going on or suspected was going on but you did not want to open your eyes to the reality of it? Or were you in a tough situation that you, at the time, could not "see" how you were going to get through it? In a lot of the dreams you are waking up. This is because your wiser inner self was hoping you would "wake up" to reality. I hate to say it but the dog park and your angry dog leads me to believe there was a loyalty issue to which you decided to close your eyes. The dreams have since stopped so the issue must now be over.

BECKA REPLIES: *You hated to say it and I hate to admit it but there was a loyalty issue. During that time my husband was cheating on me with a coworker. I did have my suspicions because he was always bringing her up in conversation and there were plenty of times he came home an hour or so later than he should have. I was so afraid to face reality that I did not share my concerns with anyone. This went on for a while until my husband finally confessed because he wanted out of the marriage so he could be with her. I wish I had been able to understand this dream sooner. I would not have prolonged that painful situation for as long as I did.*

The message of eye dreams: It is always good to have clear goals, clear focus, a clear point of view, and a clear awareness of what is going on around you. If your eyes are not in working order in your dreams then you are losing your focus or turning a blind eye toward reality in waking life. Don't lose sight of the vision you have for yourself. Your dreams don't want you to go through life with blinders on.

Hindsight should not be the only perspective that is twenty-twenty.

CHEST

In your physical body, the chest contains and protects the body's most vital and precious organ, the heart. A treasure chest also holds and protects what is valuable and precious. Therefore, the chest of your dream body represents your ability to protect your feelings. When the chest is wounded or brought to attention in some manner in your dreams, it indicates that you may be suffering from heartache in waking life.

> *I dreamed that I was getting a receipt (from a grocery store) surgically removed from my chest. I woke up from the pain and actually thought I was getting stabbed!—Bobby, 35*

LAURI: The chest is where the heart is and often is connected to your feelings in waking life. The receipt most likely represents an emotional price you have paid or perhaps is a pun on "checking out." You are having it surgically removed because your inner dreaming mind feels there is an idea or behavior that needs to be removed in order to mend a relationship or a certain situation. It may also be a pun on "getting something off your chest." Anything you need to open up about? The pain you feel upon waking is connected to the emotional pain you hold inside . . . that or you are afraid it will be painful to say what needs to be said.

BOBBY REPLIES: *My wife and I are mending our relationship. We almost got divorced a few months ago. I love her very much but no matter what I say, or how I say it, she doesn't seem to care or want to comprehend. Basically, I was packing my bags and told her she could have everything, including my bank accounts. I didn't care. I wanted out because I could not get through to her anymore. It was then she finally realized what was going on and has been changing for the better ever since.*

What I find the most interesting about Bobby's dream is the physical pain he felt upon waking. When we harbor emotional pain long enough, it will begin to manifest itself into physical pain in our dreams. We don't always realize that emotional pain needs to be treated just as seriously as physical pain. Bobby got the message. So he opened up and got the fact that he was ready to leave, "off his chest." And out of that honesty, healing began . . . and a marriage was saved!

The message of chest dreams: Your chest is your ability to protect your feelings as well as your ability to be honest. When your chest is brought to attention in your dreams, ask yourself if your emotional armor is damaged. Are your feelings in danger? Or is it time to be honest? Remember, honesty is the seed of emotional health.

HANDS

Your hands allow you to grasp, handle, and manipulate an object. They are the most active part of your body and without them there wouldn't be much you could do. This is exactly what they are to your dream body: your ability to do, your ability to "handle" the many issues with which life presents you. When something is wrong with your hands in a dream, you are very likely having difficulty with the can-do attitude in waking life.

> *In my dreams I keep getting lost in an unfamiliar house, and I have no hands. I can't open the door to leave and can't interact with anything inside.—Tyler, 25*

LAURI: The house is unfamiliar to you because you are in a situation in life that is unfamiliar, that doesn't feel comfortable anymore, and that you now want out of. You are also unable to interact with anyone because you may not be communicating your concern in waking life. Your hands are missing because you can no longer handle the issue. Your dreaming mind is most likely telling you to let it go.

TYLER REPLIES: *I am in the middle of a divorce. We were young and didn't fully understand things until we got married for two years. I do feel alone because I have very few people to talk to. This makes sense.*

Tyler's dream is a brutally honest portrayal of how he was feeling about his marriage. Tyler could no longer handle the situation; therefore his dream body had no hands. His house no longer felt like home, so in the dream it was portrayed as an unfamiliar house. Tyler's dream was showing him that he needed to get out.

The message of hand dreams: Odds are you have a lot on your plate right now or a tough situation to handle. The state of your hands in your dream is a direct reflection of your confidence in your waking life's ability to handle the issue. Swollen or huge hands suggest over-eagerness or overconfidence. Bleeding hands mean you are being too much of a helping hand to others and are not getting enough back. A hole in your hand is showing you that you can indeed handle the issue but your confidence is missing. Deformed hands may be a message that you are handling things all wrong and are messing it up. No hands at all are a good indication it's time to let go. When you listen to what your hands are telling you in your dream, you'll be able to give yourself a hand in waking life.

STOMACH

Your stomach breaks down and digests food so it can more easily nourish your body. If the stomach takes in something it cannot tolerate, it immediately purges itself of the offending matter. In the same way, the stomach area of your dream body symbolizes your ability to digest information, decide if it is healthy or not, and whether you can tolerate it or not.

> *I dreamed I was lying in bed and staring at my stomach. It turned into gooey slime and spread all over my whole body. My husband was laughing and grabbing gobs of me and wondering if he could use my goo like Silly Putty and bounced it off the walls. I was mildly curious, too, so I started slopping pieces of myself onto this novel I have on my bedside table. And yeah, it worked; then I could stretch the words and play with them . . . help me!—Suzanne, 38*

LAURI: When a woman dreams of her stomach she must first see if she can connect it to any weight or body image issues. If this is not the case with you, then the stomach is more about your ability to stomach or tolerate a waking life issue. Like the slime / Silly Putty in your dream, have you bounced back after a yucky slimy time in your life? Can you connect the novel on your bedside to what is going on in your life or within you?

SUZANNE REPLIES: *I actually have lost a lot of weight recently. Also, my husband had an affair a few years ago and I am working on bouncing back from that. The book on my bedside is about a woman being married to the wrong man and she runs off with someone else in the end. I want things to be good and sedate for my kids. We're all happy and I tell myself that I don't care, but maybe . . . according to my dream, I do. Thanks for your insight.*

Like the Silly Putty in Suzanne's dream, she is reshaping her body and her thoughts so she can stomach the past. Even though the dream was unnerving and the affair was hard to swallow, this dream is showing Suzanne that she is indeed bouncing back.

The message of stomach dreams: You've been fed some information recently. What happens to your stomach in your dream is showing you how healthy or how harmful this information or this issue is for you, as well as your ability to tolerate it. The more severe the affliction in the dream the more harmful the waking life information is to you. Just like your physical stomach, your ability to tolerate something or someone can only last so long before a serious purging must take place.

BUTT
Thankfully, like other body parts, it is not necessarily the function of the butt that plays a role in its meaning as much as the lo-

cation of the butt! The butt of your dream body is actually all about your ability to put an issue, a grudge, a problem, or a phase of life "behind" you.

> *I dreamed I was standing at a locker organizing my shoes. I felt it was time I stopped taking up two wall lockers and downsize my stuff into one. As I was bending over these men were staring at my apparently, very toned butt! I actually woke up feeling turned on by the fact that these men were so in love with my butt!—Kristen, 44*

LAURI: Organizing your shoes suggest that you are deciding what steps to take next in your life or in a particular situation. Your toned butt represents all the hard work that is "behind" you that you ought to be proud of. The two lockers are two identities you have been so used to occupying: "Kristen" and "Mom" perhaps? In what way are you downsizing your identity? Being turned on by the attention in the dream is connected to pride in yourself in waking life, so you go, girl!

KRISTEN REPLIES: *Yes, this all makes sense. I have been raising my kids for the last eighteen years. I'm having a hard time deciding who I am now that I no longer need to be a stay-at-home mom. There are so many choices available to me. It is also dawning on me about how much work I've done in the raising of my kids, and how I actually did a good job!*

This dream not only marks the ending of a phase of life for Kristen, it mirrors her positive healthy attitude and we see that in the form of her nicely toned derriere! Instead of dwelling on the empty nest, she is admiring all her hard work that resulted in well-rounded, responsible young adults.

The message of butt dreams: Time to move on and look forward, not back. Like your butt, the past is meant to be behind you.

LEGS

Whether your legs are long and sinewy or short and stubby, they offer you the ability to stand up and move forward. The same is true for the legs of your dream body. They represent your ability to stand up for yourself, move forward in life or in a particular situation, and move on from the past. But when your legs aren't working in a dream, or they are heavy or wounded in some way, then there is a serious lack of movement in some area of your waking life.

> *I had a dream that I had an open hole on my outer right thigh and could fit my hand inside. It wasn't bloody or gross, but I could touch my bone.—JoAnne, 56*

LAURI: The hole suggests that you feel something is missing in your life or missing from your own self, your behavior, or your personality. Are you having a hard time moving forward with something? Is your ability to stand up for yourself not quite all that it should be? The fact that it is your right leg indicates that you want to do the "right" thing, but are missing a substantial amount of inner strength or "muscle" to do so.

JOANNE REPLIES: *This makes perfect sense! I have struggled with weight issues my whole life and recently have felt the physical consequences of not taking care of myself. I want to start eating better and exercising, but I'm having a really difficult time even starting and do feel there is something in me that is lacking the strength to move forward in this direction. Bringing it to my attention in this manner is great. I think the more I keep that in front of me, the better.*

JoAnne's dream is showing her that her lack of conviction is like having a piece of her own body missing. Seeing her lack of strength presented this way will help her to work harder so she can move forward to that goal of a healthier body.

The message of leg dreams: You weren't put on this earth to stay in one place. God gave you legs so you could move forward physically and psychological legs so you can move toward your goals. The only one that can make those legs move is you. To quote author and abolitionist Frederick Douglass, "I prayed for twenty years but received no answer until I prayed with my legs."

FEET

In order for your legs to get you where you want to go, your feet must first take steps. And in order for you to reach your goals, *you* must first take the appropriate steps, one at a time, to get there. This is what your feet represent in dreams; your ability to take steps in the right direction or take something one step at a time, as well as your ability to stand firm in your decisions and opinions.

> *I dreamed that I was at a football game, in the front row. People were walking in the aisle in front of me inspecting my feet.—Michael, 47*

LAURI: The people inspecting your feet in the dream are the many parts of you that are trying to figure something out in real life. Are you wondering if you are taking the right "steps" toward figuring out a particular issue? The football game likely represents your frame of mind in that you are ready to "tackle" this once and for all.

MICHAEL REPLIES: *Interesting. I have been suffering from severe headaches, back pain, etc. My neurologist is trying to figure out what is causing it and says I am qualified for disability, and will assist me in obtaining it. This is a life-changing decision and I'm dreaming about it by having a bunch of strangers inspect my feet?*

Michael's dream shows us the many layers of meaning just one symbol can hold. His feet in this dream not only imply that he is trying to figure out if disability is the right *step* to take, but that he is also trying to figure out where he *stands* on this issue. Going on disability means Michael will no longer be able to stand on his own financially. Going from being financially self-sufficient to having to have government assistance is a big step, but is it a step in the right direction? Michael will have to keep dreaming on this one.

The message of feet dreams: Your dreaming mind wants you to either stand up for yourself or get going on a decision or toward a goal. The state of your feet in the dream is connected to how well or how poorly you are standing up for yourself, or how well or poorly your progress is going. But remember, as you move forward toward those aspirations to watch your step, because each one you take is a lesson learned.

GENITALS

Sigmund Freud had a lot to say about our nether regions in dreams. In fact, he was so preoccupied with genitalia that he believed just about everything from a suitcase to a landscape in a dream was in some way associated with the vagina. The truth is, much to Freud's chagrin, that even when we do dream about our genitals, it's not really about them at all.

In the waking world, a penis is what makes a man physically a man and a vagina is what makes a woman physically a woman. But in the dream world your body can often sport the wrong equipment, which can be quite shocking! As you've gathered by now, dreaming about specific body parts is rarely about that particular organ or appendage but rather about an emotional or mental ability that particular part represents. No matter your gender in waking life, a penis is your ability to man up, be assertive, and *stand up* (ahem) for yourself; it represents all the qualities associated with male energy. A vagina is your ability to be sensitive, a good listener, a nurturer, and creative: it represents all the qualities associated with female energy.

> *I dreamed that a client of mine was undressing to change for yoga class, and I saw that she had an erect penis. I told her I thought she was a woman. She said she was both, really, and trying to decide which she wanted to be. She then jumped into a swimming pool. I rarely dream of sexual issues and this was really weird!—Connie, 45*

LAURI: Don't let this dream cause you to feel awkward around your client. It's merely symbolic of something that is going on with her, or more likely, going on with you. Her penis was erect in the dream, which is your ability to exhibit male energy and "stand up" for yourself in some way. Yoga is about being flexible, yet the erect penis is about being firm and rigid. Are you having a "hard" time deciding which way to be, just as the client was having a hard time deciding which gender to be in the dream? Jumping in the pool implies that, despite the indecision, you are ready to "dive right in" and handle your business.

CONNIE REPLIES: *I think the dream is about me. I am facing some challenges in my work lately, and I am trying to change a world paradigm—not a simple task. I can handle it in different ways; I am choosing a gentle, quiet approach rather than a bold, confrontational one, hence trying to decide which gender is better. I am not giving up or giving in, so jumping in would be appropriate. Thanks for helping me to see it as more than just a weird sex dream.*

Even though in Connie's dream, the penis belonged to someone else, it still is representative of her own male energy; remember, everyone in your dream is usually a representation of some part of you. Connie's dream is a wonderful example of how we all have inner male and inner female "parts" to our personality. In Connie's situation, she is using a balance of both of these energies by *gently* (the female part) approaching those who can help make the changes she wants, all while remaining *persistent* (the male part). And so we see this nice balance in the form of a hermaphrodite!

Genital dreams don't always involve gender bending. Among other things, genitals can also be detachable, which would be connected to your ability to easily pick and choose which energy to utilize at any given time. They can be oversized, which would suggest an overabundance of that energy, i.e., being overly sensitive or overly aggressive. They can also be missing altogether, which would indicate a lack of sensitivity or a lack of assertiveness, for example.

The message of genital dreams: You have the ability to play the caring nurturer and the assertive pusher. The condition of the genitals in your dream, or who is sporting them, will let you know which gender role you are currently displaying. Ask yourself how well this part is working for you right now. If it's not helping your current circumstances, it may be time to play a little psychological gender bending.

PREGNANCY AND BIRTH

When the body is pregnant, it is working hard to build a new life that is precious and full of possibilities. When the dream body is pregnant, it reflects your ability to work hard and create a new life for yourself. That is, of course, if you are dreaming you are pregnant and are neither actually pregnant nor trying to be.

> *In June of this year, my husband passed away. Last night I dreamed that I was pregnant and gave birth to a son. I didn't feel any pain giving birth. I saw the baby come out with his limbs all folded up. I marveled at how absolutely perfect he was! He seemed to glow! The funny thing was that, after unwrapping himself, he got up and walked into the kitchen.—Lynn, 55*

LAURI: Your dream is interesting and speaks volumes about your healing process. Despite being in grief, you have managed to "give birth" to something new and precious in your life. It could be a new project, idea, or relationship, but my bet is that it is a new you! Sometimes in life we have to suffer greatly in order to find ourselves. That baby represents the *new you* that now can receive all your time and attention in order to grow and develop into something wonderful. The baby is glowing because your dreaming mind is "illuminating" the fact that you have this whole new life to look forward to. And this new you is not only "unfolding" before your very eyes but is also hungry for your attention and emotional nourishment, which is why he walks right into the kitchen!

LYNN REPLIES: *I have been thinking about going to a conference called "Celebrate Your Life" in Arizona. I finally received some life insurance money in the mail, so I think I'll go. You are correct that I am giving birth to a new me. I do plan to make time to be attentive to my own needs and to "nourish" my spirit as well.*

Lynn's dream is showing her that her new life is here, since she gave birth in the dream. Now, she needs to give it the focus and care that one would give a newborn so that she can continue to grow and reach her full potential. When something is in the works in waking life, that is when the dream involves only pregnancy rather than birth. In my research, I've found that one of the most common reasons a woman (and yes, sometimes even a man) will dream of being pregnant is when she is in school working toward a degree. In this case, it is the knowledge that is growing and developing inside of her that will eventual give birth to a new life as a respected professional with some letters behind her name.

The message of pregnancy and birth dreams: A wonderful idea has been conceived and you are now in the process of bringing it to life. How far along you are in the dream is connected to how far along you are with this growing and developing issue. If you have given birth your hard work has paid off but that does not mean you are done. It is only the ending of one chapter so a new one can begin.

There are so many parts to the physical body and the dream body that I could not possibly cover them all in this chapter, but hopefully you now have a good grasp of how to understand the language of your dream body. Remember, whenever a part of your body is brought to attention in your dream, it is rarely about that actual body part but rather the emotional or psychological part it represents. Take a good look at what the physical part you dreamed about is capable of and then try to associate that ability to an inner mental ability. A knee, for example, gives you the physical ability to bend and be flexible; therefore, the knee of your dream body likely represents your mental ability to be flexible with your schedule, to bend to others' needs, to not be so rigid or unwilling to make any changes.

You have a whole other body you inhabit when you dream, and it can really be put through the wringer. We don't often give credence to something that takes from us or afflicts us emotionally. But when something takes from us physically, such as our back going out or breaking a limb, boy, do we pay attention! And we do whatever we can to correct and heal it. This is why we'll often dream of something bad happening to our body, because the wise dreaming mind knows that if we see our emotional body as a physical thing, we can better understand how serious emotional wounds and afflictions really are, and hopefully, we'll do what is necessary to correct and heal that as well. Look at your body dreams as an X-ray that allows you to peer deep into yourself in order to get a clearer, more descriptive picture of how functional or dysfunctional, healthy or broken all your emotional and psychological parts are.

....

FASCINATING DREAM FACT: The hammer, anvil, and stirrup, the tiny bones in the inner ear, vibrate during REM sleep. This is believed to contribute to the ringing, buzzing, whispering, or crashing sound that is sometimes heard upon waking.

7

House and Home Dreams

YOUR SELF-IMAGE AND
YOUR STATE OF MIND

**House in Disrepair, Mansion or Castle,
Trailer, Haunted House, Moving, Attic, Basement,
Kitchen, Bedroom, Bathroom**

"Home sweet home." "Home is where the heart is." "There's no place like home." "A man's home is his castle." You get the idea. Our homes are our personal worlds; they are the only place where we can be completely uninhibited, completely comfortable, and completely ourselves. Our homes are also an extension of our selves. They say a lot about us, from the furnishings in each room to the pictures on the walls. Walk through a stranger's home and you get a pretty good idea of who they are and how they live.

Our dream homes say a lot about us, too, probably more than

any other dream symbol. Your home in your dream, whether it is your actual home or an unfamiliar home, is also reflective of you. It is everything about you and how you live. The style of the home, the condition of the home, what happens in the home, even the rooms in the home are connected to you and how you feel about yourself as well as what is going on inside the psyche that your body houses. The dreaming mind uses the home in order to show you yourself and your state of mind in the form of a physical structure so you can better understand your own personality construct, thought construct, and even body construct. Look at your house dreams as an honest blueprint of your current self image.

HOUSE IN DISREPAIR

An immaculate, comfortable, welcoming home in a dream is always a good sign that the dreamer is happy with himself or herself and that the inner mind is clean of any negativity or frustration, at the time of the dream anyway. However, when the home is in a state of disrepair, the dreamer ought to look carefully at any physical or emotional issues that are in need of repair and improvement.

> I constantly dream of having to redo a house I am about to move into. It is old and the walls are mildewed and the furniture is old and dusty, covered in sheets, sometimes decayed even. I am usually walking through the house, kind of afraid, telling whoever I am with about all the work that needs to be done. Oftentimes, the house has secret rooms and/or bizarre staircases that wind all over the place and lead to nowhere.—Crissy, 35

LAURI: You are probably trying to move on from something but aren't being terribly successful at it. The house is old because this is an old issue in your life. The mildew and dust point to something in your life that has been neglected. Did you ever feel neglected in your life? In your childhood? The items covered in sheets represent memories you have covered up because you don't want to deal with them. The secret rooms may even be about things in your life that you don't want others to know. The staircases that lead nowhere show us that you have not been able to progress past these issues and, to some degree, they have kept you trapped emotionally. You keep getting this dream because your inner mind wants to move on from it. Are you holding on to any resentment or anger from the past? The dreams can't move forward until you move forward.

CRISSY REPLIES: *This was very helpful. I know that I do have issues that need to be dealt with. I actually was neglected a good bit as a child. I do harbor resentment toward my mother. The reason I can't deal with it is because she is mentally ill and can't be held responsible for the way things happened in my childhood. I have been in therapy before, but sometimes these issues are just overwhelming to confront. I guess it is emotional laziness on my part. Time to revisit my therapist.*

Crissy's inner mind sometimes sees herself as an old, rotting house because she has allowed her childhood issues to reside within her psyche untouched, uncleansed, and unrepaired for too long. Her dream clearly illustrates how issues from long ago never go away; they will always remain housed within the mind, collecting dust, cobwebs, and even growing mold unless they are dealt with properly. Once Crissy goes back to therapy and starts working on uncovering those memories and improving her psychological interior, her dream houses will change and become more livable.

The message of house in disrepair dreams: Whether it is your physical state or your emotional or psychological state, your inner mind is showing you that you have not been maintaining yourself properly. Time to channel your inner Bob Vila because you've got some fixing up to do!

MANSION OR CASTLE

Marbled halls, soaring cathedral ceilings, servants quarters, *sigh*. I've been the proud owner of such lavish dwellings a number of times . . . and then I wake up. Oh well. Most of us will never reside in such opulence, in the waking world anyway. But if you're lucky enough to live in the lap of luxury in your dreams then you're likely to be far wealthier than those that actually do own such an affluent and envious abode, wealthier in spirit that is.

I dreamed I was inside a huge mansion with spacious rooms and a magnificent view of the ocean. Each window had gauze curtains that blew inside the room with the breeze. I ended up with a man in a fur vest, sitting at a massive table. Bowls of fruit and piles of spareribs and turkey legs were on the table. We ate and he toasted me with wine. I looked down and my feet were bare and my robe comfortable and I was beautiful.—Valerie, 50

LAURI: My, my, what a lovely dream! The mansion is a reflection of yourself. You must feel quite good about yourself and have grand ideas with lots of room to grow intellectually, spiritually, or perhaps even career-wise, hence the spacious rooms. The breeze is an important element to this dream, believe it or not. Wind in dreams is connected to changes that are blowing through your life, the winds of change so to speak. A breeze, however, suggests the changes are kind and gentle and are a "breeze" for you to handle.

Let's talk about the man with the vest. He is likely your male side, that part of you that has had a "vested" interest in being

assertive and taking action on this situation. All the food shows us
that your desires, your hungers are being fed. You are enjoying the
fruits of your labor, perhaps with even some to "spare," hence the
spareribs! You are toasting yourself for a job well done!! Interesting
that your feet are bare. Have you "bared" your "sole" to someone
recently? From this dream, it seems all is well!

VALERIE REPLIES: *You are right on. I have been baring my soul in
all kinds of ways, to friends, on paper, and so on. This has been an amazing career time for me with many options. I am a writer and much of the
work I have done before, the "fruits" of my labors, are beginning to blos-
som indeed and there are plenty of opportunities for me, enough to spare.
My youngest just went off to college and my older children are doing wonderfully. The winds of change are blowing in my life.*

   Valerie has reached a place in her mind where she is rich in
spirit because of the life and career she has built, and it is reflected
beautifully in the psychological structure her dream has built.
   Mansions and castles are wonderfully positive dream symbols
as they mirror a very positive self-image. However, if the mansion
or castle is dark, empty, cold, or foreboding, then you may have
an enormous amount of depression or negativity within you. Remember, the bigger something is in a dream, the bigger the waking life issue it is connected to.

The message of mansion and castle dreams: Your inner self is a pal-
ace rich in character, talent, and ideas. While you may not actually be living the *Lifestyles of the Rich and Famous,* your inner life is
certainly something Robin Leach would be proud of!

TRAILER

A trailer is a very small home and is not very sturdy as it is not built on a foundation and is vulnerable in extreme weather. It is the opposite of the lap of luxury and opulence. Unless you live in a trailer, dreaming that your home is a trailer is a sign that you are either feeling the need to simplify or you are feeling unstable and less than you used to be, depending on the context of the dream and the condition of the trailer, of course.

> I had a dream that we had moved into a trailer. When we got there the paint on the walls was all wrinkly and the doors were all destroyed. What does this mean?—Kyla, 44

LAURI: Have you moved into a lesser state of mind? Are you not feeling as good about yourself as you used to? Like the trailer, are you rundown? What in yourself or what in your life seems similar to the run-down trailer? Your dream is showing you yourself in the form of a run-down trailer so you can better understand your current state of mind. You might want to consider moving into a better mind-set. We are shaped by our thoughts; we become what we think. Buddha said that, I believe.

KYLA REPLIES: *Makes sense. There's a lot going on. I just lost my job after working twenty-five-plus years so I am feeling low about that. My mom is moving in with me because she can't take care of herself anymore, so I am taking care of everything. I guess that can make anyone run down. Thanks for helping me understand the dream. You made me feel better.*

A run-down trailer is no way to view yourself, even if you feel like one. But Kyla's dream shows us a brutally honest representation of Kyla's self-image. The good news is that just as a trailer is often a starter home, she can only go up from here.

If the home in your dream is smaller and less appealing than your waking life home, ask yourself how you are personally feeling diminished and less in your mind and body than you used to be.

The message of trailer dreams: Your opinion of yourself is not high right now. What you feel on the inside eventually shows up on the outside. No matter what limitations you are dealing with that are causing you to feel subpar, you are not. Even though you may feel like a double wide in a trailer park, you're really a mansion in Bel Air . . . you might just need a few upgrades!

HAUNTED HOUSE

Haunted houses are fun to visit around Halloween time, but in your dreams . . . not so much. Whether you believe in ghosts or not, when you dream your house is haunted you need to ask yourself what your personal ghosts are; what is it from your past that haunts you still to this day?

> Last night I dreamed my house was haunted by the ghost of a man that jumped off the stairs to his death. He was angry and you could hear him cursing. But the only time I knew the ghost was around was when I was on the phone with my husband. Finally I told the ghost to stop and get out, so he left.—Brooke, 32

LAURI: The anger in your dream is *yours!* There must be something from your past, recent or distant, that is lingering within your thoughts and haunting you to the point of anger. Does this have to do with your husband? Are your conversations with him dominated by this issue? If so, this is why the ghost only bothered you when you were on the phone with him. You tell the ghost in the dream to get out because you desperately need to get this haunting issue out of your psyche.

BROOKE REPLIES: *Yes, it is an issue with my husband. I recently discovered his infidelity and we are working to get through this issue and I am trying to let my anger go. It's pretty much dominated our conversations. That makes so much sense.*

Brooke's dreaming mind is trying to show her that she and her household are now haunted by her husband's transgression. This is why the man in her dream died and became a ghost by jumping from the stairs. Her husband, whom she held in high regard, let her *down,* and effectively killed off her high opinion of him. He has now become a man she doesn't know, which is why it was an unknown man in her dream. Brooke was successful in getting the ghost out of her house in the dream, which means she may be doing okay in getting past this issue, but if the haunted house dream comes back she is going to have to look at other options.

The message of haunted house dreams: Issues from the past that you thought were dead and buried are still lingering within your psyche. Ghosts are difficult to live with so it is time to acknowledge them and give them attention. Home, as well as the self, should feel sweet, not haunted.

MOVING

In waking life we pick up and move when a different location offers a better job, when we need a bigger or better place or when we need to downsize, basically whenever we need to reasonably accommodate our changing lives. But when we pick up and move in our dreams it's not about the location but rather the mindset.

> *My brother and I have had a pretty bad falling out. Last night I had a dream that I put my house up for sale and bought my brother's old house. While packing to move, I asked my husband, "Why are we doing this? I love this house and the house we bought is old and I'm not going to like it. So why are we moving?"—Tina, 48*

LAURI: This dream is neither about your house nor your brother's house but rather about your minds! Your dream is telling you to try to move into your brother's mind-set and understand where he is coming from. It may be that you wish you could have that old brother (from when he lived in that house) back. Maybe *you* should be the hero here and be the one to "make the move" to get things back to how they used to be even though, as you said in the dream, "I'm not going to like it."

TINA REPLIES: *I usually am the one who reaches out when we fight. I sincerely will try to do the right thing and follow the guidance this dream has given me.*

Tina's brother's old house represents the image of him Tina wants to remember and the mind-set she can understand. Actually, the fact that her dream placed her in her brother's old house rather than his current house shows unwillingness or inability on Tina's part to understand his current mind-set. But it is her nature to reach out, so thankfully this dream kick started that good nature of hers so that she and her brother can move back to the way things used to be between them. Our dreams have a pretty cool way of gently nudging us in the right direction.

Moving back into a home you used to live in, such as your childhood home is also a common dream theme. These dreams are not about the house but about who you were and your self-image when you lived in that house. Your dream may be telling you to move back into that state of mind (if you were happier and liked yourself more when you lived there) or move on from that state of mind (if you were unhappy and felt bad about yourself).

The message of moving dreams: Moving is the operative word here. This dream is telling you that your mind is moving or your perception of your self is moving. The questions is, are you moving on or are you moving back into an old mind-set or self-image? Remember, the house in your dream is all about you, what's going on in your mind and how you see yourself. Now that you have a good understanding of how the different types of homes and the conditions of the homes are connected to you and your self perception, let's take a tour of our dream homes and explore how the different parts of the house reflect the different parts of the self.

ATTIC

The dreaming mind looks at the self as though it were a house. At the top of most houses you will find an attic. The top of the self is the higher self. I know, it's kind of a new-agey term but there really is something to it. It is the part of you that strives for a higher level of awareness, of spirituality, of prosperity, of intelligence, etc. It is the part of you that aspires. To the dreaming mind, the attic is this part of you. Since the attic is where we store away items we no longer need or can't use at the moment, the dream attic is the place within your psyche where you have stored away ideas, talents, and hopes that you have either neglected or had to put on hold . . . ideas, talents and hopes that will help you to aspire to be a better you and to live a better life, once you dust them off and give them your focus.

> *I'm in an unfamiliar house, climbing into the attic on a ladder, and the ladder gets narrower the higher I climb. I reach the attic but it is just large enough for me to sit in. There is a box in the attic that voices were telling me to open, but I did not want to open the box.—Jennifer, 34*

LAURI: Unfamiliar homes in dreams suggest that we are not feeling "at home" in our life. The attic often represents the higher ideals we have for our self, sometimes even our spiritual ideals. You are climbing a ladder up to the attic because you want to rise above where you are right now in life. What are you doing to try to improve yourself lately? But the fact that it is becoming more narrow means you must be feeling crowded in your home life, making your ability to rise above more difficult. The box is most likely a gift, a skill, or a talent you have but are afraid to use. Or it represents something you may not want to "open up" about. Odds are, if you do open up in waking life, your inner attic—all that you aspire towards—will open up to you too.

JENNIFER REPLIES: *I have been married for twelve years to a man who has not worked for the last eight. I have a lot of decision making to do. I am afraid of ending my marriage, but it is killing me spiritually. I know I can't live this way anymore. In the dream, I did not want to open the box because I guess I do not trust myself. This dream is encouraging to me because it gives me the strength to speak my heart.*

Jennifer desperately wanted to rise above her unhappy life. Her voice, her ability to speak her mind is what she had boxed and stored away in her psychological attic. The attic is what is above us in a house so she had to rise above her fear in order to access her voice.

Since this dream, Jennifer did "open up" about all the feelings she had boxed in. Her life then changed dramatically. She divorced her husband, lost her fear, and actually went skydiving to celebrate her new life!

The message of attic dreams: There are hopes, talents, and ideas that have been stored away for too long in your psychological attic. Rise up and connect with your higher self so you can rise above where you are now.

BASEMENT

Like the attic, the basement is another place in the home where we store away items we no longer need or can't use at the moment, but the basement is at the bottom of the house, usually underground, and you have to go down to get to it. That is a very important detail. To the dreaming mind, the basement is the place in your psyche where you have pushed down memories or issues you don't want to deal with. While the dream attic contains hopes and ideas for your future, the dream basement contains memories and issues from the past.

> *I dreamed there were ashes in the basement that kept catching fire. Some man was down there and put it out but didn't realize there was more fire brewing underneath the ashes. They caught fire again and I was unable to warn the man that there was more fire to put*

out so I picked up a dog and some paperwork and left the
house.—Nicole, 30

LAURI: The ashes are a good indication you've been emotionally "burned" in the past. The man, your assertive, rational self
that doesn't want to feel emotion, has recently "extinguished" the
pain . . . or so you thought. It seems like it is trying to rise to the
surface again, hence the "brewing" fire. The things you try to
save are significant. The dog symbolizes someone you would consider a "loyal companion." What relationship have you been trying
to save? The paperwork symbolizes something you are currently
working on such as career, yourself, or a project. Your inability to
warn the man in your dream tells us your rational / male side does
not want to feel it or deal with it. But there does seem to be a burning issue here that can no longer be ignored.

NICOLE REPLIES: *I'm coming out of a recent breakup, which has*
been extremely painful and am working with my therapist to figure out
why I've been having these emotional issues. It's bringing up things from
my past and I don't feel I'm ready to "go there" again. Oy! I had no idea
your analysis would dig so deep!

As you can see, Nicole's dream basement contains issues from
the past she and her therapist had to dig *down* deep into her psyche
to access, and Jennifer's dream attic contains an ability (her voice)
she had to rise *above* her fear to find. Both Nicole's and Jennifer's
dreams are about something personal that has been stored away,
but in different parts of the self.

In our dreams, the basement is often a dark and menacing
place containing shadowy creatures, lots of clutter or even horror
movielike activities because many of us have dark memories or

issues from the past we'd rather forget. But the dreaming mind does not forget, so it will bring these disregarded issues up to you from time to time in hopes that you will see the state in which you have allowed your psychological basement to be.

The message of basement dreams: Time to dig deep down into your psyche. Something from your past is affecting you today. It needs to be brought back up to the surface so you can give it the proper attention it never got. Sorting out the clutter and negativity from the past clears the way for a happier, more promising future.

KITCHEN

In your waking life home, your kitchen is the place where you keep your food, as well as the place where you prepare, cook, and eat said food. But to the dreaming mind, it is the part of you that plans, prepares, and cooks up ideas. Less often, it can represent the part of you that hungers for a change or for something new. The kitchen in a dream can even refer to one's nurturing, mothering skills. So whenever your dream takes place in the kitchen, it's a good indication that you have got something in the works. The state of the kitchen and what happens in the kitchen is how you see yourself handling the planning process or—if you are a mother—how you see yourself mothering your children.

> I was in the kitchen frying eggs or something, but then the paper-towel roll that is next to the stove caught on fire, then the fire spread to the wall and on up to the spice cabinet. Whenever I managed to put it out, it would start right back up again!—Rob, 44

LAURI: Whatcha got cookin' in real life lately? What are you planning or preparing for? The fire suggests that the heat is really on! You are under some major pressure to get something done. It also seems that every time you think you have it under control and you start to relax, the pressure starts right back up. The eggs lead me to believe this may be about children. If not, then an idea has recently been hatched and you can't seem to make it happen quickly enough. The fire is letting you know that you are letting the pressure get to you too much.

ROB REPLIES: *I am under intense pressure from my wife! She's about to hit forty and wants to try to get pregnant ASAP. There have been a few times we thought she was pregnant but it turned out not to be the case, so then the pressure starts right back up.*

Rob's dream encompasses everything that a kitchen reflects about the self: being in the planning stage, hunger and desire for something, and mothering. Unfortunately, as his dream shows us, the pressure to get a bun in his wife's oven is getting to be more than he can handle. Fire in dreams is often a warning sign that some sort of pressure is getting to be too much, that it has gotten to the point of consuming you, just as a fire consumes anything it touches. Stress can affect fertility in both genders. If Rob and his wife can work on not freaking out every month they don't get pregnant, they just might find it'll happen for them.

The message of kitchen dreams: Your dreaming mind wants you to see yourself as a chef right now because there must be something you are planning and cooking up. The condition of the kitchen and what happens in the kitchen will let you know how well or how poorly you are handling the process. Time to channel your inner Julia Child so that whatever it is that is in the works will result in a magnificent feast that will feed you emotionally, intellectually and / or financially for quite some time.

BEDROOM

Our bedroom is the place in our home where we lie down to rest. It is also the place where intimacy occurs and if you are married, it is the place of the marital bed. To the dreaming mind, the bedroom—and what happens in it—is a reflection of how you see your intimate life or your marriage.

> *I dreamed of rearranging my bedroom and no matter what I tried it wouldn't work. The furniture wouldn't fit without it being cramped.—Joye, 40*

LAURI: Are you trying to rearrange your schedule or your priorities in waking life? Perhaps in your marriage? Your dream seems to be telling you that your marriage is crowded and you may need to let a few things go.

JOYE REPLIES: *I have a "relationship" with another man, which I can't let go of. My marriage is not the best. My husband is controlling and mentally abusive, and on several occasions I feared he would get physical but that hasn't happened yet. I wanted to go to college. My husband had agreed and then made me withdraw after I had enrolled. I want to get out and grow as a person, but he makes me feel shrouded by his actions. I have thought of divorce, but without a job, no money, and no education, I cannot go through with that.*

Joye's been trying to rearrange her life but, as evidenced by her dream, she can't make anything work. The marriage area of her life is obviously the problem and her dreaming mind is showing her that it has now become crowded by her husband's oppressive behavior and her extramarital relationship. Her dream is trying to show her that something has to be removed; something needs to be laid to rest so she can have the "room" she needs to grow.

When your dream takes place in a bedroom, or especially your own bedroom, compare the state of the bedroom or the action in the bedroom to your marriage or current intimate relationship. You are likely to find that the dream is pointing out, in its own storytelling way, any problems that needs to be dealt with.

The message of bedroom dreams: Time to look closely at your intimate life or your marriage. Any frustration or anger or fear felt in the dream is connected to those same emotions in your marriage or intimate relationship in waking life. Remember what Dr. William H. Masters said, "When things don't work well in the bedroom, they don't work well in the living room either."

BATHROOM

Ah, the bathroom. It is the place of great relief. It is where we can refresh ourselves by washing away the dirt and grime of the day and relieve ourselves by letting out that which our body has processed and no longer needs. Yes, the bathroom is the place in the home where we tend to go "Aahhhh." In a dream, the bathroom is also a place of relief, but it is emotional relief rather than physical relief.

I dreamed that I came home from a night out with my friends and could tell someone had been in my house. It seemed like a break-in and party happened. I walked into my bathroom to find the bathtub filled with clean, cool water. Two large plastic water jugs were empty and floating on top. I was relieved to find that, because to me it confirmed just a party went on. Then when I moved my shower curtain I saw a bloody, red smear that was missed in the cleanup. I looked up, and there was a vent above my shower with salmon-colored guts that were spilling through.—Dani, 24

LAURI: When someone breaks into our home in a dream it suggests something has recently intruded upon our usually peaceful state of mind . . . and something tells me the intrusion was caused by someone telling you something that isn't sitting so well with you. Like the tub, has someone recently "come clean" with you? Or have you been the one that's come clean? Have you or has someone "spilled their guts"? Did they or you "vent" your anger or frustration? The message of the dream is that, even though this real life situation, like the bloody guts spilling into your tub, was rather unsavory and unpleasant, the intention behind it was meant to be a cleansing relief.

DANI REPLIES: *I've been dating a guy for a few months, but any time we are to spend with each other is always on his terms. I am scared he doesn't want a relationship and I may lose him by "spilling my guts," but I also know I had to "come clean" because I deserved a commitment.*

Dani's dream takes place in a bathroom because she has to cleanse herself of something unpleasant, which appears in her dream in the form of a bloody mess. What seems like a disturbing dream is actually quite relieving and encouraging once Dani is able to understand the symbols. Her dream is showing her that the fun (the party) with her boyfriend is over and it's time to spill her guts about her concerns. Thanks to this dream, Dani did voice her concerns and is no longer seeing her boyfriend. She told me she feels as if a ton of stress has been lifted and she is excited to move on.

The message of bathroom dreams: What or who has been frustrating you lately? Your dream is telling you that it has gotten to the point of being uncomfortable and you are in dire need of relief. Time to release and wash your troubles away.

There are many other places in the home that hold significant meaning in dreams. The backyard, for example, is representative of privacy, issues or thoughts you wish to keep to yourself. Alternatively, the front yard indicates that the dream is about something everyone already knows about you or the "front" you put on for the world to see. A hallway may imply that you are currently transitioning your thoughts or opinions, as a hallway is a transition from room to room, less often it can be a play on words and suggest that you are in something for "the long haul." Finding rooms in your home you didn't know were there is the way your dreaming mind is showing you that there is a lot more to you than you are letting on or that you are utilizing. The type of room you find and the condition of the room will clue you in to what part of you that you need to start using.

In order to figure out the parts of your home that you may dream about that are not covered in this chapter, ask yourself what that particular part of the home is used for. What happens in it? How can you connect it to you? How does it reflect your current issues as well as how you are dealing—or not dealing—with your current situation?

Our dreaming minds can be master craftsmen or shoddy contractors, depending on our current state of affairs and our emotional responses to them. Just as a house is a structure that is built and designed or bought according to yours personal style and needs, so does the dreaming mind build and design your inner house according to your psychological style and needs . . . and moods. It is just as important to keep your waking life home clean, maintained, and clutter free, as it is to keep yourself clean of negativity, your body maintained, and your life free of indecisive clutter. After all, *you* are the dwelling place of your soul. You are the only you that you get to live in.

....

FASCINATING DREAM FACT: Actress Gwyneth Paltrow is reported to have recurring dreams of being trapped in a Victorian house that is being swept down a river.

8

Weather Dreams

YOUR EMOTIONAL FORECAST

Tornadoes, Hurricanes, Rain, Floods, Lightning, Ice and Snow, Sun, Rainbows

A roaring, thunderous tornado. Burning, searing heat. A torrential, pounding rainfall. . . . The weather that is so often the backdrop in our dreams isn't just there for dramatic effect; it serves a far more important purpose. Weather in dreams reflects the mood, the emotions you experienced the previous day. It is innate in us to associate various weather conditions with our various moods. Uncertainty is often described as being "in a fog." Someone who is always cheerful has a "sunny" disposition. When you have lost interest in someone or something, you have grown "cold." It is no coincidence that temperament and temperature both come from the same root word *tempus* meaning season.

Weather changes from one day to the next, even from one moment to the next, and so do our emotions. To the dreaming mind, our emotions are the weather conditions that form and flow within our psyche. Just as a meteorologist tracks the weather in order to keep us informed and prepared to handle the days ahead, so should we track and understand our psychological weather to keep us informed and prepared to handle our lives. If you pay attention, your own dreaming mind will give you the most accurate and reliable emotional forecast available.

TORNADOES

When putting this chapter together, I searched all my client files, went through all my published newspaper columns, scanned my members' forum for various weather dreams, and discovered that almost all of the weather dreams I had accumulated were of tornadoes! So I put out a query to my newsletter members soliciting for weather dreams in hopes of getting more variations, and of all the dreams sent in . . . almost all were still of tornadoes. Sigh. Needless to say, the tornado is an image imbedded deeply and firmly within our collective psyche.

The nature of the approaching tornado is what I believe makes it such a popular dream symbol. If you've ever actually experienced a tornado, or even just watched one on TV, it is the waiting and wondering over the uncertainty of its path that impacts you the most. "Which way is it going to go? Is it going to hit my house? How bad will it be? How long until it gets here?" The element of bracing for possible disaster is what plays the biggest role in the meaning behind the tornado dream.

I pretty much have the same dream about tornados that has been recurring for a few years now. It usually starts with me seeing one and

*then me trying to let everyone know that it's coming. But no one will
listen to me and the next thing I know is I'm in my grandparents' old
basement watching it circle the house.—Cole, 38*

LAURI: Tornadoes are a classic symbol for worry and anxiety
over approaching doom. The spinning of the tornado is also important as it is connected to the idea that you feel something in
your life is spinning out of control. What's been going on these
past few years that has you certain you are headed for disaster?

Notice how no one will listen to you in the dream. This is
very likely due to the fact that in waking life, you have been worried about something others are not, which also means this is an
issue no one can help you with but you.

COLE REPLIES: *We have had money issues that started up about
four years ago and it has gotten worse just this past year and has been
overwhelming ever since then. It's taken its toll on the whole family. It's
been a rough going but we're getting through it.*

Cole's tornado dreams are connected to a specific worry for which
he has been bracing for a specific amount of time: financial destruction. His tornado dreams will continue for as long as he allows
himself to worry that destruction is imminent. Once he begins to
focus on a positive outcome rather than a worst possible scenario
in his mind, the tornado dreams will stop.

Most tornado dreamers, however, are plagued with twisters
storming into their dreams their entire lives!

*I have had recurring dreams of tornados for as long as I can
remember. Last night I had a dream that I was in a trailer by myself.
There was a horrible storm and then a tornado appeared out of*

nowhere! The windows started breaking because of the hail. Then the trailer was actually picked up by the tornado and landed safely in another state!—Nancy, 36

LAURI: Lifelong recurring tornado dreams are a good indication you are a proud, card-carrying member of the worrywart club. You'll find that your tornado dreams are likely to coincide with your bouts of worry or panic. You'll also find that your bouts of worry are often over something that you cannot control, just as no one can control a tornado; it is an act of God. In this latest dream, you are in a trailer, which is the weakest structure you could be in during a tornado. This means you are not feeling very strong at the moment. Then your trailer winds up in another state! Your dream is telling you that you need to move on from this worrisome "state" of mind. Sometimes you've gotta let go and let things play themselves out naturally. When you can move into this more relaxed state of mind, your tornado dreams will have no reason to come back.

NANCY REPLIES: *Yes, I am a worrywart. I worry about everything!! I will have to start keeping track of when I have the dreams and what I am worried about at the time. I always had a feeling that's what it meant.*

As frightening as tornado dreams can be, they are actually good for you because they are alerting you to the fact that you are letting your worry and anxiety get the best of you . . . and it is often worry and anxiety over something that may not even cross your path. Your dream is showing you your own worry in the form of a tornado so that you can understand the destructive force it has on your psyche.

Whenever you get a tornado dream, ask yourself what disaster or devastation you might be bracing for. Is it something you have no control over like world affairs or someone else's issue? If so, then know that all you can do is change your reaction to it. Rather than fearing the worst, hope for the best or remove your mind from it altogether.

If your tornado dream is the result of worry over a current situation directly connected to you that you can change, then stop focusing on what you *fear* the end result may be and start focusing on what you *want* the end result to be.

The message of tornado dreams: Time to channel your inner storm chaser and meet your worries head on and think of Dorothy. On the other side of her tornado was a magical place called Oz, and once you ride out your current storm of worry, there will be a magical place for you too . . . called "peace of mind."

HURRICANES

Tornado and hurricane dreams both reflect the storm of worry that fill our mind from time to time. But there is a distinct difference between the meaning of a hurricane dream versus the meaning of a tornado dream, and the difference lies in the nature of the storms. A tornado is unpredictable, and you can see it coming but you never know if you will wind up in its path or not. A hurricane covers a broad area and its main characteristic is its powerful wind. And the wind is the key to the meaning of this dream. To the dreaming mind, wind represents the forceful changes that blow through our lives, "the winds of change," so to speak. When the wind in your dream is threatening, such as the winds of a hurricane, then the changes that are happening in waking life are upsetting you.

I dreamed my husband and I were trapped in a grocery store during a hurricane and could not find our son. It really bothered me.—Chrissy, 30

LAURI: Your inner mind must be feeling that you aren't spending enough time with your son for some reason and that is where the missing comes in to play. You "miss" him. The hurricane tells us a big change has blown into your life, a change involving your son that is upsetting to you. This all takes place in a grocery store because you are hungry for the emotional nourishment your relationship with him provides.

CHRISSY REPLIES: *My son just started kindergarten so you are right. We do not have the time together anymore that we are used to and I have been having a hard time adjusting.*

Even though we love to watch our children grow and develop, a part of us resists the changes because it means that, before we know it, our baby will be an adult and no longer in need of our cuddles and care. Chrissy's dream reflects her inner awareness of how fast the changes her son is going through are blowing through her life.

The message of hurricane dreams: The winds of change are upon you and are causing you a tremendous amount of upset. The more you resist the changes the more difficult they become, just as it is harder to walk against the wind run from it. Rather than evacuate these hurricane force winds of change, prepare for it and withstand it. And remember, the eye or center of the hurricane is the calmest point; if you can center yourself you, too, will find peace despite the changes whirling around you.

RAIN

Rain casts a gloomy and somber tone to the day. The sky is dark, the air is cold and your mood becomes dreary. When I was a little girl I was told that when it rains it means God is crying. While the rain drops may not actually be God's tears, they will represent yours when it rains in your dreams.

> *I recently had a dream that I was standing in the rain outside of my house, which wasn't really my house, to wait for my family to drive down to see me. I noticed the raindrops were much larger than normal raindrops. Then my mother and grandmother, who are both deceased, pulled into the driveway. They both appeared to be having a good time and happy to see me.—Lisa, 49*

LAURI: Your house in the dream is not your actual house because you must be in a place in your life that doesn't feel "like home," that doesn't feel familiar. The rain represents your sorrow, tears you have shed, either openly or on the inside. The harder the downpour or the bigger the raindrops, the bigger the sorrow. And you are waiting in the rain because you are waiting for the sorrow to let up.

In the end, your mother and grandmother are happy as they pull into the driveway. The driveway represents your access to others and others' access to you. Your dream is showing you that happiness is accessible and it will most likely take form in your own role as mom. Are you a mom? If so, whatever your sorrow may be, you can always access some level of happiness when you focus on your children.

LISA REPLIES: *My sorrow is that two months ago my husband Jack suffered a massive heart attack in his sleep and passed away. I am so very heartbroken that he is no longer with me because he was the light of my life. Yes, I am a mother of two adult children and I absolutely am able to find happiness in them. Thank you.*

The message of rain dreams: Just as rain falls down, down, down, something has you feeling down, down, down, too. Let the tears flow because a good cry will cleanse the psyche the same way a good rain will cleanse the air.

FLOODS

The nature of a flood is its rising, overwhelming water, which causes an increasingly hazardous situation. As the water continues to rise, the situation becomes more and more urgent. In that same vein, if a flood comes pouring into your dreamscape, you can bet it is connected to a situation in your waking life that is getting increasingly worse causing you to feel increasingly overwhelmed and in increasing need of help.

> *I was at home and I could see the rain and wind through the windows. As I walked up the stairs, the water followed me, overtaking me inches at a time. My heart was racing as I hit the top step and by then the water was to my waist. I went into the bedroom and climbed onto the top of a dresser. The water was overtaking the room. The drawers to the dresser floated out on their own. I placed my cats in the drawers so they could float to safety.—Mary, 56*

LAURI: You must be dealing with something that is getting increasingly worse and causing you to feel increasingly overwhelmed. Seeing rain in the dream indicates that this situation has caused many tears. The cats are also an important element to the dream as they likely refer to your own sexual / reproductive energy *or* your ability to be independent and prideful. Is there a situation or a person you need to break free from before it is too late?

MARY REPLIES: *I have a grown daughter and two grandsons who are in a less than desirable situation. Her husband is not a good provider. My daughter works very hard, but even working two jobs, she is unable to provide for herself and the boys. It's a very frustrating situation and I listen daily to her problems. I am not wealthy, and was hoping for retirement within the next few years, but will not be able to do that. I am constantly sending money to her. Despite the emotional stress and the increasing financial burden, it is a situation I now see I need to find a way to break away from.*

The message of flood dreams: Whether it is a worsening state of affairs or an increasing amount of responsibilities you are being flooded with, this dream is warning you that the situation is threatening to sweep you away and overwhelm you to the point of drowning in your misery or obligations. Find a way to lighten your load or find someone or something that can serve as a life vest and keep you afloat. And fear not, just like in an actual flood, waters eventually subside and so will the feelings of being overwhelmed.

LIGHTNING

Often, when we dream of storms, lightning is an expected part of the ensemble. But when the lightning in your dream stands out and is a major focus, that is when you know it has a meaning all on its own.

Lightning is sudden, brilliant, unexpected, and electrifying. They say it never strikes twice in the same place, but when lightning strikes in your dream it is often connected to something sudden and unexpected you are excited about. It could be any-thing from a sudden, brilliant idea to a sudden and unexpected turn of events. In other words, the tingling excitement you feel coursing through your veins will show up in your dreams in the image of lightning.

The first part of my dream I was in a bathroom popping a pimple in the mirror. It squirted on the mirror, the ceiling, and the floor! I cleaned it up and then I was driving a car in the country by a cornfield. There was a lot of lightning. The lightning strikes the cornfield, with a huge explosion causing the corn to start popping into popcorn!—Nicole, 24

LAURI: The pimple represents a small unattractive problem in your life that is causing you to worry about how you may look to others, which is why it squirted all over the mirror. You popped the pimple in the dream, which means the problem has been re-solved. The dream suddenly switches to you driving in a corn-field. When dreams suddenly switch scenes like yours did, it is showing you how one thing leads to another. You are suddenly in a cornfield, which either represents your career "field" or "playing the field," as in dating. The lightning suggests there has been a sudden and unexpected turn of events or a sudden and unexpected brilliant idea, which has excited you, electrified you! The fact that this lightning strike created popcorn leads me to believe this may be more about dating than career because popcorn is a popu-lar treat to be had at a popular dating activity . . . going to the movies.

NICOLE REPLIES: *I have recently been asked out by a coworker. I was hesitant about it at first because I was worried about what other coworkers might think. Our entire company ended up having a meeting about employee conduct and employee dating was a topic that came up. To my surprise, no one thought it was bad, which really took a weight off my shoulders and excited me!*

The message of lightning dreams: A stroke of genius, a flash of inspiration, a bolt of energy and motivation . . . something brilliant has suddenly struck your life causing untold excitement. Now it is time to channel your inner Ben Franklin and harness that energy while it's hot!

ICE AND SNOW

When your dreamscape takes on the form of a frozen tundra, it does not mean you are dreaming of a white Christmas. Snow, hail, frost, ice, anything below 32 degrees in a dream is usually related to the fact that your emotions have cooled toward something or someone, or something in your life has become frozen, stuck, and is no longer progressing.

> *In my dream I am with my husband. It is snowing and there is ice stretching as far as the eye can see. I step on a mound I know a polar bear is buried underneath. Crying, I turn to my husband and say, "Why do they have to die?"—Roxanne, 43*

LAURI: Your dream points to one of two things: you have grown emotionally cold toward someone or something lately or some area of your life is frozen, on hold, not moving. Have things gotten cold between you and hubby? The polar bear is your tendency to insulate yourself from the chill that has taken over your marriage. The polar bear is dead, which means *you* are now feeling the cold harsh conditions between the two of you. You are no longer numb to it. The comment you make to your husband suggests that you aren't sure why things are the way they are. Even though it is directed toward your husband in the dream, it is really a question you are asking yourself. It is also now time to ask yourself what role you can play in bringing warmth back into this marriage.

ROXANNE REPLIES: *You are right on. My relationship with my husband has grown very cold. Your interpretation has definitely brought some light to the situation and has forced me to reexamine the role I am playing in it. Thank you for your help.*

Like Roxanne's dream, our dreams will often call us to action. This dream illustrates how devastated Roxanne truly is about the current chilly conditions of her marriage. With this being brought to light, she can now—and hopefully will—work on melting the ice that has formed between her and her husband.

The message of ice and snow dreams: There is a cold front running through your life. Are you the one giving off the cold vibes or is someone giving them to you? What area of your life has frozen to a standstill? It is time to figure out if it is worth the effort to break the ice or move on to something or someone with a warmer climate.

SUN

Nothing lifts your spirits like a warm, sunny day. We naturally equate sunny days to happiness and even tend to draw sunshines with smiley faces on them. When the sun shines in your dreams, odds are you are beaming with happiness in waking life.

I was out by the pool at my parents' house, which is the house I grew up in. There was a party going on and it was a warm sunny day. The sun felt so good that I took my top off and sunned right there in front of everybody! The thing is, I would never take my top off in public and I haven't sunbathed in I don't know how long as I am worried about skin cancer.—Carol, 26

LAURI: The party, the warm sunshine, even your topless sunbathing suggests something in your life is worth celebrating. I'm guessing you opened up and got something off your chest as open honesty in waking life often translates into happy nudity in dream life (grin). Did you open up to your parents about something? Did you break the news that you are going to be a parent? Whatever it is, you are now basking in the glow of this joy just as you were sunbathing in the dream. Don't worry. The dream sun contains no UVA or UVB rays, so bask away.

CAROL REPLIES: *I am in shock at how intertwined this dream is with my real life. No, I'm not about to become a parent but I did finally open up to my Catholic parents that the man I've been seeing for six months now is Jewish and they didn't have a problem with it at all and are actually eager to finally meet him. I've been dancing on air ever since because it truly has had me worried to death.*

Usually when the weather stands out in our dreams it's pounding, hammering rain, or a coming tornado that's destroying everything in its path, so it's awful nice when our dreamscape is clear and sunny and warm like Carol's dream. Her dream shows us how the sun in a dream not only reflects happiness but can also point to honesty. The sun gives us light as well as warmth. When we want to find something out or learn something we "shed light on it." Carol had been keeping her boyfriend's religion in the dark.

When she finally shed light on it, happiness ensued and she basked in it.

I am out in a boat and the sun is extremely warm and enjoyable but within a short amount of time I am in a storm that is extremely scary with high winds and heavy rain. I am alone and confused. I cannot see any land and am wondering where the sun went.—Tammy, 46

LAURI: The warm sun represents your happiness and feelings of warmth and comfort in your life. But alas, it seems the good times and senses of comfort were short lived before things got stormy! The high winds seem to suggest there were sudden and strong changes in your life. The boat is your ability to navigate through and stay afloat during this emotional time. The heavy rain is the sorrow that soon followed and the tears that were shed. The fact that you are unable to see land is connected to your inability to see the silver lining around the cloud, your hopelessness so to speak. You are all alone in the dream. Did someone leave you in real life? Are you feeling like no one understands or cares? Whatever the case, being alone in a dream is the way you are showing yourself that you, and you alone, are the only one who can pull yourself out of this dark time. Whether it is working to refocus your thoughts or surrounding yourself with people who make you laugh, *you* are the one that can steer yourself in the right direction.

TAMMY REPLIES: *This all makes sense. My youngest sister, who was also my best friend, died of cancer a couple years ago. We spent lots of warm, happy times together raising kids, chatting on the phone daily, vacationing together every year, etc. Soon after her death, my oldest son became addicted to oxycontin then turned to heroin. I have spent many days and sleepless nights trying to understand it all and wondering where the sun in my life went. Not being able to see land is truly how I feel.*

If the sun in your dream goes away, like the sun did in Tammy's dream, know that your inner joy is still very much there but is being blocked by clouds of uncertainty or gloom. Clouds always move out of the way to reveal the sun and so will your gloom eventually make way for your happiness. The sun is always there, clouds are not.

The message of sun dreams: In the same way the Earth is anchored to and depends on the sun for life, your personal world is anchored to and needs joy to sustain your life. When the sun shines in your dream, things are good. Your outlook is bright. Remember, the sun is for all to share so spread your cheer.

RAINBOWS

In the story of Noah's Ark, God uses a rainbow to represent his promise to mankind that He would never again destroy the world by way of flood. This story seems to resonate in our collective psyche that rainbows equal hopes of a brighter future. But even if you aren't from a Judeo-Christian background, to see a rainbow in the sky, you can't help but feel it is an omen of good things to come. After all, rainbows often appear after a dark and gloomy downpour. So when a rainbow appears in your dreams, t'is a good sign that you are feeling hopeful.

I'm driving in the car headed to an amusement park. Directly in front of me I watch a huge beautiful rainbow start to go up and over me. The sky has some gray clouds but it's clearing up. The ground is wet

*from the rain. I am in awe of the rainbow but realize I need to watch
the road to avoid a crash.—Pam, 44*

LAURI: The clearing gray clouds and the ground being wet from
a recent rain suggest that depression or sadness is clearing out of
your life. The rainbow is your hope about brighter, cheerier days
ahead, about color being brought back into your life. This is why
you are headed to the amusement park in your dream . . . you are
headed to a more carefree time in your life! In the dream you realized you needed to keep your eyes on the road. Any realization in
a dream is a revelation you need to take with you into your waking life. Your realization is: stay focused on this new path you are
on, this new direction you are headed, so as to avoid another mess
of a situation.

PAM REPLIES: *We just lost a family member, my sister-in-law, to
cancer and complications with pneumonia. Also my husband has been
out of work for a while but has been interviewing and applying. Things
that are brighter about both is that I know my sister-in-law is no longer
suffering and my husband had an awesome interview. Looks like he has
the job!*

Our emotions are an ever-changing force within us just as the
weather is an ever changing force in the atmosphere. When you
are able to recognize the various weather patterns in your dreams
as the various emotions you experience in waking life, you will be
able to keep yourself in check, as they say. Your weather dreams
serve as an emotional barometer and thermometer, helping you
to measure your emotional pressure (your level of stress), and
measure your emotional temperature (your emotional highs and

lows). Your dreams can warn you when you are letting your worry overpower you, hence the tornado dream, and let you know when you are in a clear and positive state of mind, hence the sunny dreams. Thus, you are then able to stay on top of and take control of your emotions rather than having your emotions control you. Accomplishing this allows you to "weather" anything life may throw at you.

....

FASCINATING DREAM FACT: The dreaming mind has the ability to seamlessly incorporate a barking dog, a car horn, a rainstorm, or any other real world noises into the storyline of a dream. These dreams are called "outside interference" dreams.

9

Sex Dreams

THE URGE TO MERGE

The Mystery Lover, Cheating, the Ex, the Coworker,
the Boss, the Friend, the Same Gender, Oral Sex,
Your Parents, Masturbation

Of all the dream themes we experience, there is none as emotionally polarizing as the sex dream. These dreams will either leave you with a spring in your step or an inability to look others in the eye the next day.

Back in the Middle Ages, sex dreams were so shameful that people attributed them to incubus or succubus, male and female sex demons, who would molest the unwary while they slept! This far-fetched idea was likely due to a need to absolve oneself from the perversion felt upon waking . . . "Wow, that couldn't possibly have come from my mind! Why that must have been a horny little demon trying to wreak havoc on my pure and Godly thoughts! Yeah, that makes sense. I'm going with it."

Nowadays, sex dreams are not quite as taboo; in fact, according to a recent study at the University of Montreal, sex dreams make up about 8 percent of all dreams for both men and women. Society's openness regarding sex coupled with our growing interest in understanding dream content has taught us that, surprisingly, sex dreams are rarely about sex at all—no matter how saucy they might be.

Whether you are dreaming of a passionate tryst with Brad Pitt on the beaches of Puerto Vallarta with the rhythm of the waves matching the rhythm of your bodies, or you're getting it on with the geeky guy—or gal—in the cubicle behind you, it's important to remember that sex, to your dreaming mind, is not about a physical union you want, but rather a psychological union you need!

In this chapter, as we explore the more common sex dreams and what they mean, you'll not only begin to feel more comfortable about your sex dreams, you'll also discover how the dreaming mind cleverly uses sex to show you—not *who* but *what*—you desire and need to merge into your own personality.

THE MYSTERY LOVER

The mystery lover is the most common of all sex dreams. Many of us wonder if this dream is actually a glimpse of our soul mate who might be out there somewhere waiting for us. Alas, t'is not so. But what is so is that the unknown, faceless man or woman that often appears in our dreams does indeed hold significance. As you may remember in Chapter 2, our dreams have a cool way of showing us the different parts of our *person*ality in the form of a *person* so we can gain a deeper understanding of ourselves and what makes us tick. That being said, the mystery lover in your dreams is the embodiment, the *person*ification of the qualities we tend to associate with that gender. If you are a woman, the mystery man represents your male *person*ality traits, the part of you that can be assertive, speak your mind, bring home the bacon, handle your business and even squish the spider in the tub.

> *I have had this dream several times where I am having very graphic sex with an unknown man. He is everything I have ever wanted and very kind. I reach orgasm in these dreams and I always wake up very satisfied, but I never see his face.—Tammy, 40*

LAURI: You are attracted to this man in your dream because your dreaming mind wants you to be attracted to your own male, assertive, money-making, take-charge qualities so that you will use them to improve your life. Your dream is showing you that this part of you is very much a part of who you are and a part of you that you like. It's a *very good* sign that you are having these dreams as it means you have successfully merged your male self into your life and have achieved darn near perfect balance of male assertive energy and female nurturing energy. The orgasm is like extra credit for a job well done in waking life. Your body doesn't know the difference between a dreaming event and a waking event, so it reacts the same. During the sex dream, your brain sends messages to the nerve endings in your little lady down there that sex is happening so she responds in the same explosive way as if it were real!

TAMMY REPLIES: *I am a single mother and I do everything! I bring home the money, fix the plumbing, paint, mix cement, etc. I have been divorced for thirteen years now and I do feel I have finally found myself. I am proud of myself and am very excited that I can do what some men don't even know how to do when fixing a house. It saves me a lot of money.*

Tammy's dream is a great example of a woman who has embraced and merged with her male side. Notice how satisfied she is from these dreams. That satisfaction is not just physical; it is emotional and psychological satisfaction as well.

Whenever a woman needs to assert herself or take charge in some form or fashion such as when she is up for a promotion, when she is a single parent and has to play the role of both, or when she needs to speak up for herself during the day, these are the times when the mystery lover will pay her a visit at night.

If you are a man, the mystery woman represents your female qualities . . . yes, even the hairiest and burliest of men have at least a touch of feminine wiles within. Female qualities are the traits we usually associate with women, such as sensitivity, creativity, being a good listener, nurturing yourself and those around you. From time to time in a man's life, it will do him well to acknowledge and utilize these softer qualities.

For about a year now I have been having dreams where I am shrinking each time I thrust into my lover. I get smaller and smaller and my lover (always the same girl but someone I do not know) gets even more aroused. I go from five feet ten and I shrink slowly until I end up the size of a doll or toy. While I am shrinking in the dream I do my best to please my lover, sometimes having to change positions as I get smaller.—Jared, 33

LAURI: You've been having the dream for about a year so it is commenting on something you have been dealing with for about a year. There has been a shift or merger happening in your personality lately. A big part of you is diminishing while another part of you, symbolized by your mystery lover, is becoming more powerful and demanding. Your mystery lover is the embodiment of the personality traits typically associated with the female gender: sensitivity, being a good listener and nurturer, etc.

In the dream you have to change positions frequently, which is a good sign that you may find yourself being more flexible and willing to bend in order to accommodate others, or even in order to accommodate yourself in waking life (they say only a woman is allowed to change her mind; I say, "Feh!"). Perhaps your flexibility and willingness to change your mind is the female attribute that you are merging with lately. Notice how pleased she is in the dream? That is confirmation of a job well done in waking life, my man.

JARED REPLIES: *I started a new job about the time this dream started. In my former job I was in a position where many people looked up to me, but there was some restructuring and I lost my job. Therefore I had a feeling I was diminished and would have to start over again, leaving me feeling "small." However with my new job, I have to be a jack-of-all-trades, often switching my mind-set at the different obstacles presented before me. You are right on.*

The mystery lover dream is so common because it is a subset of a larger category of dream, "the unknown man and unknown woman dream" that we discussed in Chapter 2. The message it holds is so powerful because it guides us toward a balanced and whole personality. According to Carl Jung, one of the creators of modern depth psychology, the male and female mystery lovers are representations of the animus and anima that can be found in each of us. The animus is male energy and the anima is female energy, similar to the female yin energy and male yang energy discussed in Chapter 2.

Throughout life we struggle to incorporate the right balance of each into our personalities and behavior. A man wants to be caring and understanding, yet he doesn't want to be a sissy. A woman wants to assert herself, yet she doesn't want to be labeled the B word! Our mystery lover dreams are guiding us toward that perfect balance of firm and gentle, bold and caring, yin and yang.

The message of the mystery lover dream: Time to recognize the male assertive energy or the female nurturing energy within you. Merge these opposite qualities into your personality just as you merged your bodies in the dream so that you can be courageous and take charge when you must, and be tender and compassionate when you want.

CHEATING

Cheating dreams can be infuriating, worrisome, and the cause of many a slap across the face first thing in the morning. In fact, in a recent survey I conducted with over 5,000 participants, the cheating dream came in as the number one most common dream! As upsetting as these dreams can be, the good news is that they rarely indicate that your mate is getting his or her pleasures elsewhere. They do suggest, however that something rather than someone is taking the time and attention from your mate that you feel you deserve.

> *I keep getting these dreams about my boyfriend of five years cheating on me. It's like he doesn't even care and has no emotion in the dream. I'm 99 percent sure he would never do that. I just don't understand why I keep having these dreams and why they are so constant. Is it about a trust problem?—Brenda, 24*

LAURI: Did anything happen that would give you a good reason to be distrustful? If not, then let's figure out the other reason you are getting these dreams. Is he doing something that you are a bit jealous of? Is he working too much? Spending too much time with friends or on some project or hobby? What is he doing that makes you feel like he should be with you instead?

BRENDA REPLIES: *He always spends time on the computer. When he comes home from work he goes straight on the computer and does his fantasy baseball thing. When I start to tell him about my day he won't even listen and it makes me feel like he doesn't care.*

Brenda's dream is a clear indication that her boyfriend's fantasy baseball league has taken on the qualities of a mistress in her mind. And the fact that the dream is so constant means it is a constant issue in their relationship. He should be tickling her, not the keyboard! Plus, the apathy he displays in the dream is directly connected to the apathy he shows her in real life. These dreams will keep happening until Brenda is able to work this out with her boyfriend.

Sometimes, *we* may be the ones having extracurricular sex with someone other than our mate. These are the dreams where you are very much aware that you are cheating and the feelings of guilt are often included. When you are the one straying in your dreams you need to ask yourself what you may be doing that is taking your attention away from your mate. The guilt you feel in the dream is a telltale sign that, deep down, you are aware that this may not be sitting well with your significant other.

Cheating dreams can be very upsetting and they rarely mean an actual affair is going on. In fact, when understood, they can actually fan the flames in your relationship. Once you can pinpoint what it is your mate is "cheating on you" with, or what you may be guilty of giving too much time to, it's time to compromise. Offer to give up or cut back on something your mate isn't a big fan of if he or she promises to cut back on the activity that is causing you to feel left out. If you both stick to the compromise, you'll find that the dreams will stop.

The message of the cheating dream: Something has become a third wheel in this relationship. Time to merge more time for each other into your schedule . . . no matter how busy you may be!

THE EX

The ex is a very popular character in our naughty dreams. Even though it may be light years since you were with this person, he or she *still* continues to appear in your dreams, bringing those old feelings back to the surface that leave you wondering if you still may be holding a flame.

> *I keep having recurring dreams about getting back together with my ex boyfriend. Sometimes we're just hanging out and other times it's downright filthy sex! However, I am married and haven't spoken to him in over ten years.—Jennifer, 37*

LAURI: Was he your first love? Strangely enough, we continue to dream of our first loves, even if we've moved on into a happy marriage. Don't worry, it's not that you want him back, it's that you want what he represents back: excitement, bubbles, passion! You are likely to get these dreams when your marriage gets a little too routine and humdrum, as all marriages do from time to time. Your dream is using your ex to remind you of the passion that is still alive inside of you. These dreams are actually good for you and are alerting you to the fact that the passion department doesn't want to become a thing of the past. Might be a good idea to get thyself down to Victoria's Secret and buy something red and lacy.

JENNIFER REPLIES: *It makes so much sense now. He was my first love. While I was with him, there was lots of excitement and passion. We would do things so spontaneously. And I wasn't as self-conscious as I am now. I can see now that I don't get involved in new things like I did before. You're right; I do need to spice things up, in my life and in my marriage. You've made me see things in a different light.*

Jennifer's marriage, like millions of marriages before hers and millions of marriages yet to be, has become complacent. Complacency is easy because it takes no effort. Like Jennifer, as we settle into the land of humdrum while awake, our dreams become restless while we sleep. The dreaming mind doesn't forget the excitement and thrill from long ago, so it will bring those feelings back to you in the form of the person you first experienced those feelings with. These dreams aren't about the person, they are about the feelings.

The most common meaning behind the "sex with the ex" dream is a need to rekindle the excitement in your intimate life. Once you take action on your dream's gentle nudging, and continue to change it up and keep it interesting, the ex won't need to pay you another visit . . . that is, unless the ex still has a role in your life, such as an ex-spouse. If you deal with the ex-spouse on a regular basis then that person is not likely to be a symbol, rather your inner mind is alerting you to an issue with that specific person and, as always, you will need to look at what happened the day before the dream in order to pinpoint the issue.

I have this sex dream, and I've had it about four times now. It usually takes place in my old house and it is me having sex with my ex-wife, not my current wife. I do not get along with my ex. Why am I dreaming of having sex with her?—Nick, 35

LAURI: Are there children involved? If so, they are the reason. Let me assure you that these dreams do not mean you have a secret desire to bed the ex. What they do mean is that you have a secret desire to . . . ahem . . . "come together" with her on some level, for the sake of your kids. Deep down you know it is unhealthy for your kids to know that Mommy and Daddy hate each other. Just as two bodies during sex come together and work in rhythm, like a well-oiled machine, so do you and the ex need to work together in rhythm like a well-oiled parenting machine. When you are able to do this, the dreams will stop.

NICK REPLIES: *Makes sense. I get it loud and clear. I think I can pull this off. Thank you!*

The exes we tend to have naughty dreams about the most are our first love, an ex we still have ties to because of children or other circumstances, or the ex that most recently broke our heart. Dreaming of the ex that broke your heart can be a sign that you are stuck emotionally and have not allowed yourself to move on. These dreams are a clear indication that you have not healed in which case the dreams will continue until you let go and leave the past in the past. It is impossible to move forward while you are still holding on to what is behind you.

The message of the ex dream: Depending on which ex you shagged in your dream, it is either time to merge the passion of long ago into the relationship of now or time to merge your efforts together for the sake of a common goal such as your children. If the ex is someone you are still pining for, then it is best to de-merge and realize this person is an ex for a reason.

THE COWORKER

The coworker dream can make work a very uncomfortable place to be. Unless your coworker causes your heart to skip a beat and your mind to wander into naughty-naughty land, then your sex dream(s) about him or her are nothing to cause you concern. However, understanding the dream is well worth your while because odds are, that dream is actually trying to help you improve yourself at work.

I've had several dreams of having sex with my coworker ... whom I hate! In the last one, as we were going at it, my phone rang and some voice told me my father had died.—Leslie, 31

LAURI: Your dreaming mind is telling you again and again that you need to "come together" on some level with this guy, for the sake of work. In this latest dream you are even giving yourself a stern warning in the form of a phone call. When the phone rings in a dream it is your dreaming mind calling you to attention. There is a message for you in your father's death. Your father is the part of your personality that knows what is best (Father knows best, as they say) and how your ability to bring home the bacon. What this dream is trying to get across to you is that your very livelihood is at stake. If you don't put on that plastic grin and make the best of it, your ability to bring home the bacon will die off, and come to an end!

LESLIE REPLIES: *Wow. That makes perfect sense. There are many projects he and I have to work on together so yes, this would be in my best interest.*

Leslie's dream shows us how sex dreams can mean we need to
have a meeting of the minds in order to make coexisting and co-
working more efficient. But what if you don't really have much to
do with a particular coworker during the day but you find yourself knocking boots at night? All you need to do is ask yourself
what stands out about that person. Is he really good with comput-
ers? Does the boss seem to favor her? Maybe he's easygoing and
doesn't seem to have a care in the world. There is very likely a quality he or she possesses that your dreaming mind feels you would
do well to take on as your own.

The coworker dream can also be more about your job than
the coworker herself.

*There is a woman at work whom I am very attracted to. In my dream,
we were at work and she told me that she wanted to have sex with
me but I would have to take off my shirt. Then she progressed
through each article of clothing until I was at work and completely
naked. After I was completely naked she kept adding requirements
for having sex with me. So she started telling me I needed to run
some numbers for her first and finish a project for her while I was still
naked. We never had sex but I did get a lot of work done.—Sean, 37*

LAURI: As Freud would say, "Sometimes a cigar is just a cigar." It
is possible this was merely a compensation dream allowing you to
live out a hidden fantasy safely within the confines of your head.
But there is an awful lot of focus on work in this dream so that
leads me to believe this dream is actually commenting on your
job. Notice how she asks you to take your shirt off first. Is there
anything regarding work that you need to "get off your chest"?
You wind up completely naked at the end and to no avail. Is this
how you feel at work lately? Are you working your tail off and not
being rewarded for it?

SEAN REPLIES: *This was insightful . . . I do feel like I am working my tail off and not being appreciated. I think I will try cross-dressing and see if that helps.* ☺

While Sean's dream didn't quite get to the sex act, it did focus on sex—or rather the lack of it—to drive home the message that he is not getting the satisfaction from all his hard work that he would like. And his dreaming mind is using a coworker he desires but cannot have to correlate the satisfaction he desires but is not getting. Seeing his work situation from this point of view will help Sean to get this issue "off his chest" and will hopefully bring about the appreciation from his bosses that he deserves.

Work is a social setting so there are many politics involved. It is also vital to our livelihood, which is why you will find yourself dreaming of work more often than you would like. Your dreaming mind is figuring out your work-related issues for you so you can feel comfortable there and advance yourself on up the ladder. The sex with a coworker dreams are the most important of all work-related dreams because they are showing you who you need to focus on getting along with as well as what you can add to your own personality or behavior in order to better yourself and more easily reach your career goals.

The message of the coworker dream: Whether it's a meeting of the minds or a quality of theirs you should take on as your own, there is a lot to be gained by merging with your co-worker.

THE BOSS

Shagging the boss at night can sure make it difficult to come into work the next day. If this is the case with you, remember, sex dreams are not necessarily about the person but rather about what he or she represents. In the case of your boss, it is most likely power, authority, management skills, decision making, etc., that you need to merge into your own life.

> *I dreamed that I was at a casino with my boss. He told me there was an urgent situation he needed my help with and took me into some back room and we then proceeded to have sex, which was very enjoyable. I was disgusted and embarrassed when I woke up.*—Pam, 38

LAURI: The setting of your dream is always a good place to start when analyzing it. What have you been thinking about "taking a chance" on? What seems like a "gamble" to you? Sex with your boss either means you need to unite his decisive and authoritative qualities into your self *or* you need to unite with him, have a meeting of the minds, in order to raise the odds of this situation working out.

PAM REPLIES: *I have been thinking about breaking out on my own and starting my own business and be my own boss so this makes perfect sense. It would indeed be a gamble but my boss is very organized and decisive so if his qualities were my own, I think I'll do well!*

Do you need to take on the role of boss at home and better manage those unruly kids? Are you facing a tough decision? Do you need to fire or get rid of a certain element, person, or behavior in your life? Or perhaps you simply need to merge with your boss psychologically in order to deal with a client or project.

The message of the boss dream: Time to take charge! Being decisive and authoritative would suit you well right now.

THE FRIEND

This dream often brings up the question, "Am I secretly wanting to move beyond *the friend zone*?" Could be! T'was the case quite some time ago when I was having dreams that started with a good friend of mine buying me pizza topped with dog kibble and ended in a red hot, mind-blowing, heaving . . . well, you get the idea. Anyway, eighteen years later I now call that friend "hubby"! So you may want to go ahead and examine your feelings toward this friend. Very often, your dreaming mind knows better than you.

But if being more than friends is not even within the realm of consideration, fear not. As always, there is a perfectly reasonable and helpful explanation of why you may be dreaming of knockin' boots with your bud.

The other night I dreamed that I was lying down on my stomach outside in a field. Then my guy friend who I am not romantically involved with lay on top of me and hugged me from behind. I felt him get hard! I was sort of uncomfortable but it felt good to have someone intimate with me. But then he ejaculated. I didn't want to embarrass him because other people were around, so I acted like nothing happened. Then when he got up my pants were wet but it didn't show that much.—Michelle, 21

LAURI: What you might be worried is a sign of a hidden attraction is actually a confirmation of a good friendship. The two of you must have recently shared an intimate moment of conversation where he was able to "unload" on you and in doing so, put some issues between the two of you "behind you." This is also why the dream took place outside, because he got some things "out in the open" with you. Notice how you didn't want to embarrass him in the dream? That is directly connected to how you must have made him feel comfortable enough to open up to you in waking life. It is being shown to you in the form of ejaculation because your dreaming mind is equating it to the satisfying release of an orgasm. This was something that may have been "hard" to do at first but wound up feeling good because he needed that release. There is not much evidence on your pants in the dream because in waking life, it turned out not to be such a big mess after all.

MICHELLE REPLIES: *This is exactly right. My friend opened up to me about his attraction to a mutual friend of ours. We had a very long and intimate talk about the situation, his concerns about how it might affect our friendship, and so on. And yeah, he definitely unloaded!*

Anytime you are "more than friends" with a pal in a dream ask yourself first if the two of you have united on a psychological level. Did you two really "connect" recently? If not, then odds are there is something about that friend you need to merge into your own life or your own behavior. Perhaps he or she is a social butterfly and you wish to be more sociable. Or maybe he or she speaks their mind, in which case your dream would mean you ought to stop beating around the bush so much. Just pick the first three words that come to mind when you think of this person and then apply them to yourself. You'll find that at least one of those qualities would look awful nice on you as well.

The message of the friend dream: Something about this friend, when merged into yourself, is going to make you a better person in the end!

THE SAME GENDER

Girl-on-girl action may be exciting for a guy, but when we of the fairer sex dream about it, it can be a bit unnerving. And guy-on-guy action is particularly upsetting for a man who is an avowed skirt chaser. If you are not gay and you have a gay or lesbian dream, it does not mean you have a hidden desire to bat for the other team. What it does mean is that you are indeed proud of being a member of said team.

The sex with the same gender dreams are cousin to the mystery lover dreams in that the meaning is most often focused on gender roles. For example, when a woman does something that makes her feel particularly feminine, such as mothering a sick friend or getting cat calls from a construction crew across the street, she could very well be the proud recipient of a lesbian dream that night! When a man does something particularly manly, such as getting a raise or replacing the timing belt in his car, he, too, may very well find a man loving up on him that night

> During the last trimester of my pregnancy I had dreams of having sex with other women. I have had numerous dreams like this. I am not a lesbian. I don't know why but I would have sex with women I don't know and have orgasms that felt so real.—Jaymie, 29

LAURI: Believe it or not, lesbian dreams are *very* common during pregnancy! When a woman dreams of being with another woman, it's because she is feeling very proud of her gender . . . and there is nothing more female than creating and carrying life inside of you. It is what our bodies were designed to do. You are putting the womb in woman to use. These dreams were merely a celebration of your woman-power.

JAYMIE REPLIES: *That makes a lot of sense now. I have had many miscarriages and this time I finally made it to the last trimester. It is amazing, and empowering that we women can create another being inside of us.*

In my research and experience it seems it is much easier for women to admit to lesbian dreams than it is for men to admit to gay dreams. But when a man does fess up to me, he's always glad he did because he discovers that his gay dream is actually a reflection of his own manliness.

> *This is hard for me to admit, but last night I dreamed about this bully from grade school. We were in the locker room and no one else was around. He came toward me like he was going to pick on me or slam me into the locker like he used to, but instead he put his hand on my shoulder and leaned in and kissed me. Ugh! I am sure you can guess what happened after that. I can't even bring myself to type it!—Barry, 41*

LAURI: Well, I commend you for your bravery in owning up to this dream. Keep in mind that dreams cannot be taken literally. Like I always say, you can't look *at* your dream; you have to look *into* your dream. Let's start with the bully. Since you have not seen him since grade school, he is not playing himself but has now become a part of you. He could be the part of you that beats yourself up over silly things but because of the intimacy in this dream I'm thinking he is the positive side of that, meaning he is probably standing in for the part of you that has toughened up and made something happen or learned to take it on the chin. The sex that takes place in the dream symbolizes the uniting of this tough, masculine quality into yourself. This takes place in the locker room for a reason. The locker room is where we change, indicating that a change has taken place with you! In what way have you toughened up and made changes?

BARRY REPLIES: *Okay. Feeling* much *better now, thank you! I have indeed toughened up . . . after months of beating myself up actually. I have been on a baseball team sponsored by the company I work for and all season I've been basically a worthless player adding nothing to the game. I finally got tired of being mad at myself so I really buckled down and practiced, practiced, practiced. The day before I had this dream I scored the winning point for my team.*

There are many reasons you might have turned gay in your dreams because there are so many reasons to be proud of being a woman or a man. Each gender has attributes we are happy to display and utilize. Women are often proud of their curves, men of their brawn. Nurturing tends to come more naturally to women whereas being a warrior and protector is often an easier role to take on for a man. Accomplishing or displaying an attribute specific to your gender can often lead to a gay dream, not because you desire your own gender but because you have embraced it and merged its specific qualities into your waking life behavior . . . and your dreaming mind is pleased.

The message of sex with the same gender dream: Your gender offers you powerful tools in life. When merged into your personality positively, your feminine wiles or your manly guile will get you far.

ORAL SEX

Anything having to do with the mouth in a dream is all about communication, because we use our mouths to communicate. Oral sex in a dream is often connected to communication you have had with someone else that has brought the two of you closer psycho-logically or emotionally. If you are the one performing oral sex in your dream, look at what *you* have communicated recently. If you are on the receiving end, then look at what has been communicated to you. If the oral sex in the dream is gratifying, then that is a good sign the communication in waking life was gratifying as well.

> I recently had a dream of performing oral sex on my current
> boyfriend, whom I have not even met in person yet. In the dream as
> I was performing the oral sex he went from erect to not erect and
> stood up and walked out. I never have sex dreams so this is very
> confusing to me.—Sandra, 37

LAURI: The oral sex represents the fact that you have had only oral communication with this guy. I believe the fact that he lost his erection and walked out is your fear that when you two finally meet, it will be "a letdown" for either you or him or both.

SANDRA REPLIES: *You are definitely right. I have told him on at least two occasions that I hope once we meet that he is not disappointed.*

The sex aspect of Sandra's dream reflects her desire to unite with her cyber boyfriend. The oral aspect is all about what *she* has communicated to him, "I hope you're not disappointed." And be-cause of the message she is communicating to him, her dream is showing her that she is already setting herself up for *his* dis-appointment.

> Last night I had a dream that my wife and I were having sex. We
> were doing everything from extremely hot and passionate oral sex to
> banging each other's brains out. In reality, our sex life is not like
> that. My wife won't even go down on me orally. I find it weird that in

one part of my dream she was going down on me with such passion
that I actually had a wet dream!—Bryce, 30

LAURI: I noticed an awful lot of . . . ahem . . . oral activity going on in this dream. This may in fact point to communication in waking life. Do you recall, at the time of this dream, you and your wife having a very open, honest, intimate, and gratifying conversation? The fact that you actually ejaculated is connected to some form of emotional release in waking life on your part. This dream seems to suggest that the two of you "came together" on some issue, perhaps really going at it at first and then both reaching a meeting of the minds, which resulted in relief and satisfaction. Consider this dream a sweet reward for a conversation well done.

BRYCE REPLIES: *My wife and I have been going through some financial issues, so we sat down and figured out the things we both needed to change, and now we are a little better off. I think you are right on.*

Bryce's oral sex dream was with his wife so obviously the waking life issue was concerning her as well. When you get an oral sex dream it is important to pay attention to whom your partner is. If it is someone you deal with regularly, then odds are the dream is about communication between the two of you. If it is not someone you deal with regularly then the dream is most likely about the way *you* communicate in which case you will want to use the basic rule of thumb that I have been using throughout this book where you pick three things that first come to mind when trying to describe this person. Once you have them, apply those words to yourself and see if you can connect any or all of them to the way you have been communicating lately. If you merged one of those qualities into yourself, would your communication be more effective?

The message of the oral sex dream: Like oral sex, if done right, open and honest communication can be very satisfying.

YOUR PARENTS

Keep in mind, the dreaming realm is a place in which ethics don't necessarily apply. In fact, you have to throw your ethical standards out the window in order to understand dream language because sex in a dream is rarely about sex and your parents in a dream are rarely playing themselves.

> *My father died ten years ago. We had a very good relationship and I still miss him terribly. Last night I had a dream that completely confused me and disturbed me. In my dream my dad was very sad. He told me he was dying and that the only way I could save him was if I had sex with him! So I did. I am very upset by this dream.—Mary, 29*

LAURI: Don't worry. This dream doesn't mean there was ever anything inappropriate between you and your father. In fact, your father isn't even playing himself in this dream. He is standing in for your ability to make decisions, run your household and manage your finances . . . basically, your dream is giving form to all that you associate with the role of Dad. He's sad in the dream because your finances or your household must be in a sad state of affairs right now in waking life. Even though he has already passed in real life, he is dying in the dream because your inner mind is warning you that your finances must have one foot in the grave right now. Yes, the sex part has major "eew!" factor but that is the solution your dream is giving you. Remember, sex in a dream is not about a physical union you want but a psychological union you need. Unite the breadwinner mentality into yourself and this will ensure that your income will live long and prosper.

MARY REPLIES: *I feel so much better! This totally fits my life right now. I have so much credit-card debt from spending recklessly right out of college that I have been at a loss as to how to handle this. Unfortunately, I don't have Dad around to help with this mess so I am looking into money managers so I can find someone to help me get it under control and plan for the future.*

If your dad dreams are creeping you out, first ask yourself if you and your dad need to or have recently come together on some level, had a meeting of the minds, or formed a singular opinion. If not, then turn the dream inward into yourself and into your life. What qualities of dear old Dad do you need to integrate into your behavior or mind-set in order to better yourself?

Unfortunately, some Dads were less than stellar, in which case the dream may be a warning that you have taken his negative behavior on as your own.

Sex with Mom dreams are also common and very rarely point to an Oedipus complex. In fact, in my research women seem to have this dream more than men. Just like Dad in a dream, Mom is not always playing herself. For both genders, Mom in a dream tends to stand in for the part of your personality that nurtures and mothers others as well as yourself. And if you are a woman and are a mother, she often stands in for your role as mom, and how she behaves in a dream is reflective of how you are mothering your children in waking life.

I have begun to have these very *disturbing dreams of having sex with my* mother! *Please help me.—Roberta, 38*

LAURI: Don't freak out. Your mom probably is not playing herself but instead represents something you desire to bring into your own life. Are you a mom? If so, your dream suggests you want to be more like your own mother in how you nurture your children. If you are not a mom, do you want to be? Perhaps that is what you wish to merge into your life. Your dream may also indicate that you have taken on a mothering and nurturing role lately. The dreams do not suggest anything is wrong with you but rather that mothering in some form or fashion is on your mind.

ROBERTA REPLIES: *Wow. I have been trying to become a mom for years. I am at the age now where my husband and I are feeling it will never happen if we don't take drastic measures so we have begun IVF treatments. Whew! What a relief.*

An interesting little fact is that at the time of this dream, Roberta was pregnant and did not know it. It is very likely this dream was revealing to her that her union into motherhood had indeed taken place.

Sex dreams can be disturbing enough without throwing family members into the mix. But knowing that these dreams are not literal but rather symbolic of you, much relief and insight is to be had.

The message of your parents dream: While this dream may be hard to digest, keep in mind that your inner mother and father know best!

MASTURBATION

Choking the chicken, auditioning the finger puppets, beating around the bush, call it what you will, this is not only a popular indoor activity, it is also a popular dreamtime activity. And just as masturbation in waking life is about pleasing one's self physically, masturbation in a dream is about *being* pleased with one's self.

My boyfriend and I were sleeping in the bed. I woke up to the house
shaking so I woke my boyfriend. He didn't feel it and told me to go
back to sleep. It happened again, this time I heard a woman's voice
calling his name. I looked out the window and saw a leg swaying
from the roof. My boyfriend went outside and his friend's girlfriend
was straddled over the peak of the house, riding it and getting off.
She was naked and calling his name in between moans. He just shut
the door and said it was nothing. I went out but couldn't speak
because she had grown four legs!—Kristi, 27

LAURI: That's quite a dream you've got there! You begin by waking up in the dream, which means this is a "wake-up call" to you.
Your wiser dreaming mind wants you to realize something. The
house shaking suggests that your relationship with your boyfriend is a little shaky. Just as you tried to make him realize this in
the dream, is he in denial in waking life?

This girl on your roof may not be playing herself. What is she
like? What can you learn from her personality in real life? She's
masturbating and calling your boyfriend's name, which means
your dream is calling your attention to something about him.
Masturbation in a dream is usually about being either self-centered
or needing to please yourself rather than worrying about everyone else's happiness. Are you not looking out for your own happiness enough in this relationship? Do you need to please yourself
more?

You're unable to speak in the dream which points to a communication issue. Your dream may be telling you that you aren't
doing a good enough job of getting your point across. What you
are saying is falling on deaf ears.

What's the most interesting to me in this dream is the girl
growing more legs. Legs are all about your ability to move forward

or move on . . . a good indication that it is time to move on from this relationship.

KRISTI REPLIES: *You have hit me like a ball. My relationship is shaky, and I have a hard time talking to my boyfriend about it because if I do bring something up it turns into a heated debate, and I back away. For the girl in my dream, she is very self-centered, which was really funny that was brought up. So I guess I need to be more like her and care about me. Also, the part about the legs, this is the way I have been feeling, just up and run away, not looking back. I guess the more legs the faster.*

As you can see, no matter who is doing the masturbation in the dream, it will always point to being self-centered or wanting to please the self.

The message of the masturbation dream: It's all about you right now. Time to look at your current circumstances and determine whether it's been a little too much about you or perhaps not about you enough. Recurring masturbation dreams signify that you may be too self-involved, whereas the once-in-a-rare-while masturbation dream suggests a need to focus on your needs or may even be a pat on the back for a job well done.

Spicy or awkward, your sex dreams play an important role in your life's journey. In a nutshell, they show you what you lack. In waking life, sex begins with desire, proceeds to a merger, and ends in completion and satisfaction. The dreaming mind uses this same process to help you bring what you lack into your life. If you desire to be able to speak your mind, your dream will use someone you know that has that ability, will create a desire for them in your dream, merge your bodies together to symbolize bringing that quality into yourself, and in most cases, complete the merger, and give you satisfaction, i.e., orgasm, which is not only representative of the satisfaction of having that quality be a new part of you but is also icing on the cake!

 FASCINATING DREAM FACT: During REM sleep, blood rushes to the genitals of both men and women no matter whether the dream content is sexual in nature or not. For men, this causes nocturnal erections. When men wake up with "morning wood," it is because they had just awakened from REM sleep.

10

Nightmares

IGNORED, MISHANDLED, AND DIFFICULT ISSUES

Being Chased, Falling, Your Death, Death of a Loved One, Murder, Trapped, End of the World, Zombies, Blood, Paralyzed, Ending Nightmares

You suddenly jolt awake, gasping for breath, sweat dripping onto your sheets, and your heart is pounding inside your chest so hard it hurts . . . You have just had a nightmare! A nightmare can shake you to your very core. The imagery can be so disturbing and the emotions so upsetting that you may wonder if something is wrong with you. "Why would I dream something like that?" you ask yourself.

Of all the different types of dreams we have, the nightmare is the most mysterious. Why so violent? Why so gross? Why so frightening? Why *me?* Most of us consider ourselves to be decent people so it's hard to understand why our own minds would sometimes create such horrific stories. Why do we do this to ourselves?

The answer is simple. We get nightmares when we have ignored or mishandled an issue for far too long. The nightmare is the way our wiser, inner mind slaps us into reality and says, "Enough!" You see, nightmares don't suddenly come out of nowhere; they build. When you've got a tough issue during the day, you will dream about it at night to find a solution to it, but if you don't get the message or if you don't act on the message, then the dream will come back. Sometimes it will come back in the same form, hence the recurring dream, and sometimes in a different form but the same message, hence the recurring themes. The longer you ignore the message or the longer you mishandle the issue, the more hostile your dreams become . . . until they reach nightmare status! The dreaming mind neither likes complacency, nor does it like to be ignored.

BEING CHASED

The most common nightmare, or perhaps the most common element in a nightmare, is being chased. It is also the most common recurring nightmare, especially for women! In general, chasing dreams are caused by "fight or flight" situations where you choose "flight" or avoidance rather than "fight" or confrontation.

> *I have had this reoccurring dream for about four months now where I'm being chased by a guy I don't know. I always seem to find a place to hide but he always finds me. In the dream I am screaming for my husband but he can never find me. It all happens in a maze of some sort, full of secret rooms and closets and basements. It builds to the point where I wake up screaming and crying. It's very scary!—Julie, 28*

LAURI: Has something been going on for four months that you have been avoiding dealing with? Is there something you are hiding or are trying to keep private? The maze suggests that there is confusion over this issue. The secret rooms, the basements, and the closets all point to secrecy in waking life. What are you "keeping in the closet"? Your husband is never able to find you or help you in the dream because this is probably your issue and your issue alone and not something he can really do anything about.

JULIE REPLIES: *I have some student loans that are in default and they took my taxes last year for them. My husband and I just got married so he didn't know about them until we went to go get our taxes done this year. I feel guilty about not being up-front about them. The closer it was getting to tax time this year, the more I knew I couldn't hide it any longer. It amazes me how much this affected my dreams! Thank you so much. Hopefully now I won't have that dream again!*

Julie's recurring nightmare illustrates her *fear of getting caught*, of getting found out. Julie avoided telling her husband about her financial issues for too long and her inner self was none too happy about it. Through these dreams it was trying to show her that the longer she avoided the issue, the more complicated it was going to get, hence the maze. Julie's mismanagement of the truth is what created the dream. Allowing the issue to go on for as long as it did is what created the recurrence, and her building guilt is what turned it into a nightmare. Julie chose flight . . . and look what it got her!

The message of being chased nightmares: There is an issue right now you are running from rather than facing. Is it a confrontation you need to make? An obligation you want out of? An issue you don't know how to deal with? Or is it something from the past you are afraid will catch up with you? You can't run forever. Avoidance is never a good way to handle an issue. All it does is prolong the pain and anxiety. These dreams will stop when you face and deal with whatever it is you fear during waking hours.

FALLING

Have you ever heard that if you dream of falling and you hit the ground, you will die?! I sure heard that a lot as a kid, and even today I am frequently asked if that is true. Let me clear that up right now; I have never spoken to a single dead person who told me that they were having that dream at the point of their death. You cannot die from your dreams. I do have a theory however, on why this is such a common belief, or old wives' tale. Falling in a dream is terrifying! You are plummeting through the air to certain death, and since the body doesn't know the difference between a dreaming event and a waking event, it reacts in the same manner. Your adrenaline rises, your heart beats rapidly, and your body goes into freak-out mode! This extreme psychological and physiological reaction often jolts you awake before you go splat. In other words, the majority of people throughout history, when experiencing a falling dream, have never hit the ground because they wake up. Couple that with practically no reports whatsoever of people who did hit the ground, well, it's only natural to assume that hitting the ground doesn't happen . . . and if it did, the shock of it may kill you!

I have in fact heard many reports of folks who dreamed of falling and hit the bottom, and they did indeed wake up with a pulse. A couple of them even bounced. Nonetheless, the falling dream is terrifying and is not to be taken lightly, as it is one of the most common warning symbols the dreaming mind sends us when something in our life is going rapidly in the wrong direction.

I'm driving and I cannot see anything in front of me. It is pitch black,
very scary and my heart is beating fast. I suddenly find myself going
off a cliff, and as I'm falling I wake up. I have had this dream several
times for a couple weeks now.—Edwin, 45

LAURI: Driving your car often refers to how you are currently
driving down your road of life or how well a path you have chosen
to take is moving forward. You are unable to see in your dream,
which means you are feeling very uncertain of your future, of what
lies before you. Going off the cliff is a horrible experience, isn't it? It
is reflective of your fear that something in your life may be rapidly
going in the wrong direction. We want to find ourselves going up
in a dream because that means things are progressing; going down
points to regression. Falling can also mean a fear of failure or can
even be connected to suffering a letdown. The dream came to you
more than once because the issue has not been resolved and your
inner dreaming mind is nagging you to find a way to redirect this
situation—or at least your emotional reaction to it—immediately.

EDWIN REPLIES: *I had several interviews lately at my job and every-*
one that I had, I did not get, so I am beginning to feel as if I cannot go any
further with the company. I have been feeling like a failure but I refuse to
give in or up. Thank you for clarifying this for me.

Edwin's real-life situation encompasses just about all the elements
that trigger falling dreams: fear of failure, suffering a letdown,
and some area of life going in the wrong direction, i.e., his career
path. You see, falling is a downward motion, so when you are
feeling down, when things aren't looking up, when you don't feel
you have anyone around you to support you, to hold you up, or
whenever something happens that causes your emotional state to
fall, you are likely to find yourself falling in a dream.

The message of falling nightmares: Something in your life is going in the wrong direction, and fast! Hang in there; you haven't hit rock bottom yet. It is time to redirect this situation immediately . . . or at the very least, redirect your emotional reaction to the situation. Chin up! You can do it.

YOUR DEATH

While you cannot die *from* your dreams, you certainly can die *in* your dreams. It's really a fascinating experience, as none of us have ever died before, yet when we die in a dream we can literally feel ourselves slipping out of our body. Of course, who knows if that is what dying will actually feel like, but the dreaming mind certainly has an impressive way of creating the sensation! And it is the vividness of the dying dream that makes it so terrifying, so much so that we tend to wonder if the dream was giving us a glimpse of our future.

Nay! T'is not the case at all. If that were true, not a single one of us would live out our entire natural life. But what is true is that the dying dream is indeed connected to the end of life, not the end of your life as a whole but rather the end of your life as you now know it.

I was in a building and it was filling up with water. I was trapped and couldn't get out, even though there was no top to the building. It was open on top but I just couldn't get out and I died.—Annie, 32

LAURI: You are good testimony to the fact that if you die in your dreams you do not actually die in real life. I assume you still have a pulse. That being said, rising water in a dream can often be connected to a situation in waking life that is getting increasingly worse, to the point that it is absolutely overwhelming you. You can't get out in the dream because you must not feel you can get out of the situation. Your dream is showing you though, that you can get out. "Keep looking up," is the message (hence the open top). In other words, stay positive about it. Dying shows us that this issue has changed you. Perhaps you had enough and decided to make some changes in your own attitude or behavior and let the "woe is me" mind-set die off so you can have a new life.

ANNIE REPLIES: *I have goose bumps reading this. I can't believe how much this dream fits what's been going on in my life! My fiancé is a heavy drinker. After we got engaged he seemed to be getting better. But in the last six weeks it has gotten worse and worse, to the point that he went missing one night. I've tried to get him to go to rehab. I've begged, I've pleaded. I've tried to get his family to help me with an intervention but they won't. The day before I had that dream I had decided to pack my stuff and leave. I can no longer feel responsible for him. And I am staying positive, for my new life.*

The message of nightmares of your own death: Something within you is changing. Like death, change can be scary because—also like death—we do not know what is "on the other side" of the change, which is why the dreaming mind equates change with death. Your life as you know it is ending. But fear not, you are simply letting go of the old so that the new can emerge.

DEATH OF A LOVED ONE

Dreaming of the death of a loved one is possibly the most horrific nightmare to have because the feelings and thoughts that flow through you in the dream are very likely exactly what you would experience were it an actual event. It seems kind of cruel that we should have to go through such trauma unnecessarily. So if dreams and nightmares are our own creation, why would we do this to ourselves? Well, the limbic system (the part of the brain that associates emotions with sensory information) is highly active in the dream state, so emotional reactions from what happens in the dream will be very strong and are *sometimes* a by-product of the message. What is the message when someone we love dies in a dream? Again, it has to do with changes, with something about that person or even a part of you that is like that person, changing or coming to a close.

> *I dreamed that my sixteen-year-old daughter committed suicide. I saw a stream of blood going down the gutter in my front yard. I couldn't find my daughter, but my sister showed up and found her. By the time I found them, my daughter had "left" and I thought, "My sister made her clean up the mess." I finally saw her ghost, and I was crying, saying, "I just want to hold you." She walked up to me and said, "It's too late now. You did this." And I woke up crying.—Tami, 45*

LAURI: As unsettling as it is for a parent to dream of their child's death, it is actually very common. These dreams tend to happen most when the child has reached a milestone, such as learning to walk, learning to drive, starting a new grade, etc., or when they suddenly act or appear older, at which point the inner mind wonders where that younger child went. It is kind of like a little death, and so we mourn the rapid passage of time in our dreams.

In your case, your daughter has committed suicide but blames you! In what way has your daughter changed lately? Suicide is death by one's own hands. What is she doing that is causing you to wonder where the younger, more dependent and loving daughter has gone? The confusion between her taking her own life and you being the cause is likely connected to your inner awareness that she is the one forcing the change but you may not be handling the change well . . . therefore causing the change to be a negative one.

You say that all you want to do is hold her. This may be connected to your feelings of wanting to hold on to the daughter that she was before she changed. Her appearing as a ghost suggests that there may be some things going on right now, behaviors perhaps, that you fear will haunt you in the future. All the blood is a warning you are sending yourself that this change is taking an awful lot out of both of you; it is draining. You may want to ask yourself if this change is something natural that you should allow or is it a change that you need to handle differently? Because as evidenced by the dream, you are resisting it.

TAMI REPLIES: *We are looking at colleges and she is definitely becoming more and more independent, which makes me happy, but of course I still feel the loss that is around the corner. We argue a lot and I know I need to back off because she is a good kid, but wants to do things her own way instead of the right way (which, of course, is my way)! I think her blaming me in the dream is because I know I'm pushing her away by not giving her more space and being too critical, so I really am trying to back off. It definitely has been draining for us both and I think we both miss the more relaxed relationship we used to have before she had so much independence and responsibilities. You said I'm not handling the change well so it is going to be a negative experience. That makes perfect sense and is exactly true. When I back off, she tends to come and snuggle up with her mommy like the old days.*

Like Tami, we don't always handle changes well, especially when it is our children that are growing and changing so much. It's hard to let go of the swaddled, precious infant in order to make way for the toddler. And with the same defiance, we have to eventually say good-bye to our cute, pudgy little toddler in order to make way for the preschooler, and it goes on and on and rips and tears at our heart every step of the way. We don't realize it, but we do need to mourn the passing of each phase of our child's life, so the dreaming mind takes care of that for us and allows us to express our grief in our dreams.

The message of death of a loved one nightmares: Changes are happening either with this person, with your relationship with this person, or with your perspective of this person. It is also possible the change is within you, in which case it is the part of you that is similar to this person that is changing. As difficult as these dreams are to experience, it is important that you understand a natural ending-beginning process is taking place. Your dream is telling you that it is time to let go of what is passing so that you can look forward to what is coming.

MURDER

Just last week I was doing one of my regular radio appearances when a listener, who was too embarrassed to call in, e-mailed his dream instead. In his dream he had murdered somebody and then proceeded to chop up the body in order to hide it. He was obviously disturbed by this dream and wanted to know why he would dream something so disturbing and graphic. I reassured him that he was not alone in performing this gruesome, bloody act and that at some point in our lives almost all of us become sadistic, homicidal maniacs in our dreams! The reason is because at some point in our lives, almost all of us have to put an end to something before it goes on for too long. Death in a dream is connected to something naturally changing or ending, whereas murder is a forced change or ending. The more difficult the change or ending is to implement, the more disturbing the dream.

I dreamed that my husband murdered two people then stuffed them into my desk at work! I was upset with him because he didn't finish the job. So I flipped a switch on my desk and, basically, a garbage disposal finished them off. I woke up screaming!—Rachael, 32

LAURI: This dream is commenting on an important issue. What are you and hubby trying to "dispose of" in your life? Two bodies indicate there are two issues, behavior patterns, or attitudes that need to be "killed off." The fact that the bodies were in your desk at work may mean that this is something that you will need to "work on." Won't be a piece of cake. However, you are both in on it . . . partners in crime, so to speak. That means you are each other's support system in this purging.

RACHAEL REPLIES: *I think you are right about the meaning. My husband and I want children but have made a pact to quit smoking and drinking first. He's quit drinking but I'm still doing both. Yes, I will certainly need to work hard on this.*

Ending a habit, addiction, or recurring behavior pattern is very difficult to do. Rachael had been ignoring her need to end hers for too long, which is why her dreams became disturbing. But her dream, as gross as it is, is also giving her encouragement by equating her bad habits to *garbage,* hence the garbage disposal. Even in the most grisly of dreams you can find a positive message.

While committing murder in a dream is connected to intentionally forcing a change or ending in your life, being murdered is connected to a change or ending being forced upon you, usually against your will just as murder is a forced death upon someone against their will. You may dream of being a murder victim when your spouse is forcing you to change or quit a behavior or habit, when someone breaks up with you, when you lose a job, or when

outside influences or unforeseen circumstances force you to make
an unwelcome change somewhere in your life.

*I just woke up from one of the worst dreams I ever had in my whole
life. I have a four-year-old son and I dreamed that there was a man
that murdered us. He hit me and I fell through the closet doors. I
screamed and reached for my phone to call 911 but couldn't. I could
hear my son screaming and crying. The man dragged me by my
ankle back into the room and stabbed me three times, all on my left
side, one near my collar bone, one in the lungs, and one in the
stomach. I watched myself die and was floating above the scene
and I watched him murder my son with the same wounds that he
inflicted on me. I then watched my dead body float down this street
that was flooded with black dirty water.—Jessica, 30*

LAURI: Being murdered means a change has been forced in your
life, and it may be a change that has seemingly been dragging on
for some time, the way you were dragged in the dream. What are
you feeling pressured to end or change? Is it your weight? I ask because you were stabbed in the stomach. Actually, there were three
wounds. When there is a specific number of something in your
dream, it is directly connected to that same amount in waking life.
Are there three changes you are dealing with? Whatever it is,
making these changes has been difficult for you, hence the distress
in your dream. It is also something that you need help with since
you tried to call 911, but perhaps in real life you haven't had the
courage to ask for that help since you never were able to call. The
black water points to depression. Do you suffer from depression
and worry your son will suffer, too? Your son receiving the same
wounds means you worry that something that afflicts you in waking life is or will afflict him as well. But notice how, despite the
carnage of the dream, you float above it and watch. Believe it or

not, this is a fairly common dream occurrence and what it means is that your inner self wants you to rise above your current fears and concerns and look at the big picture. Step outside of your situation and observe as a third party. Suddenly, things will become much clearer.

JESSICA REPLIES: *Several things have been changing: work, weight, and home. I just got approved for lap band surgery. I'm both excited but very scared. I fear that I will not get the support I need from my family, etc. The main thing that I have been depressed about is my dating life, or really lack thereof, and am feeling serious pressure from my friends to start dating again even though I don't want to. Doesn't really matter to me if I have a boyfriend, but I worry about my son growing up without a father. I'm also depressed about work because I feel there are issues there that will not be resolved due to lack of proper management. In the terms that you have presented, this dream is not nearly as scary and makes more sense. You helped me see the lessons my subconscious was trying to teach me.*

As we see in Jessica's dream, the more difficult or afraid we are of the changes, the more frightening the dream. The dating pressure and the work changes being forced onto Jessica are not of her doing, and while the lap band surgery is her choice, it is a physical change that will take place due to someone else's doing . . . the surgeon's. This is why I believe her dreaming mind chose to use a knife as the murder weapon, because she will be going under the knife soon and that's what is causing the most anxiety for her. Not to mention that it will also be the biggest change, as her body will change rapidly and dramatically. All these changes and pressures combined are telling Jessica it's time for the old, heavier, single, and depressed Jessica to "die" so the new, slimmer, happier, dating Jessica can have a chance to live.

The murder weapon and the means of death in your dreams can be major clues as to what changes and issues are being forced upon you. Strangulation is a sign that you are being forced to hold back your words in some way, that you are not being allowed to voice your opinion or thoughts. Getting shot may indicate that someone is shooting you down verbally with wounding remarks and criticism. And being stabbed can also point to someone's stabbing remarks. If the knife is a major focus of the dream then it may be telling you there is a behavior, issue, or person you need to "cut out" of your life.

The message of murder nightmares: Something has been going on for too long and it is now time for it to change or come to an end. If you are the murderer, you are in control of that change or ending. If you are the victim, the ending or change is controlling you, which means it's time to decide if you should allow the change to happen or not. Do you want your life, as you now know it, to continue on as is or is it time to let it end so a new life can begin? Author and actor Orson Welles said it best: "If you want a happy ending, that depends, of course, on where you stop your story."

TRAPPED

In my research and experience, being trapped comes in as the sixth most common nightmare theme. The waking-life issues that cause this nightmare are the complete opposite of what causes the various death-themed nightmares. While death nightmares reflect changes happening in our life, trapped nightmares reflect a lack of a much-needed change. The needed change doesn't happen because we are afraid to do what is necessary to implement the change, which causes us to be essentially trapped in a situation we need to free ourselves from.

*I was in my bedroom when the power went out, and the lightbulbs
burst. It was dark except for the moon shining through the window. I
was scared and tried to get out but I couldn't because a baby gate
was in the doorway. Then I saw spider webs everywhere. Dead-
looking dolls with mouths stitched closed were falling from the
ceiling. I was really scared. I tried again to get out but was trapped,
because of the baby gate. Then my dog opened my door. She was
really sick and looked like she was about to die.—Ryan, 14*

LAURI: From your dream it seems like you are in some sort of
situation, or even a state of mind that you want out of. Is there
someone around you that you think isn't being honest? Or is
there something you haven't been honest about? I ask because
spider webs in a dream often suggest one is trapped by a web of
lies. The lights go out in your dream, because you are "in the
dark" about some issue. Or you need to "shed some light" on an
issue . . . perhaps the lies that are going on. The dolls indicate that
you are being "played" or manipulated and their mouths are
stitched closed because *you* must not be speaking up. You are also
trapped by the baby gate, which suggests that you or someone
else is "being a baby" about things, thus causing you to be stuck
when what you really need to do is grow up and handle this situation so you can free yourself. In the end of your dream, your dog
is very sick. The point at which your dream ends is usually the
main message of the dream. Your dream is telling you that your
loyalty to this situation or deceitful person is very unhealthy . . .
something's got to change here.

RYAN REPLIES: *A family member of mine is not being honest and
it bothers me a lot. They are lying and stealing. I'm not speaking up
about it. I do feel I would be disloyal if I spoke up. And, yes, sometimes I*

do feel like I'm manipulated. I will have to think about how to talk about it. Thanks so much.

Ryan's definitely in a tough situation that he clearly wants out of. Ratting out a family member is not at all easy. But since he is mishandling this situation by not speaking up, or at least telling this family member that he will rat them out if they don't fess up themselves, Ryan is trapping himself. He knows what the right thing to do is, but since he's not doing it his inner mind is becoming frustrated and is communicating its frustration in the form of a nightmare.

The message of trapped nightmares: You are in a situation or a mindset right now that you need to get out of. Time to be honest and ask yourself what you are doing that is contributing to the situation you are now in as well as what you can do to free yourself.

END OF THE WORLD

From the Book of Revelations, to Nostradamus's predictions, to movies like *The Day After,* it's no wonder that when we get an "end of the world" dream we wonder if we are actually seeing the future demise of our planet! Thankfully, nothing could be farther from the truth. End-of-the-world dreams are very common and come to us when our own personal world, as we now know it, is ending or changing. I'm sure you're starting to see a theme here, changes and endings seem to cause nightmares. Keep in mind, it is only the changes and endings that we resist or that we fear that induce nightmares. As far as end of the world dreams, the change or ending is much more vast and encompasses a massive part of your life.

I dreamed that I was outdoors watching some sporting event. All of a sudden, missiles began dropping from the sky and one exploded right on top of us! I knew this was Armageddon. I felt the explosion ripple through my body and I literally felt my body dissolve. I also heard the sound very loudly, but did not wake up until it was over. It felt so real!—Christina, 25

LAURI: What sort of major shift or change is happening in your life? Your body disintegrated because there must be some major physical changes happening with you. Sometimes, explosions in dreams can indicate an emotional explosion is about to happen. It is a warning that if you don't get rid of certain stresses or frustrations or angers in your life, you are likely to have a serious emotional outburst. Whatever the case, this dream seems to be an indicator that your personal world around you is undergoing massive change . . . let's hope it's a change for the better!

CHRISTINA REPLIES: *I did just have a baby and I was having the dream before the baby came! We also just moved into a new house at the first of this month. So what you said about my personal world undergoing massive change makes sense.*

A new baby and a new home are substantial changes, yet positive ones, so why the nightmare? As any first time Mom will tell you, a new baby is scary! So many things to worry about: Am I going to be a good mom? What is this going to do to my body? Is labor going to really hurt? Is my baby going to be healthy? Your world changes when you become a parent for the first time . . . and it's scary because it's the biggest undertaking of your life. Your world no longer revolves around you. Through this dream Christina's inner mind bid adieu to the world, and body, she left behind.

Our own personal worlds are the reality that revolves around us; it consists of the people who are immediately around us such as spouses, children, coworkers, and best friends. Our daily or repetitive surroundings such as our home, place of work, favorite hangout, place of worship or gym, and our daily and repetitive behaviors, beliefs, and self-image. When any of these areas change dramatically, or is essentially wiped out to the point that serious and focused adjustment is required, an end-of-the-world dream is likely to occur. It is the way the inner mind says, "Well, that's the end of that."

The message of end-of-the-world nightmares: Your life probably seems so different now, to the point that you may be feeling it doesn't belong to you. Whether these considerable changes that have happened—or need to happen—feel devastating or exciting, it's not the literal end of the world. Just as there are many more worlds in this universe to explore, so are there many, many more worlds you can create around yourself.

ZOMBIES

I've only ever dreamed of zombies once, and that was over fifteen years ago, so it always surprises me how often zombies stagger into the dreamscape of others. But knowing what zombies actually represent to our collective unconscious, it makes sense as to why they frequent our dreams as much as they do. Think about what a zombie is: it's a dead body that still has life to it. It is decaying and falling apart, yet it walks and eats and tries to survive even though it ought to be dead and buried. It does not belong in the land of the living. In that same vein, many of us tend to keep certain issues or grudges alive even though they came to an end some time ago.

I consistently dream that the world is being overrun by zombies. I always manage to avoid getting bitten or whatever the case may be, but they usually find a way to get inside and I find myself cornered in either an attic or closet and trapped.—Chris, 31

LAURI: You may get these dreams whenever you feel like your personal world is being crowded or overrun with issues from the past that you can't seem to let die. The zombies are likely grudges you can't let go of, issues that ought to be dead but that you are keeping alive. You are always cornered in a closet or attic. Both of these are places are where we store things away in real life, which, to the dreaming mind, represent the places in your psyche where you have stored away memories, issues, feelings you don't want to deal with. Your dreams keep forcing you in there because you haven't properly dealt with your feelings about them. Have you tucked them away in a nice little corner inside of you instead of letting out the rage? If so, this could be yet another connection to the zombies; they may represent the numbness and lack of feeling you are allowing to overtake you.

CHRIS REPLIES: *I'm having trouble letting go of my wife. She blindsided me, pretty much told me we lived a lie for the last few years and each time she told me she loved me was a lie. My life that I had is gone, swept away and hidden like dirt under a rug, and I don't feel the forgiveness I need to yet. I have trouble letting things go and this is the hardest thing I've ever had to go through. And I am afraid to let out the rage. I'm pretty easy-going and try to keep a lot locked away. I'm the funny fat guy! Ha ha! So yeah, I'm hiding a lot.*

Chris's dream encompasses everything that zombies represent: keeping alive an issue that ought to be dead and trying to go about life void of emotion. It's certainly understandable to respond that way after what his wife did, but his inner dreaming mind does not agree with this choice, which is why it continues to nag him with the zombie nightmare. Chris is mishandling the emotional aftermath of his marriage so his dreaming mind has to keep reminding him that he really needs to allow this to die so he can bury it and move on. Too often we allow our hardships in life to become our identity rather than an opportunity to improve and strengthen our self. Heartache should not define you, it should teach you. When Chris learns to bury the past and become alive again, the zombies will stagger out of his dreamscape for good!

The message of zombie nightmares: You know how zombies must eat brains? There is an issue that is eating away at your mind right now, and it is an issue that—in reality—is dead, but you are keeping it alive by giving it your energy. You need to let it go so you can live with healthy peace of mind, not a mind consumed with grudges.

BLOOD

It's frightening to bleed in real life, let alone in a dream! When you bleed, whether it is in the dream world or the real world, it means you are being drained of something you vitally need and the draining process must be stopped immediately. In most cases, blood in a dream represents one's own energy or essence and to bleed means too much of your energy or too much of you is being exerted and you are not receiving enough back in return. Even if it is someone else in the dream that is bleeding, it most likely represents your energy, your essence that is being drained.

The other night I dreamed that a friend and I were talking and all of a sudden I ran away from her because my face was bleeding and I

couldn't get it to stop. I remember waking up and then quickly
falling back to sleep.—Dana, 34

LAURI: I'm surprised you were able to fall back asleep after that one. Your face, in a dream, usually refers to something in your waking life that you need to face. Is there anything or anyone you are afraid to face and deal with? Or is something going on that is causing you to feel that you need to "save face"? Are you losing someone's respect? Are you perhaps overly concerned about how you may appear to others? All the bleeding is a warning your inner mind is sending you that you are wasting a lot of time or energy on this issue. There is a lot more of you going out than you are getting back in return.

DANA REPLIES: *My dad recently passed away and this will be the first holiday season I'll have to "face" without him. I will also have to "face" my sister whom I feel I need to "show the perfect face" to. She is always putting me down and telling me I don't know what I'm doing in life. I often feel that no matter what I do it isn't good enough in her eyes.*

Dana's dream is showing her what she allows her sister to do to her. Her sister's criticisms suck Dana of who she is. It's very painful and draining to have to face someone who doesn't treat you very well. I believe this is why the beginning of Dana's dream started out with a conversation with a friend. In a healthy relationship, adult sisters are also friends that build each other up not bleed each other of their very essence. Dana's dream also shows us that she feels helpless to stop the emotional and psychological bleeding. But notice how she chooses flight instead of fight? As long as she makes that same choice in waking life instead of confronting her sister, the bleeding will continue and she will continue to lose her sense of self every time she and her sister are together.

The message of bleeding nightmares: You are allowing too much to flow out of you and you are not getting enough back in return. Are you putting too much of yourself into a relationship? Too much time and energy into a project? Are you bleeding financially? Or is someone sucking the very life out of you? Time to stop the bleeding and reclaim what is yours before you are nothing but an empty shell.

PARALYZED

Another very common nightmare that gets reported to me is the paralysis nightmare, or what some believe to be a haunting or even demonic possession. It is such a vivid and terrifying experience because the dreamer is certain they are awake. He or she is lying in bed, aware of their surroundings but unable to move. Often there is a strange buzzing, ringing, or whispering that accompanies the experience. And then . . . there's the presence, the dark sinister figure that enters the room. This demon, this ghost: what does it want? It holds the dreamer down, and slowly begins to press on the chest stifling the dreamer's breath. The dreamer is completely and utterly powerless to move or even scream and is certain he or she is going to die when suddenly, the presence is gone, the heaviness has lifted and breath and movement are fully restored. Whew! What the *heck* just happened?

My dreams scare me. I am always in my bed and I cannot move. Then I see someone. Sometimes they have a bright light behind them; sometimes it is black around them. I try to wake up but it takes some time. I try to yell out but that does not work, either. This has been a problem for me since I can remember and it's getting worse. It absolutely terrifies me and it has gotten to the point where I think I need help.—Melissa, 30

LAURI: What you are experiencing are not dreams but rather physiological episodes of sleep paralysis, also known as the Old Hag Syndrome! The latter name comes from the superstitious belief that a witch—or an old hag—sits on the chest of the victims, rendering them immobile and often unable to breathe. What's really happening is that you are getting stuck in hypnagogia, which is the first stage we enter when we fall asleep and the last stage before we wake up. It is a transitional state between wakefulness and sleep, which is why you are aware that you are in your bed.

Here's what happens, when we enter the dreaming state (also known as REM), the brain releases a chemical that literally paralyzes our skeletal muscles so that we do not get up and act out our dreams. It's a safety mechanism. Sometimes, when we are having a fitful night of sleep, or aren't getting enough good solid sleep allowing us to go through all the sleep phases, we may start to wake up before the brain can reactivate our muscles (most people don't realize what a complicated process it is to simply fall asleep and to wake up). This can cause us to get stuck in hypnagogia and experience sleep paralysis, where your mind is mostly awake but your body is still paralyzed.

For some reason, it feels like there is a dark sinister presence in the room, often at the foot of the bed. We'll often feel pressure on our chest and have a hard time breathing. Other symptoms include shaking or hearing strange sounds. Some people feel like they are leaving their bodies. Why it is so frightening is uncertain but researchers have discovered that the amygdala, which is located deep inside the brain and is the body's fear center, is highly active during REM sleep. Couple this high activity with awakening paralyzed while still in the dream state, and you have a recipe for terror. But it never lasts too long and is completely harmless. Rest assured, there is nothing wrong with you. The best way to cure yourself is to make sure you establish a normal bedtime routine. Go to bed at the same time every night; the body loves and adapts very well to routine, and make sure you get at least seven hours of sleep straight.

MELISSA REPLIES: *Thank you so much! I was thinking there was something wrong with me, and it is true I do not get much sleep. I own a bar and have two kids so by the time I get to bed I average only four to five hours of sleep. I will try my best to get more sleep.*

I have had this experience before, once as a child and once when I was in the third trimester of pregnancy. At that point, due to my body being a very large incubator, good, solid sleep was not easy to come by. When people report this experience to me, after I explain the science of what is going on, I tell them not to fear it but embrace it because it is actually a way cool state of mind. You are awake and aware while in a dream state at the same time! You see, once you understand what is really going on, it takes the fear factor out of it so that you can explore the wonders of hypnagogia. At this point you could will yourself back into sleep and remain lucid so that you can control what happens in your dream. Or you could simply ask the presence in the room a question such as, "What is the meaning of life?" and see what sort of answer you get. You could will yourself to float up and out of your bed and see if you can move through the wall. There are really no limits to what you can do because waking life rules do not apply!

While paralysis is a by-product of this fascinating physiological experience, it is not to be confused with dreams where paralysis is part of the story line. If you have a dream where some part of your body is paralyzed, for example, the popular dream where you are trying to run from a pursuer but your legs won't move, then you need to ask yourself what in your waking life has become stagnant? Paralysis is an inability to move, therefore in a dream it is connected to something in waking life that is stuck and no longer progressing. The part of the body that is paralyzed will give you insight into what the issue is as well as how you may be playing a part in the lack of movement. Please refer to Chapter 6 to refresh yourself on what your various body parts mean.

Demonlike presences in the bedroom are also a by-product of sleep paralysis; they can appear in our dreams and nightmares, too, in which case we need to examine them closely. A demon or the devil would represent your own personal demons, such as drinking, smoking, indulging in some way that takes away from your life and from you. Demons or the devil may also refer to something you have "demonized" and grown afraid of or resentful of. In either case, your dream is showing you the negative impact the issue, behavior or person is making in your life and is a call to action to exorcise the problem out of your life before it completely overtakes you.

While nightmares are no fun, they are good for us because they alert us to what is being mishandled or what is being ignored. They force us to take action to correct what is wrong and they will be relentless until we do. It's important to remember that the nightmare is a very tangible tool that can be used to overcome the past, to face our fears, and to become a more powerful individual. Don't fear your nightmares; embrace them because they are giving you the opportunity to conquer and persevere.

I have had dreams and I have had nightmares, but I have conquered my nightmares because of my dreams.—Dr. Jonas Salk, developer of the polio vaccine

How to End Recurring Nightmares

Nightmares are a terrifying experience and are often hard to shake. They can leave you feeling uneasy for days. Most of us experience a nightmare only once in a while, but some are plagued with them . . . almost every night! This makes bedtime the most dreaded time of all. It doesn't have to be this way. Nightmares do not have to imprison you. The best way to end a recurring nightmare is to pinpoint the issue that is causing the nightmare and do what you can to correct the issue. Sometimes it's as simple as stepping outside of your comfort zone and asserting yourself in some way that puts an end to the issue. Other times it may require professional help, depending on how deeply rooted and severe the issue is. No matter what the case, a nightmare is a cry for help from your inner self. It is letting you know something is wrong in your life and needs attention.

Write Down Your Dream. Write down your dream when you are sitting in bed, right before you turn out the lights. It's crucial you do this at bedtime because it needs to be fresh on your mind so that when you go to sleep your dreams will work on it for you. Write down your dream in as much detail as you can remember, including all emotions and thoughts you had in the dream. As you write, certain details may come back to your memory that you had forgotten. Writing down the dream in all its gory detail will help desensitize you to the horror of it and when you can step outside of the emotions you can look at the dream more objectively.

Add Conversation to the Dream. This is a very therapeutic exercise. Whomever the antagonist is in your dream, whether it is a creature or a person, whether you actually know the person or not, they represent the waking issue that is causing you to feel powerless. Somewhere within the context of the dream, you need to fit in a conversation with the bad guy. Write out what you would love to say if that person or creature were actually sitting in front of you. Write out what is on your mind, how they make you feel, what you'd like them to know. In some cases, you may be the bad guy in the dream doing harm to someone else. Write out a conversation with yourself. Take up as many pages as you like. Get it all out of you and onto paper. Once you get going, you'll be surprised what comes out of your pen. You'll find that you'll even write out what the bad guy says back to you. Doing this helps you to connect with that part of you that is consumed by the fear, anger, or guilt that is causing the dreams. It opens up a dialogue between yourself and your inner self. It also helps you to sort out your innermost thoughts and feelings, which you probably push down while awake . . . yet they are screaming for help while you dream.

Change the Ending. Remember, this is your dream, your creation, you gave it to yourself therefore you can rewrite it. When you get to the end, or to the most frightening or desperate point, change the dream to how you would like it to turn out. Be creative. It's dreamland so no rules apply! Just make sure you give yourself the power and make sure you take control of the dream scenario because, ultimately, it is a sense of feeling powerless against our issues that causes nightmares. This also reprograms your subconscious mind to give you the outcome you want.

When You're Done, Rip It Out of Your Journal and Throw It Away. This symbolizes that the nightmare and the issue that is causing it are no longer useful to you. It is garbage and, like garbage, needs to be taken out of your life. The inner subconscious mind speaks in symbols so it will understand this gesture. After that, turn out your light and see what kind of dream you get. Odds are, you will get a dream that shows you are beginning to move past the issue. Whatever dream(s) you get, make sure you write it down when you wake up or it will be gone after breakfast. You will then need to apply what you have learned from this book to the dream so that you can figure out the message you are giving yourself through the dream.

You may have to do this technique several nights in a row in order to make the nightmares change and stop. If you are consistent, it will absolutely work. But most of the people I have taught to use this technique get results the very first night. This very same technique has proven to be helpful in helping war veterans overcome their recurring post-traumatic stress disorder dreams and I know you'll find it to be unbelievably helpful to you too.

Once you've been successful in changing or ending the nightmare, you'll find that your emotional connection to the waking life issue will change too. If it's an issue from the past you haven't been able to get over, you'll find that it doesn't carry as much weight as it used to. If it's a current issue you have been mishandling or ignoring, you'll find it's not quite as frightening anymore and you will feel more apt to take care of it correctly. What you are doing is working from the inside out rather than working from the outside in.

This technique will work for you and will work especially well for children. If you have a child that has a recurring nightmare, know that it is connected to something happening in their life they feel powerless to control. I recommend you have your child draw the scary part of the nightmare, older children can write out the nightmare or even draw it in comic book form. Then ask them to be creative and redraw or rewrite the ending, the way they would like it to play out. Doing this gives the child a sense of power and control, which they feel they lack in waking life. Once the dream changes or stops you'll see big positive changes in your child because he or she will feel accomplished and empowered!

FASCINATING DREAM FACT: The "mare" in nightmare is not about a female horse. It comes from the Old English *mare* meaning "goblin."

Final Checklist

RULES TO REMEMBER

In the introduction of this book, I assured you that by the time you were finished with it, you'd never dismiss your dreams again. I can only assume by now that you are more than convinced of the power of your own dreaming mind and are eager to find what answers and guidance await you in your dreams tonight, as well as in all the dreams that are yet to come.

I've put together a final checklist for you of points you need to remember when figuring out your dreams. As random or bizarre as dreams often seem, they do play by certain rules. The following list outlines those rules for you and if you apply them to your dreams, you'll be surprised how easily the message in your dream reveals itself to you.

1. Dreams speak in metaphors. "She's the apple of my eye." "Dad was boiling mad." "He's the black sheep of the family." Metaphors compare two seemingly unlike things in order to make a point. Our dreams work the same way, which is one of the reasons they are often so bizarre. Make it a habit to ask yourself how the characters, the objects, the actions, and the settings in your dreams are comparable to yourself and the events in your waking life. How is your dream last night a metaphor for your life right now or for how your day went yesterday? Does the raging storm in last night's dream seem like the current state of your marriage? Does winning the lottery in your dream remind you of how you felt when you recently got that promotion? Like a metaphor, your dreams illustrate what's going on in your life and how you truly feel about it. When you can find the metaphor, you have found the message.

2. Dreams love to use puns and figures of speech. Sometimes the figure of speech or the pun in your dream will be as plain as day, for example if you dream of lots of bugs then obviously something is really "bugging" you in waking life. Or if you dream you're walking along train tracks that turn to the right then it's pretty clear the dream means "you're on the right track." But if you were to dream of crabs, oysters, and clams, it may take some digging before you realize that your dream is showing you that you have been acting *shellfish* lately. It does take a certain level of creativity and knowledge of word play but, like the metaphors, if you can find the pun or figure of speech then you've found the message.

3. Your dreams are always connected to the previous day. Whatever happens in your life today, whatever thought runs through your mind, whatever accomplishment you make, whatever conversations you have, whatever frustrates you is likely show up in your dreams tonight in some form or fashion.

Be sure to ask yourself how your dream last night reminds you of yesterday. Keeping a day journal in tandem with a dream journal will help you to connect the dots between the imagery in your dream to the events and thoughts and conversations of the previous day. Write down all TV shows, books, etc., that you read, saw, or talked about that day. You never know when your dream will borrow something you saw or read in order to help it make its message.

4. Your dreams are all about you! When we dream, we go inward and focus on the self. Think about it: your eyes are closed, your room is dark, the outside world is shut off, so *you* go in to yourself and focus on *you* and all the things that *you* are dealing with right now.

Our dreams will show us ourselves in the guise of different people or animals or even objects so that we can gain a better understanding of ourselves and our current behavior.

Everything in your dream is you. The exception to this rule is when you dream of someone you deal with closely on a daily basis, such as your roommate, your spouse, your boyfriend or girlfriend, your children, your coworker. The best way to determine if someone in your dream is playing his or herself, rather than representing some aspect of you, is to ask yourself if there is a current concern or issue you have with the person or are they involved in the same situation with you. If the answer is no, then odds are, the person is indeed a representation of some part of you.

So start with yourself first—how is this creature, this person, this object like me? What three words first come to mind when you think of that person, creature, etc.? Can you connect any of the words you chose to yourself and your life and behavior right now?

If the dots don't connect, then work outward. How is this creature, this person, this object like my spouse? My best friend? My child? Etc. Do this and those dots are sure to connect. There is always a link. Nothing and no one in your dream is random.

5. The emotion you feel in a dream is directly connected to how you currently feel about something in waking life. The emotional centers of the brain are highly active when we dream, which is why our dreams can sometimes be intensely frightening or profoundly awe-inspiring, but that's not to say those emotions should be disregarded. They are definitely connected to waking life issues that make you feel the same way, but perhaps not as exaggerated.

If your dream is filled with anger, ask yourself what or who is angering you right now in real life. If you cry in your dreams, ask yourself what, in waking life, is causing you sorrow. You'll be able to make the connection, and when you do, know that the emotion is being expressed while you sleep because you may not be expressing it effectively while awake.

6. Whatever is said to you in a dream is advice you are giving yourself, and whatever question is asked of you in a dream is a question you are posing to yourself. Remember, dreams are a conversation with the self. During the day we often ignore that little intuitive voice in the back of our head that is constantly nagging and advising us. When we go to sleep and enter the dream state, that voice rises to the surface and takes on the form of someone in our dream and gives us the message again in hopes that this time, we'll pay attention. But of course, what is being said to you in a dream may not be in literal language, but symbolic dream language. By now, you should be able to decipher that language so you can get the message.

This same rule applies to questions you are asked in a dream—whether the question is coming from you or someone else—it is a question you are really asking yourself. The questions in your dreams are often rhetorical, meant to provoke thought or are a call to action, action that needs to be taken in your life in order to improve your current circumstances.

7. The objects in your dream tend to represent your skills and abilities. We *use* objects to accomplish something just as we use our skills and abilities to accomplish something. We use a phone to communicate, we use a car to go somewhere, we use a toilet to . . . you know . . . relieve ourselves. So the objects in your dream, and how well or how poorly the objects work, are connected to your waking life skills and how well or poorly you are using them.

A phone that won't dial is showing you that you aren't communicating well enough with someone in waking life. A toilet that is backed up is showing you that your ability to relieve yourself of frustration or negativity isn't working.

Just as our dreams give form to the different parts of our personality, so do they give form to our abilities, skills, and our inner tools.

8. Numbers and amounts in a dream are directly connected to that same number or amount in waking life. If a certain number shows up in your dream, then you need to put your thinking cap on and go through all the numbers in your life such as birthdates, addresses, salary, how many years you've been married, etc. Odds are, you'll be able to connect it to something in which case you'll then need to ask yourself how that connection—if you connect the number in your dream to your ex-boyfriend's address, for example—is relevant to your life right now. Do the same thing when there is a specific amount of something in your dream. If you dream of three eggs, then there are likely going to be three ideas or projects in your waking life that are about to hatch.

9. When a dream suddenly switches scenes, it is showing you how one thing did or could lead to another in waking life. Sudden scene changes often make dreams hard to follow and understand, but that doesn't mean there isn't a clear message in there somewhere. The best way to figure out a dream that seems to jump all over the place is to take it scene by scene. Start with the first scene as though it were a dream by itself and decipher the setting, the symbols, action, etc. until you feel you have found the message. Then move on to the next scene and do the same. As you move from scene to scene, you are likely to start finding a common thread that ties it all together. If not, then once you've got all the meanings and messages figured out, ask yourself how the message of the first scene could lead to or could be connected to the message of the next scene. Keep using the thought process of *this* then *that*: "if *this* happens, then *that* will happen" or "if I do *this,* then I'll do *that.*" You'll be able to string it all together and tie it up with a nice bow when you're done. And what a gift that message will be.

10. The end of the dream is often the point your dreaming mind wants to leave you with. That is, if your dream ends naturally and you aren't awakened by an alarm clock or the dog licking your face. Just like a good story, the moral is found at the end. The same is true with dreams.

For example, if your dream ends just as your car goes off a cliff, then the main point your dream is leaving you with is that you have steered some issue in your life off track and if you don't get back on course it's going to be a downward spiral for you.

Although the ending may not always be happy, it does give you something to focus on and work with so that you can take control of your life and steer it where you want it to go.

Remember, your dreams can be your best friend once you know how to communicate with them. You may not always like what they have to say but, like a best friend who only wants the best for you, they will be brutally honest when they have to yet consistent in their wisdom and guidance.

After all, your dreams are your deepest, most focused thoughts. They are the most powerful part of who you are. Now that you understand the ways of the dreaming mind, I hope you will have a lasting relationship with yours because no matter how difficult an issue life may hand you, once you dream on it, you'll know what to do.

Dream Glossary

✦

This glossary of dream symbols was designed to be used as a quick reference that will aid you in your continued dream work. Many of the symbols in this glossary can be found throughout the dreams that are discussed in this book. You will find a reference after the definitions of those symbols that directs you to the chapter or chapters where you can read that particular symbol in an actual dream. Each symbol may not hold the same meaning for everybody. The definitions in this glossary are the most common meanings for each symbol and should help you realize the true meaning for you. Happy dream working!

ADULTERY: Something has become a third wheel in your relationship. Is your loved one doing too much of something that takes away from the relationship? Your subconscious mind may see it as a "mistress" or another man. Your dream is telling you that you are feeling "cheated" out of your loved one's time and attention. If you are the one cheating, ask yourself what you may be doing that is taking away from the time your mate needs from you. Is it a new baby? Is it your job? Your friends? Traveling? These dreams are telling you that you and your mate need to find a way to appreciate one another more. (**Ch. 9**)

AIRPLANE: A path you have chosen may be taking off and reaching new heights, getting you closer to the high goals you have set for yourself. Usually points to career but could symbolize anything you want to keep "up" such as finances, a relationship, your self-esteem, etc. If your dream airplane is crashing, it could mean you fear something in your life, or within you may come crashing down around you, or that you have recently suffered a letdown. (**Ch. 4**)

ALIEN: Symbolizes something you are unfamiliar with, something you have never encountered before. Unfamiliar territory. What issue in your life seems foreign to you right now? (**Ch. 4**)

ALLIGATOR: Verbal expression. The large mouth and sharp teeth often point to sharp biting remarks. Have you or has someone else around you been saying some harsh things? Have you or has someone around you been snappy? (**Ch. 2**)

ANIMALS: Symbolize our basic instincts and behaviors. Are you behaving or do you need to behave like the animal in your dream? Is there anyone around you that is behaving like the animal in your dream? What characteristics does that animal have and how can you connect them to you or someone around you? (**Ch. 5**)

ANKLE: Your ability to be flexible. Have you been too flexible lately allowing someone to take advantage of you? Or do you need to be more flexible right now in order for a situation to progress? **(Ch. 5)**

ANTS: Typically, any bug in your dream indicates that someone or something is really "bugging" you. Ants in particular are hard workers and store away for the winter and therefore may reflect your own industriousness.

ARGUMENT: Do you have a real-life issue, disagreement, or unhappiness with the person you argued with in the dream? If so, then pay attention to what you both said. There may be something very enlightening within the dream argument. If you have no beef with the person in your dream, then ask yourself what you may be angry with yourself about. Odds are, your dream argument is about an inner struggle you are trying to sort through.

ARM: The way you express yourself and/or reach out to others. Your ability to do something. Is your arm afflicted in the dream? If so, you may be feeling incapable right now. Could be pun on "arm yourself."

ATTIC: Mental place where you store your higher and spiritual ideals and goals. Is also a place in the home where things that are no longer needed are stored and therefore represents the place in your psyche where things you have forgotten or do not want to deal with are stored. Your dream is placing you in the attic because there may be something you need to confront or bring back into your life. **(Ch. 7)**

BABY: Something new in your life that needs lots of care and attention in order to reach its full potential, such as a new relationship, new job, etc. Can also mean you are going through a rebirth. Are you reinventing yourself? Have you gained a new awareness? What is new about you? Are you starting over or do you need to start over? Can also refer to someone in your life who you are "babying" or who is acting like a "baby." **(Ch. 2)**

BACK: Your strength, your ability to carry a heavy burden. Can also mean you need to or you have put something behind you, or that you have turned your back on something/someone. Or is there something you need to get back to in your life?

BACKSEAT: If you are in the backseat, then you are not in control of some area of your life, you always want to be in the driver's seat in your dreams. Whoever or whatever is in the backseat represents something you need to put behind you for now until you can get back to it. **(Ch. 4)**

BACKYARD: Symbolizes things you like to keep private, to yourself and away from the prying eyes of others. Can also sometimes represent the past, that which is behind us. **(Ch. 7)**

BAG: May refer to fear of losing your job: getting "sacked." May indicate that you or someone around you has something to hide: "Don't let the cat out of the bag."

BALL: May be telling you that the ball is in your court, it's your turn to take action. Can mean childishness or competitiveness. Time to play hard ball. The type of ball is also significant.

BAR: A need to relax, let go of inhibitions

BASEMENT: Mental place where you store memories, attitudes, behaviors, etc., that you would like to forget about, that you keep below the surface. Can sometimes symbolize the past. If your dream takes place in a basement, it means there is likely something from your past you tried to keep buried but need to bring to the surface and deal with it. **(Ch. 7)**

BATHROOM: Do you need to cleanse yourself of negativity, or frustration, or a destructive behavior? If the bathroom is filthy or unusable, then you are not properly relieving your frustrations. Your dream is telling you that you are holding in too much. **(Ch. 7)**

BATTLE: What are you battling in waking life? Weight? Smoking? An illness? Self-esteem issues? Someone else? What are you trying to overcome? The battle in your dream reflects how you are winning or losing the battle in waking life. **(Ch. 3)**

BEACH: May mean you need to take a break and relax. On a deeper level, could symbolize your own power; the tremendous energy of the ocean, the land and the sky all coming together. Your creativity. How are you feeling inspired lately?

BEAR: Is there anything going on in your life right now that is un-*bear*able? Bears can also symbolize someone around you—or perhaps a part of you—that has inconsistent emotional energy, sweet and cuddly like a teddy bear one moment, and then harsh and aggressive, like an angry mother bear another moment. Could also point to someone who is overprotective. **(Ch. 5)**

BEDROOM: You may need more rest. May be commenting on private, intimate matters, particularly with your mate. Is something keeping you up at night? A *childhood bedroom* often points to the beginnings of your hopes, ideals, fears, etc. It may be time to examine them and ask yourself if you are where you thought you'd be by now. **(Ch. 7)**

BICYCLE: A need for balance in your life. Like the two wheels on a bike, what are you trying to balance in waking life? Family and career? Business and personal? The way you ride the bike tells you how well you are or aren't balancing your issues. **(Ch. 4)**

BIRD: Your ability to soar, to rise above where you are now. Can also refer to your ability to break free from something that has you feeling caged in. **(Ch. 5)**

BITE: Has someone around you said something hurtful or critical that wounded your feelings? Are you the one saying hurtful things? Biting can also point to something that is a bad situation, something that "bites," so to speak. **(Ch. 4)**

BLACK: Mysterious, unknown, can sometimes symbolize negativity.

BLIND: You may be turning a blind eye toward something. This dream is telling you to open your eyes and take a good hard look at what is really going on in your waking life. You are not seeing something for what it really is. **(Ch. 6)**

BLOOD: Your energy, your life force, that which keeps you going. If you see a lot of blood in your dream then you are wasting or losing energy or someone or something is draining your energy. Too much is going out of you and you aren't getting enough back in return. Are you bleeding financially? **(Ch. 6)**

BLUE: Often points to depression or "the blues."

BOAT: Your ability to navigate through an emotional situation. If the boat is sinking it means you are getting emotionally overwhelmed, perhaps sinking into a depression or you are getting in over your head. Boats and ships can also point to a romantic relationship: the love boat, two ships passing in the night, etc. The boat in your dream will reflect if your current situation—particularly romantic situation—is smooth sailing or rocky and sinking. **(Ch. 4)**

BOMB: Wiping out a massive part of your life. Can also point to an enormous emotional outburst. Bad news. Has someone "dropped the bomb" on you?

BONES: Something you need to bury for good and stop bringing up. A dog bone may be referring to a relationship. Are you rewarding your partner fairly or are you leading them on, making them perform for you before you reward them? Or are they doing this to you?

BOSS: Is there an issue with your boss right now in real life? If not, then your boss represents your ability to take charge and make decisions. Ask yourself where you need to be more authoritative in your life. If dreaming of a former boss, ask yourself if there are any qualities that boss has that you could take on as your own right now to improve your current situation. May also be a reference to that time in your life, who you were when you worked for that person. Have you progressed since then? **(Ch. 2)**

BOX: What have you been holding in lately? Your opinion? An idea? Your frustrations? A secret? A box usually represents our ability to contain something; it is something that ought to be released. Do you need to open up and break out of your box, or think outside the box? If you find a box or someone gives you a box, then what is inside the box will very often represent your God-given gifts or abilities that you need release upon the world or on those around you. **(Ch. 5)**

BOY: An unknown boy in your dream may represent your child self, the part of you that needs to be carefree and likes to have fun. Sometimes unknown children in dreams can represent a project or something else in your life that requires your attention and focus, something that—like a child—is not yet fully developed. A boy can also be an undeveloped aspect of your own personality, specifically undeveloped male qualities such as your assertiveness and ability to make firm decisions. **(Ch. 2)**

BREASTS: Your ability to nurture and mother yourself and those around you.

BRIDGE: Transition, getting from point A to point B. Are you trying to cross over into some new area of your life? If the bridge collapses or you fall off the bridge then you are worried you are not going to make it through this transition in your life.

BROKEN: If something is broken in a dream then you need to ask yourself what in waking life has been broken. A promise? A relationship? Your trust? A deal? A hope? Or has there been a recent breakthrough in some area of your life as far as a communication breakthrough, a breakthrough at work or with a goal, etc.

BROTHER: Is there a current issue with your brother that you are concerned about? If so, this dream is giving you some guidance with this issue. If not, your brother may represent a part of you, a part of you that is like your brother. What qualities does your brother have? Do you need to utilize those qualities in your own life?

BUGS: It's time to deal with something or someone that is "bugging you." The more bugs in the dream the more of a problem the issue is. Do what is necessary to "squash" the issue once and for all. **(Ch. 5)**

BUILDING: A building symbolizes something in your life you have already built. What is the building like? Is it huge and towering? This indicates success. Is it under construction? It is something that is not yet finished. Is it falling apart or abandoned? It then symbolizes something in your life that you have been neglecting and needs more attention . . . or perhaps needs to be demolished. **(Ch. 4)**

BURNED: How are you feeling burned out lately? Are you exhausted or tired of something? Or have you been emotionally burned? Has someone's anger hurt your feelings recently?

BURY: Ask yourself, "Do I need to bury this issue and move on?" "Is this issue dead to me?"

BUS: One of the slowest means of getting from point A to point B. Are things going slowly for you? Can also symbolize conforming, going along with the masses. If missing a bus, you may be missing an opportunity in waking life. **(Ch. 4)**

BUTT: Time to put something "behind" you. Can also refer to your recent past. **(Ch. 6)**

BUTTERFLY: Transformation. Just as a caterpillar changes into a butterfly, you are changing into a higher form or a higher awareness.

CAKE: Time to celebrate. Cakes, cookies and other treats are telling you it's time to treat yourself for a job well done. If watching your diet in waking life, to dream of cake is the way your inner mind tries to get what it can't in waking life.

CANCER: What is eating away at you right now? Like a cancer, something is consuming you. Your dream is letting you know there is something or someone unhealthy in your life that needs to be removed. **(Ch. 6)**

CAR: Shows how you are traveling through life or through a particular situation or how well you are reaching your goals. Can also refer to your "drive" or motivation. **(Ch. 4)**

CASINO: Is there something you are considering taking a chance on? Your dream may be showing you if it is worth the gamble or not. **(Ch. 2)**

CASTLE: Dwelling places in dreams almost always represent the self. So the castle in your dream is *you*. It suggests that you have very grand plans for yourself or feel very good about who you are. You are rich in talent and/or in personality. A castle can also mean that you feel you are "in a very good place" in your life. (**Ch. 7**)

CAT: Feminine sexual energy; "sex kitten." A cat biting you can mean a call to intimacy. A sick or starving cat can mean you are having a dry spell. Can also point to independence, aloofness, gossip, or "cattiness," balance or any other qualities you associate with a cat. A predatory cat is your ability to protect your best interests as well as go out on the hunt and get what you want in life. If the cat is a threat in your dream then this part of you is trying to get your attention because it wants you to utilize it in your life. (**Ch. 5**)

CAVE: Caves are for exploring. Usually a cave in a dream is about exploring your inner self, discovering what makes you tick. Was it scary in your dream cave? If so, that may mean there is something you have buried deep within you that you are afraid to deal with. A cave in a dream can also be a pun on "caving in." Are you or is someone around you about to cave and give up?

CELEBRITY: Your ability to shine and perform. What the celebrity is doing in the dream may reflect how you are acting in life or in a particular situation. What is your dream celebrity best known for? What qualities do you associate with that celebrity? Perhaps it is a song they sing or a role they play. If you applied those qualities to yourself, would you shine in life? (**Ch. 2**)

CHASING: If you are being chased then you are running from some issue or confrontation in waking life. What or whom are you avoiding? If you are chasing something or someone then you may be up against a deadline in waking life, perhaps even a self-imposed deadline. (**Ch. 10**)

CHEATING: *See* Adultery.

CHEETAH: Predatory cats represent your ability to go out on the prowl and bring what you want into your life. A cheetah in particular can sometimes refer to someone who is a "cheater" in real life. Cheetahs are also known for their great speed and may be a nudge from your subconscious to hurry up and finish something. (**Ch. 5**)

CHEF: Your ability to plan and prepare, to cook up a scheme. Can also represent your ability to provide emotional nourishment to others.

CHEST: (part of the body): The chest is where the heart is and often refers to your emotions, or your love for somebody or something. If the chest is afflicted in your dream then you may be going through a heartache or are losing your feelings toward someone. (**Ch. 6**)

CHEST: (furniture): A chest such as a treasure chest symbolizes the place within your psyche where you store treasured memories or beliefs that are valuable to you. It may also symbolize something you have recently discovered that could prove to be valuable in your life like a new talent or skill.

CHICKEN: Have you been afraid to deal with something lately? Or has someone around you been too "chicken" to do something? (**Ch. 2**)

CHILD: Unknown children in your dream most often symbolize your inner child, the part of you that wants to have fun,
that doesn't want to grow up and deal with responsibilities. Do
you need to pay attention to your inner child and have some
fun in your life? Are you being too childish about something?
Unknown children can also refer to a project, idea, or endeavor
of yours that is not fully developed and still needs your care
and focus. (Ch. 2)

CHIN: Your ability to be tough, to "take it on the chin" or to
"keep your chin up" despite what might be going wrong.

CHOKING: Are you choking back your words? Is there something you want or need to say but can't bring yourself to do it
or are being forced by someone else to keep quiet? Your dream
is showing you that not speaking up or voicing your thoughts
is harmful to you. If you frequently dream of choking and wake
up unable to breathe, you may want to get checked for sleep
apnea as waking up choking is a common symptom.

CHURCH: Your moral foundation. Are you dealing with a moral
dilemma right now? Your dream may be reminding you of your
morals in order to deal with the issue at hand. It may also be telling you to have faith and believe that things will get better or
what you are praying for may happen for you.

CIGARETTE: If you have recently quit smoking it is very
common to dream that you are still smoking cigarettes. It often
takes about seven years for these dreams to taper off, so hang in
there! If you are not a smoker or haven't smoked in more than
a decade, then a cigarette may represent a bad habit or negative behavior pattern of yours or of someone around you. Ask

yourself if you have been habitually doing something that is not good for you or if someone around you is doing this.

CLASSMATE: An old classmate isn't playing himself or herself in your dream but rather something you have in common with that person, or a personality trait of theirs that you need to use in your life right now. Sometimes an old classmate can be referring to who you were back then. Do you need to leave that old state of mind in the past or do you need to bring it to the present? (Ch. 2)

CLASSROOM: Time to learn a lesson or educate yourself on certain matters. You may be feeling tested or that you need to pass a particular situation with flying colors. Do you have a fear of failure? If searching for a class, you are directionless in some area of your life. If you are late for class, you are afraid of missing an opportunity or are feeling unprepared. (Ch. 3)

CLIFF: Are you on the verge of something? Are you afraid you are about to fall into a depression? Has something come to a sudden end in your life? If you are being pushed off a cliff, then you are feeling that you are being pushed over the edge in real life; you have finally had enough. If you are jumping off a cliff then you may be jumping into something too quickly. Look before you leap! (Ch. 4)

CLIMB: If you are struggling while you climb in your dream, then there is something in waking life you are having a hard time overcoming or a goal you are finding difficult to reach. Your dream is encouraging you to keep moving toward your goal because when you finally reach it the "high," you experience will be well worth it.

CLOCK: Usually, a clock or a watch in a dream means you are under some sort of deadline in waking life. What deadline are you trying to beat right now? Is it a self-imposed deadline? A clock for a woman can point to her biological clock. Has it started ticking? Are you beginning to worry time is running out? What is causing you to feel impatient?

CLOSET: The place in your psyche where you store ideas, feelings, behaviors, etc. that you don't want others to know about. Pay close attention to what is in the closet in your dream and ask yourself if it represents something you need to open up about. **(Ch. 3)**

CLOUDS: Your thought forms that are constantly changing. Fluffy white clouds symbolize positive thoughts. Dark clouds mean negative or depressing thoughts. If you are watching a cloud change shape, it suggests you may be changing your mind about something. **(Ch. 8)**

COMPUTER: How are you computing or processing certain information you've recently learned? Can also represent your means of communication.

COOKING: Cooking up ideas and schemes, something is in the works. What are you preparing for in real life? Can also show up in pregnant women's dreams. **(Ch. 7)**

COWORKER: Is there a current issue with your coworker right now? Your dream may be showing you how to sort it out. Was your coworker helpful or harmful to you in your dream? Or was your coworker helpless? If harmful you may need to address this in waking life. Sometimes your coworker will be standing in for a part of your personality that is like him or her. What quality or fault do you have in common with this person? Or what quality of this person would you like to have for yourself? **(Ch. 2)**

CRACK: Are you or is someone around you beginning to crack under the pressure? If something is cracked or cracking in your dream, then it suggests that something in your life may be starting to crumble. What needs your attention right now? What do you need to mend or rebuild? If you are peeking through a crack, then you may be on the verge of new knowledge about something.

CRASH: May be referring to a mistake you have made recently. What in your life is a mess? Are you headed for an emotional crash? This could be a warning you are sending yourself not to veer off course. **(Ch. 4)**

CROCODILE: *See* Alligator.

CROWD: Where in your life are you feeling crowded or overwhelmed? Do you have too much going on? Are you feeling unorganized? Many people can also symbolize all the different aspects of your personality or your life. An unruly crowd indicates chaos or anger in waking life.

CRYING: If you are crying in a dream, then there is something in your waking life that is upsetting you and that you may not be allowing yourself to cry over. If someone else is crying, this could still point to your own sorrow. But you should also look at the people around you in waking life. Is there anyone around you that is depressed? **(Ch. 2 and Ch. 10)**

CUT: Desire or need to cut someone or something out of your life, a separation. Can also point to cutting, painful remarks. Criticism.

DARK: To be in the dark in a dream means you are "in the dark" on some issue in waking life; there is something going on you need to shed some light on. What are you uncertain about right now? Can also mean depression. (**Ch. 3, Ch. 8, and Ch. 10**)

DAUGHTER: If you are dreaming of your own daughter, ask yourself if there is a current issue with her that you are concerned about. If not—and especially if she is no longer under your roof—then your daughter may be standing in for some aspect of yourself that is like your daughter. What part of you do you see in her the most? That is most likely what she represents in your dream. If you don't have a daughter in real life, then your daughter in your dream is most likely some project, some relationship, or even some part of you that is still growing and developing, something *you* are responsible for. (**Ch. 2**)

DEADLINE: Are you up against a deadline in real life? Have you imposed a personal deadline on yourself? How do you feel like time is running out in real life? Are you worried about missing out on an opportunity?

DEATH: Change, the old dying off in order to make way for the new. The end of an issue or relationship. A part of yourself, a part of your life, something in your world coming to a close. Fear not. Rebirth is around the corner. Dead people in a dream usually refer to issues that are dead, that you should no longer give any energy to. Ask yourself if you are holding a grudge that you need to let die. (**Ch. 10**)

DECK: A porch or deck is an extension of the house so it may reflect your ability to extend yourself to others as well as your ability to be "open" and honest. A back porch is behind the house and can either represent something in your very recent past or something you prefer to keep private.

DEFORMITY: Uncertainty. Something in your life is not what it ought to be. Do you have a distorted view of something? Some aspect of yourself or of your life has not been allowed to grow and develop in a healthy and normal manner.

DESERT: Where in your life is there a lack of productivity? Where in your life have you hit a dry spell? **(Ch. 3)**

DEVIL: An evil / negative force. Something around you or within you that tempts you to do the wrong thing, to blame others, and to be naughty. Could be a warning to clean up your act. Devils and demons in dreams are often referring to your own personal demons such as addiction, a bad behavior or attitude, a weakness, etc. **(Ch. 10)**

DIAMOND: Jewels in dreams often refer to jewels of wisdom. Has someone given "valuable" advice recently? Is someone around you or is some project or idea a "diamond" in the rough? A diamond can represent your ability to shine and dazzle others.

DIGGING: A form of searching. Dig deeper into the issue. Dig deep into yourself or into your past to discover the answers or insight you need. Maybe you are being too nosy. Can reflect a fear of something from your past being dug up. Can also mean you are digging yourself into a deeper hole, a worsening situation.

DIRT: Dirt and filth in a dream often refers to negativity, frustration, or depression as these are things that "dirty" an otherwise clear psyche. **(Ch. 3 and Ch. 10)**

DISEASE: Is something or someone eating away at you? Is something getting progressively worse? Are you or is someone around you exhibiting a behavior that is unhealthy or imbalanced? Your dream is telling you it is time to heal the situation. **(Ch. 6)**

DIVORCE: If you are currently going through a divorce or are recently divorced, then dreaming of divorce is extremely common because your dreams are trying to help you cope. If you are not recently divorced or going through one, then to dream of divorce means there has been a separation of ideas lately between you and your spouse. What sort of disagreement have you had lately? Has something like a job or a project or a person come in between the two of you? Divorce, even if you aren't the one getting divorced in the dream, can mean there is something or someone you need to separate yourself from.

DOCK: Is some area of your life that was in motion and moving forward now parked? Do you need to park it for a while and reevaluate? A dock or a harbor can also represent something or someone that gives you a sense of security and need to stay put for a while. **(Ch. 4)**

DOCTOR: Time for emotional, spiritual, or physical healing. The part of you that knows what's good for you. Your ability to heal yourself or a particular situation. Are you in an unhealthy situation or relationship? Pay attention to the advice your dream doctor gives you. **(Ch. 2)**

DOG: Symbolizes someone you feel is a loyal companion. Usually refers to your mate but could also be a friend or coworker. Could symbolize responsibility, as pets are responsibilities. Could symbolize a fear if you are afraid of dogs. May also symbolize your need or desire to buckle down and train yourself to behave. Look at the type of dog in your dream. What is that type of dog known for? **(Ch. 5)**

DOLL: Is someone toying with you or manipulating or belittling you? Or are you doing this to someone else? If you are cuddling a doll in your dream then your dream may be telling you that you are acting childish *or* you may be giving your love to someone or something that cannot reciprocate it. A doll can also refer to someone you think is "a doll," someone who is very sweet. **(Ch. 10)**

DOLPHIN: Dolphins are playful and intelligent and thrive in water, therefore they often stand in for your ability to thrive and enjoy an emotional situation such as a relationship. Dolphins can also represent your creative or spiritual ideas. You want the dolphins in your dream to be thriving and to play a helpful role. If they are injured you need to ask yourself if your emotional self or creative self is wounded in waking life.

DOOR: An opportunity. A locked door symbolizes your inability to get through to somebody or an inability to progress. An open door is telling you to move forward. The sound of a doorbell in your dream is a means by which your inner self is trying to get your attention. Is there an opportunity knocking? Are you answering your "calling" in life? Or perhaps you need to "open up" and be honest about something or open up and let someone in to your trust zone. **(Ch. 2)**

DRAIN: Something is draining you either of your energy, your emotions, or perhaps your finances. May also suggest that something isn't working out and is slipping away from you. If dirty water is going down the drain, then this is a good sign that depression is lifting.

DRIVEWAY: Your ability to venture into something new. If you are leaving the driveway you are beginning a new journey in your life, or a journey is coming to a close if you are coming into the driveway. If your dream takes place in the driveway and you never leave it, then ask yourself what area of your life is on hold. **(Ch. 8)**

DROWNING: Often means you are sinking into depression. Can also mean you are feeling overwhelmed or that you may be in over your head, or have gotten in too deep into a situation. **(Ch. 10)**

DRUNK: You or someone around you may have a distorted perspective of the current situation. The need or desire to numb yourself. **(Ch. 3)**

DUST: To see dust in a dream means you have been neglecting something, an issue, or perhaps a part of yourself. Are you not using all your skills and talents right now? To dust means to get back down to business. What are you refocusing on lately? Are you cleaning or clearing up an issue? Something turning to dust means you feel something is becoming less relevant in your life.

EAR: Your listening skills. Are you listening to your partner or someone else in your life? Time to pay attention to what someone is trying to say to you.

EATING: Hunger for intellectual or emotional nourishment. Take a good look at what you ate in your dream. If you ate something unusual, then you may have a hunger to take in a particular quality that you associate with that thing. Could be pointing to your diet. May also suggest that something is "eating away" at you. **(Ch. 3)**

EGG: Most often an egg in a dream symbolizes a rebirth, something new coming into your life. Can mean that you are hatching an idea. If you are pregnant or trying to get pregnant, eggs are very common dream symbols as they are commenting on your fertility. **(Ch. 3)**

ELEPHANT: Elephants are known for their memory. Did something or someone from the past recently jar your memory or give you a blast from the past? Is there a lesson happening in your life right now that you need to remember? Elephants are also very large so your dream may be using the elephant's size as a message. What is a really big deal in your life right now? Do you have a really big opportunity before you? In some cultures an elephant is considered good luck. Are you feeling lucky right now? In Hinduism, the elephant is the deity that blocks obstacles.

ELEVATOR: In what area of your life are you trying to move on up to the next level? Progression or regression depending on whether the elevator is going up or down. Elevate your mind and spirit. Your ability to rise above where you are now. If the elevator won't work or is going sideways or falling, then you are having a difficult time progressing in some area. Your dream may be telling you it's time for a different strategy. **(Ch. 3)**

EMPTY: What is missing in your life? Are you feeling emotionally empty? Are you out of ideas? This dream may be telling you it's time to find fulfillment in your life. (Ch. 3)

ESCAPING: What situation are you trying to escape in waking life? Often means a desire to improve current conditions. A need to get out of an undesirable situation. (Ch. 2)

EX: Is the ex you are dreaming about your first love? If so, he or she has become a symbol to you for passion and excitement and has appeared in your dream to tell you it's time to bring the passion back into your current relationship or into your life. In other words, it's time to spice things up or it's time to end your dry spell. If there are—or were—serious issues with your ex, then you may be dreaming of him or her because you have not been able to move past these issues. Part of you still feels attached. These dreams are telling you it's time to let go. You don't want to bring your past issues into your current or your future relationship. It's impossible to move forward when you are holding on to what is behind you. (Ch. 2)

EXECUTION: What are you feeling forced to put an end to in real life? Are you feeling guilty about something?

EXPLOSION: Emotional outbursts. Anger. A warning you are headed for an explosion. A huge idea. Sometimes we'll dream of explosions when there is a major shift going on in our lives. (Ch. 8)

EYEGLASSES: Focus your attention. Look closer at the issue. What is your "point of view" of your current situation? Are you or is someone around you turning a "blind eye" to what is really going on?

EYES: Open your eyes and take a closer look at your situation. Your perception or point of view or ability to focus on an issue. If something is wrong with your eyes, then your dream is telling you you aren't seeing a current issue for what it really is or you aren't giving enough focus and attention to a current situation. **(Ch. 6)**

FACE: Face the issue, face the past, face the facts, etc. If there is no face, then it may mean you are afraid to face something or it may symbolize a part of yourself that you do not recognize. What difficulties are you facing right now in waking life? Your dream will show you how you are handling those difficulties. **(Ch. 9 and Ch. 10)**

FAIRY: The part of yourself that believes in unseen forces in the world and unseen forces within yourself. The part of you that is light-hearted and playful, or could represent someone around you that is like this. May also indicate that you are feeling very small and are up against something that you feel is bigger than you are.

FALLING: Fear of failure, of losing status, or of losing control. Something in your life is going rapidly in the wrong direction: Your finances? A relationship? Your career? Your self-esteem? Time to redirect this situation immediately! Sometimes falling can point to falling into a depression. **(Ch. 2 and Ch. 10)**

FAT: Often points to abundance, having an enormous amount of a certain quality: overly friendly, overly angry, etc. It can also mean that you or someone else is exaggerating the truth. It can also point to a poor body image.

FATHER: Is there a current issue with your father? If so, your dream is showing you how you feel about the situation and may even be showing you what you can do. If there is no issue, then your father is not playing himself but instead is standing in for your fatherlike abilities: your ability to make decisions, to make money, and to be assertive. If there is something wrong with your father or if he dies in your dream then ask yourself if you feel you have lost your ability to make money or make a firm decision. If you are a father yourself, then your dad is standing in for your own role as a father. (Ch. 2)

FECES: May refer to what you feel is a crappy situation. What in your life really stinks right now? Has something in your life become a big mess? Whatever it is, your dream is telling you that it is something you need to get rid of, flush it away.

FENCE: Are you "on the fence" about something in real life, not sure what you should do? A fence can also mean you have put up an emotional barrier that does not allow people to get too close to you. (Ch. 2)

FIELD: In what area of your life is there enormous potential for growth? A barren or dried-up field points to lack of growth, nonproductivity. This can also be a reference to "playing the field," or your career "field."

FIGHTING: What or who are you battling in waking life? Weight? Smoking? An illness? Self-esteem issues? Someone else? What are you trying to overcome? The battle in your dream reflects how you are winning or losing the battle in waking life. (**Ch. 2, Ch. 3, and Ch. 5**)

FINDING: Finding something in a dream means you are discovering something new about yourself or about your world around you. Whatever you find, whether it be an object, a person, or an animal, it symbolizes something you need to recognize in waking life. Usually it is something positive you need in your life but sometimes the discovery is unpleasant, in which case you must find a way to turn this unpleasant element in your life into something positive.

FINGER: Can often refer to blame, "finger pointing." Have you been blamed for something? Or do you blame someone else? More than one finger represents your ability to "grasp" a concept or hold on to something. You should also pay attention to which finger your dream is using. The **pointer or index finger** = guilt or blame, but could also be about your ability to make a point. The **ring finger** = commitment. The **thumb** = approval or disapproval. The **middle finger** = your ability or need to tell someone to f**k off , and the **pinky** = are you being too delicate or sensitive right now?

FIRE: Often means rage and anger or burning passion. If house is on fire it's a warning of frazzled nerves, a nervous breakdown. A destructive or consuming force in your life. (**Ch. 7**)

FISH: Is the fish dying? You may need to realize that there are plenty of "other fish in the sea." Are the fish thriving? If so, then your creative ideas or a creative project is probably doing very well! Did you catch a fish? There may be someone in your life you consider "a good catch!" Can also symbolize creative or spiritual ideas. A symbol for Christianity. A common symbol in pregnant women's dreams as well as it refers to the fetus. (**Ch. 3**)

FLOATING: Ability to rise above the ordinary or to rise above a tough situation. If floating and can't get down could be your subconscious telling you to come back down to Earth, ground yourself, stop hanging around, etc. Hovering suggests that you or some issue in your life isn't moving forward, or backward. Where is there stagnation in your life? (**Ch. 10**)

FLOOD: A worsening situation. Overwhelming emotions. Something is becoming more than you can handle. You need to find a way to stay afloat. Also a common symbol in women's dreams about once a month relating to her menses. (**Ch. 8 and Ch. 10**)

FLOOR: Most often, the floor reflects how stable or secure you are feeling right now in your life or in a particular situation. The condition of the floor is directly related to how confident you feel.

FLYING: Ability to break free from Earthly woes and from things that bring you down and make you feel heavy. Your ability to soar to new heights and reach a higher level in life than where you are now. Can be a pat on the back from your subconscious for doing a good job. What's happening right now that makes your spirit feel like soaring? (**Ch. 4 and Ch. 5**)

FOG: Inability to see a certain situation clearly. An unclear or cloudy idea or situation. Uncertainty. (**Ch. 8**)

FOLLOWING: If something or someone is following you in a dream, then there is very likely something you are having a hard time putting "behind you" in waking life. Is there a grudge you need to let go of? An issue you haven't dealt with properly? A reputation you can't get rid of? If you are following something or someone in a dream, then that thing or that person represents something you want to obtain in real life. Are you wanting to follow in someone's footsteps?

FOOD: What are you "hungry" for in real life right now? Do you crave emotional nourishment? Spiritual nourishment? Intellectual nourishment? The food in your dream very likely symbolizes what is available to you in waking life that could "feed" a particular need you have. A lot of food would suggest that there are many things available to you right now that would fulfill your needs. Scarce food would mean that you don't feel there are many options available to you at this time. Food in dreams can also refer to a weight issue. If you are trying to or need to lose weight, it is common to dream of food. (**Ch. 3**)

FOOT: Your ability to stand up for yourself, stand your ground, and move forward in life or in a particular situation. (**Ch. 6**)

FOOTBALL: Football is a competitive sport. Are you feeling competitive in any area of your life right now? In what way are you wanting to score? Is there something you need to "tackle"? Can also refer to dating as in "playing the field." (**Ch. 6**)

FOREIGNERS: Foreign people in a dream often symbolize aspects of your own personality that you do not recognize as your own or that you are not yet familiar with. Have you or has someone around you acted in a way that seems unfamiliar or "foreign" to you? A foreign land or a foreign place in your dream means you are dealing with foreign territory in waking life; you are in a situation you have never been in before that may be causing you to feel lost as to what to do.

FROZEN: Is something frozen in your life, no longer moving forward? Has someone around you been cold emotionally? Is there a project or idea you need to put in cold storage for now? (**Ch. 8**)

FRIEND: Can sometimes be playing themselves or can symbolize a particular quality the two of you share. If it is not a real person but just a friend in the dream, then it symbolizes a part of yourself that you like, a quality within you that is being helpful to you in your life right now. Our dreams will show us the different parts of our *person*ality in the form of a person so we can gain a deeper understanding of ourselves. (**Ch. 10**)

FRUIT: Most often refers to the fruit of your labor. Have you been working hard on something and it is finally becoming fruitful? Fruit is also a common symbol in pregnant women's dreams because the pregnant woman is becoming "fruitful" and multiplying. (**Ch. 7**)

FUNERAL: What has ended in your life? What sort of change is going on? The dreaming mind equates change to death because— like death—we do not know what is on "the other side" of that change. A funeral also suggests it may be time to put something to rest and move on such as a grudge, an issue, a behavior, a project, a relationship, etc. It is okay and healthy to mourn the ending of certain things. (**Ch. 2**)

FURNITURE: Most often refers to thoughts that furnish the mind. Antique furniture represents old-fashioned, conservative thoughts and attitudes. Sparse furniture suggests a lack of ideas right now. Rearranging furniture means you are rearranging your priorities. Moving furniture means you are trying to move on from something but you may need to ask yourself if you are still holding on to certain feelings, insecurities, or beliefs from the past. Modern furniture points to new ideas. **(Ch. 7)**

GALLERY: Time to display your gifts and talents and knowledge. A reminder to preserve your memories. Don't forget your life lessons.

GAMBLE: Where in your life are you taking a chance? Is it worth the risk? **(Ch. 2)**

GARAGE: What in your life is temporarily "parked" or on hold? **(Ch. 3)**

GARDEN: Something is in bloom in your life. Time to cultivate a new relationship, talent, or skill. Your ability to nurture and grow aspects of your life.

GATE: An open gate is an opportunity available to you right now or can mark the beginning of a new journey or phase in your life. It can also represent your ability to get through an obstacle or a barrier you are currently facing. A closed gate may suggest that you or someone around you needs to "open up" about something in order to "get through" a current issue. It can also mean you are feeling closed out or unwelcome by someone. **(Ch. 10)**

GHOST: A ghost in a dream suggests that something from your past is still haunting you today. Something you thought was over is still lingering within your psyche. Time to face the ghosts of your past so you can move on. It is impossible to move forward when you are hanging on to what is behind you. (Ch. 3)

GIANT: Something in your life or some part of your personality has been blown out of proportion. What seems overpowering or overwhelming to you? Can also point to an abundance of something. (Ch. 4)

GIRL: Usually symbolizes your childlike carefree self. Could also be your immature, naïve self. Unknown young children in dreams often symbolize a project, idea, relationship, or something else in your life that is not yet fully developed. An unknown girl can represent your sensitivity and/or your nurturing ability. (Ch. 2)

GRADUATION: Your ability to move on up to the next level in life, in career, in relationship, in your personal goals, etc. If you are afraid you aren't going to graduate in your dream, then you must be feeling unsure of your ability to progress in some area of waking life. This dream is probably telling you to work a little harder and be more prepared for that deadline. (Ch. 3)

GRANDMOTHER: The wisdom you have gained through age and experience. Can mean a need to be pampered and spoiled. Could symbolize passage of time or old, outdated attitudes and behaviors. May mean something is getting old, you are growing tired of something. If you dream of your grandmother that has died, it may actually be a contact dream! What advice is she giving you?

GRAVEYARD: Could be a pun on a grave situation. Often indicates you have buried some issue . . . or some issue or grudge needs to be buried so you can move on. You don't want to see anything coming out of that grave as that would mean old, dead issues are rising to the surface again.

GROCERY STORE: Time to nurture and nourish yourself and those around you. **(Ch. 3, Ch. 6, and Ch. 8)**

GUM: Are you in a "sticky" situation? Usually, gum dreams are telling you that you need to speak up, there is something you need to "spit out" already! **(Ch. 6)**

GUTS: Gut feeling. Spill your guts. **(Ch. 7)**

HAIR: Thoughts and ideas because, like hair, it comes from the head. What's been on your mind lately? What plans or ideas are sprouting from your head? If you get a *haircut,* then you may need to cut an idea or mode of thinking short. *Tangled hair* indicates confusion over some issue; *hair falling out* means a lack of ideas or uncertainty; and *long hair* means you need to expand on an idea or represents lots of ideas. **(Ch. 6)**

HALL: What transition are you going through right now? Is your hallway long? If so, it is telling you this is going to be a long "haul." A dark hallway means uncertainty as to how you are going to get through this transition. Lots of doorways mean there are many options for you right now. **(Ch. 7)**

HAND: Your ability to "handle" a situation. It's in your hands now. Do you need to lend a hand? Ask for a helping hand? Also a means of expressing yourself. If there is something wrong with the hand in your dream, you may be feeling incapable of handling something in waking life. (**Ch. 2 and Ch. 6**)

HANG: This may suggest that some area of your life is "suspended," not going anywhere. If you are being hung or you see someone else being hung, it is most likely referring to choking off your voice. Is there something you are not speaking up about?

HAT: Are you or is someone around you covering up or hiding their thoughts and ideas? Could also symbolize the role you choose to play in this life.

HEAD: A head in a dream represents intellect, knowledge, ideas. If something is wrong with the head in a dream then there may be something wrong with your thinking. Is something a bad idea?

HEEL: Most often the heel of your foot refers to your own vulnerability. Have you been a little too vulnerable lately? The heel (even the heel of a shoe) can also be a pun on "healing." Is something going on where you need to heal emotionally or physically? (**Ch. 2**)

HELL: May symbolize a very difficult time you are having to go through. Fears, anxieties, feeling trapped. An evil force.

HIDING: A good indication you are avoiding an issue, you are afraid of confrontation, or perhaps you are hiding a secret? What is it you don't want to be "found" out? (**Ch. 10**)

HILL: Most often represents an obstacle that you need to overcome. The steeper the hill, the more difficult you feel your waking life obstacle is. If you are going down a hill, it may suggest
that things are getting easier now, "all downhill from here." A
hill can also be a reference to where you are in your life. Are
you feeling "over the hill"?

HOLE: A hole suggests something is missing in your life. Where
the hole is will give you a clue. Most often a hole indicates
you are lacking a certain ability that you need at the moment.
(Ch. 6)

HOMOSEXUAL: To have a homosexual affair in a dream (if
you are straight) means you are admiring your own femininity
or masculinity. Being proud of your gender. When men get
a raise, land a client, score a hot date, etc. they may get a man-
on-man dream because they did something particularly manly
that day in real life. Women often get lesbian dreams when they
are pregnant as that is the epitome of being female. Ask yourself what you have done that has been particularly manly or
feminine lately. (Ch. 9)

HORSE: Strength, nobility. Your ability to get back in the saddle
when life knocks you down. Can also refer to your health.
An injured or sick horse may mean that you are not feeling
strong enough or perhaps healthy enough to handle something.
(Ch. 5)

HOSPITAL: Some area of your life is in need of healing, either
emotional or physical. Is it a relationship? Is it your own self-
esteem? Or is it a physical ailment? Your dream is telling you it
is time to make things better. (Ch. 3)

HOTEL: A hotel suggests that you are in a temporary situation or are going through a transition since we only stay in hotels for a short amount of time. **(Ch. 3)**

HOUSE: No matter whether you dream of your actual house or some random dream house, it symbolizes *you*, your state of mind, the dwelling place of your soul. The state of the house reflects yourself at the time the dream. If it is a house you used to live in, then it may not be about the house but who you were back then. If you are trying to find your way back home, then you are probably trying to get things back to normal in waking life. **(Ch. 7)**

HUG: To hug someone in a dream means you are welcoming or embracing something into your life. Is it a new attitude or belief? A new regimen? A new person? If someone is hugging you, then ask yourself if you are feeling welcomed in your life. If someone you don't know in real life is hugging you, then ask yourself what you need to embrace. An unknown man would suggest you are embracing your male, assertive energy. An unknown female would suggest you are embracing your feminine, creative, nurturing energy. Hugs are almost always a positive sign that you are feeling closer to someone in waking life or that you have embraced a new attitude or outlook. **(Ch. 9)**

HURRICANE: Have you or has someone around you had an emotional outburst? Are there strong, sudden changes happening in your life? A hurricane can also point to someone's rage or extreme worry. If they or you can "center" yourself, you will find "calm," just as the eye of the hurricane is the calmest point. **(Ch. 8)**

ICE: Frozen emotions or a frozen situation. Something's on hold or someone is giving you the cold shoulder. **(Ch. 8)**

INFECTION: *See* Disease.

INTRUDER: The intruder most likely represents something that has intruded upon your peaceful world or has invaded and disrupted your usual routine. It could be an invasive thought. Intruder dreams are common among pregnant women as the body perceives the fetus as an intruder.

ISLAND: Are you feeling isolated and alone? How are you feeling separated or cut off from others? An island in a dream may also mean it is time to relax and rejuvenate.

JAIL: You are currently stuck in some area of your life. What do you think is holding you back? In what way might you be imprisoning yourself? **(Ch. 3)**

JAR: You are holding things in, keeping things bottled up. Perhaps you should open up!

JUMP: Are you about to "jump" into something too quickly in real life? How are you taking a "leap of faith"? May also mean you need to jump on a certain idea or opportunity before it is too late.

JUNKYARD: Discarded, unused, and negative ideas, attitudes and behaviors. Are you currently dealing with issues in your life that are of no use to you? Time to discard what you no longer need.

KEY: Your ability to open doors of opportunity. An idea or solution. The "key" ingredient to what you need for your life right now. Ask yourself how you are feeling enlightened or more certain lately. **(Ch. 5)**

KISSING: Anything having to do with the mouth points to verbal expression. Kissing often means communicating because— like kissing—it takes two mouths to communicate. Who are you kissing in your dream? Have you been communicating well with them? Do you need to find a better way of communicating? If someone is blowing you kisses, then someone around you is trying to get your attention and tell you something.

KITCHEN: What are you preparing for in real life? Are you cooking up an idea or a plan? A kitchen setting can also suggest that you are "hungry" for emotional, intellectual, or spiritual nourishment. **(Ch. 7)**

KITTEN: For a woman, a kitten often refers to her inner sex kitten, her sexuality. For a man, a kitten may refer to a female in his life that he finds attractive. Can also symbolize your playful, young self. Or an underdeveloped independence. **(Ch. 5)**

KNEE: Your ability to be flexible. Do you need to be stubborn or should you "bend" a little right now? **(Ch. 6)**

KNIFE: A need or desire to cut or sever ties, to separate yourself from a particular issue or cut out a particular behavior, idea, or person. Harsh, cutting remarks, cuts like a knife. Criticism. **(Ch. 10)**

LADDER: Your ability to succeed. Time to progress. A step-by-step process.

LAKE: Your emotional depths. An emotional issue. Hopefully, the water is clear and inviting. Murky water points to depression or an emotional issue you can't see through. Bodies of water in women's dreams are common about once a month as it refers to her menses. **(Ch. 4)**

LATE: If you are running late in a dream, ask yourself what deadline are you up against in real life. Is it work related? Or is it a self-imposed deadline? Is there something you are afraid you might miss out on? You are telling yourself through this dream to get your act together and focus!

LEFT: The left side usually refers to what has been or what needs to be "left" behind. Can also imply that you are feeling left out. **(Ch. 4)**

LEG: Your ability to stand up for yourself, to stand your ground, or to move forward. If something is wrong with your legs, then there may be an inability on your part to stand up for yourself or progress in some area. **(Ch. 6)**

LIGHTNING: A flash of inspiration. A sudden and bright idea. A huge burst of energy or momentum. Sometimes a spiritual symbol as it comes from the heavens. **(Ch. 8)**

LION: Courage, bravery. It may be time to roar, show who is king of the jungle. Can also symbolize your predatory self, your ability to go out on the hunt and get what you want. Less often, it may be a play on words. Is someone around you lyin' to you?

For women, a lion can represent her sexuality, her inner "sex kitten." For a man, a lion may refer to a female. (**Ch. 5**)

LIPSTICK: Draws attention to the mouth, therefore points to verbal communication. Is there something that needs to be said? Have you exaggerated or enhanced a story lately? Could also be a pun on make up, or time to make up with someone.

LOCKER: If you are unable to find your locker or unable to open your locker in a dream, then ask yourself what you are feeling unprepared for in waking life? Are you feeling un-equipped to deal with something or someone right now? The locker can also represent your identity as it is where you keep your personal belongings, in which case not being able to find your locker would suggest that you are not sure of your place in life or perhaps in career or even in a social circle. (**Ch. 3 and Ch. 6**)

LOST: Where in your life are you feeling directionless? It may be time to map out a plan for yourself. Nothing lasts forever. Learn to appreciate what you have. Perhaps you need to let go of something. You may be feeling that something is missing from your life. How are you feeling empty? May be a call from your subconscious to find something that fulfills you. (**Ch. 2**)

LUGGAGE: Often symbolizes a burden you carry around with you in waking life. Have you brought unnecessary baggage into your current relationship or current situation? Or does some-one around come with a lot of baggage? If you are having a hard time closing your suitcase, then your dreaming mind is telling you that you need to let go of certain issues so you can travel through life more easily.

MAIL: Your ability to communicate. Where in your life are there communication issues? Are you paying attention to the messages someone is trying to send you?

MALL: Many options are available to you right now. You may also find yourself in the mall when you need some pampering or are searching for something to make you happy. What are you trying to bring into your life right now?

MAN: Your masculine self; the part of your personality that is assertive, takes action, makes decisions, and makes money. If an unknown man is attacking you, it is because you are ignoring your assertive male self. If an unknown man is attracted to you, then you are beginning to recognize and unite your male qualities into your life. **(Ch. 2)**

MARRIAGE: A union of qualities or opinions. Who are you marrying? You need to unite with a quality or opinion of your dream bride or groom, until "death do you part." If marrying an unknown bride or groom then you need to merge the qualities of that gender into your psyche. An unknown or faceless groom means it is time to commit to your assertive male self. An unknown bride means it is time to commit to being more sensitive and caring in your life. Where else in your life do you need to commit? A marriage can also refer to a commitment or obligation you have recently made or need to make. **(Ch. 3)**

MASTURBATE: Masturbation often means one is being self-serving in waking life rather than thinking of other's needs. It can also mean that you are very pleased with yourself for a recent accomplishment. **(Ch. 9)**

MAZE: Somewhere in your life you are feeling uncertain and directionless. What or who is causing you confusion? Your dreaming mind wants you to find your way out of this situation. **(Ch. 10)**

MILITARY: Time to buckle down, be disciplined, and be responsible. Could also mean overly disciplined and strict. May also mean it is time to stand up and fight for what you believe is right.

MIRROR: What is going on right now that has you concerned about how you have appeared to others? Like a mirror, our dreams are reflections of our self. To see your reflection in a dream means you need to take a good hard look at your self and your behavior in waking life and ask yourself if you like what you see. **(Ch. 8)**

MISSING: If an item in a dream is missing, it most likely represents something in your life or something within you that is missing. Where in your life is there emptiness? If a person is missing, it may mean that you "miss" that person. Often, parents will dream their child is missing. This is because the parent and child are growing apart. Missing a bus, plane, etc., indicates a fear of missing out on opportunity *or* can refer to a deadline you face in real life. **(Ch. 8)**

MOLD: Mold or mildew in a dream suggests some issue in your life has gotten old or something has been neglected. Just as mold and mildew eat away at things that are left for too long, there may be something that is eating away at your peace of mind because you have allowed something to go on for too long or have neglected to deal with an old issue. **(Ch. 7)**

MONEY: Your self-worth or how you value others. Very often money in dreams means you need to realize your own value. If coins, you may need to make a change in your life. It's common to dream of finding money or obtaining money when you have financial difficulty in waking life.

MOON: The moon and other celestial bodies often refer to one's high hopes or high expectations. Traveling to the moon would suggest things are in motion toward reaching a high goal you have set. *Many moons* represent many high aspirations. A *half moon* may mean you are only giving half your effort toward that goal. If the *moon is very close,* you may be getting closer to that goal. Less often, a moon can reflect one's mood. A *bright moon* is optimism. A dark *low moon* can be depression.

MOTHER: Unless there is a current issue with your mother, then your mother in a dream will stand in for your ability to know what's best, to nurture yourself and others. If you are a mom, then your mother symbolizes your own role as mom. If your mom is dying or hurt in the dream, examine your own mothering skills. Also pay attention to the advice Mom gives in your dream because it is coming from your own intuition. **(Ch. 2)**

MOTORCYCLE: A need for freedom from a relationship, job, or other situation. You are ready to travel down a certain path alone. **(Ch. 4)**

MOUNTAIN: Can symbolize a goal you wish to reach or an obstacle or setback you need to overcome. The bigger the mountain the bigger the goal, obstacle, or setback. You always want to find yourself on the mountaintop or climbing toward the top as that means progression and success. Can also symbolize spiritual heights.

MOUSE: Something or someone has been irritating you or gnawing away at you. A **rat** can also point to irritation you are dealing with but more specifically the irritation would be caused by someone you think is up to dirty tricks.

MOUTH: Any dream having to do with the mouth points to verbal communication. Take a good look at the things you say, have said, or need to say. **(Ch. 6 and Ch. 10)**

MOVIE: Whatever is going on in the movie is a direct reflection of how you have been "acting" in real life. It can also be a direct reflection of what you see for yourself in the big picture . . . in the long run.

MOVING: Unless you are actually moving in real life, moving in a dream means a need to move on from some situation or a need to move on from the past or to move into a new mind-set. It is impossible to move forward if you are hanging on to what is behind you. **(Ch. 7)**

MURDER: If you are doing the killing then there is a need or desire to kill off, to put an end to something in your life such as a relationship, a behavior, a situation, etc. If someone is trying to kill you, then ask yourself if you are feeling pressure to make some changes in your life or to put an end to something. If someone you know is being killed, ask yourself what sort of change they may be going through right now, *or* perhaps your relationship with them is changing or is endangered. **(Ch. 10)**

MUSEUM: *See* Gallery.

NAKED: What is causing you to feel embarrassed, vulnerable, or unprepared in real life? Are you going to be or have you recently been in a situation where all eyes are on you? Have you "revealed" a little too much about yourself or about something? Maybe you need to reveal the truth or get down to the bare facts. **(Ch. 10)**

NECK: Have you stuck your neck out for somebody? Are you feeling competitive with somebody, as though you are "neck and neck"? Usually, anything having to do with the neck or throat in a dream is all about your voice, something you need to say . . . or wish you hadn't said.

NEEDLE: Your ability to create something, to pull strings in order to make something happen. Your ability to mend something. May also imply that someone around you is "needling" you, irritating and annoying you.

NEWSPAPER: What information have you learned recently about your personal world? If you are having a hard time reading the newspaper, then you may be having a hard time accepting this recent tidbit of info.

NUMBERS: Numbers point to specific things in our life. Compare the numbers in your dream to the numbers in your life, such as birthdays, addresses, finances, telephone numbers, etc. **(See more in Ch. 11's Final Checklist)**

OCEAN: Your emotional or creative depths. Something may be deeply affecting you emotionally. Your dream may be telling you that there are plenty of fish in the sea. There is vast opportunity for you. (**Ch. 4**)

OLD: Is something in your life starting to get "old"? An old person in your dream may point to your own wisdom you have gained through age and experience. May be referring to old, outdated attitudes and beliefs.

ORGASM: To orgasm in a dream means your body did in fact orgasm! The body does not know the difference between a dreaming event and a waking event so it will react to a dream as if it were real. Orgasms in dreams are more common for women than for men . . . sorry, guys! If you orgasm in a dream, it may imply you are not having an active enough sex life. A sexual release needs to happen one way or another! But it can also mean there is a need for an emotional release. (**Ch. 9**)

OUTSIDE: The outside in a dream often refers to getting something out in the open. If you're trying to get something out of your house, car, etc., it may mean that something has intruded upon your personal world, your peace of mind, and you need to find a way to get it out of your life or out of your thoughts.

OVEN: Are you planning something? What ideas are you cooking up? Is some area of your life starting to heat up? If you dream of a *grill*, it may mean that you feel someone has "grilled" you with too many questions. The oven is also a common symbol for the womb and often appears in pregnant women's dreams. (**Ch. 7**)

OWL: Owls are known for wisdom and therefore represent your own wisdom and knowledge . . . or perhaps someone around you that you consider to be wise. Is anything going on right now where you need to draw upon your own wisdom and know-how? Do you need to seek the advice of someone wise? Have you learned something new that you can add to your banks of wisdom? Owls are also nocturnal so it may refer to staying up all night.

PAIN: Often points to emotional pain. What part of the body is afflicted? Pain in the chest means hurt feelings. Pain in the head means hurt ego; pain in the feet means you're having a hard or painful experience getting where you want to go in life. **(Ch. 6)**

PAINTING: Painting in a dream suggests you are either trying to create something, enhance something in your life, *or* you may be trying to cover something up. To paint a picture means you are trying to express yourself in waking life or you are trying to create what you "picture" for your life. You should also ask yourself if you are trying to influence someone else, or is someone around you trying to influence you.

PANTS: Your ability to be in charge, to "wear the pants" in a relationship or other situation. If your pants or someone else's pants are missing or are too small or don't fit, look at the different areas of your life and ask yourself where you are ineffective or uncomfortable being in charge. If the pants fit or look great on you, then you are doing well with being authoritative and in charge. Can also be referring to being caught with your pants down!

PARALYZED: Where in your life are you not making enough movement in order to progress? In what way are you feeling stuck? If you wake up and can't move, you have probably experienced an episode of "Sleep Paralysis," which can be very frightening (often includes the feeling of a dark presence in the room and pressure on the chest). It is completely harmless and means you were stuck in the Hypnogogic stage of sleep for a brief time. You can't move because when you are in REM sleep your brain paralyzes your muscles so that you don't get up and act out your dream. Sometimes (when you don't get enough good sleep) you'll wake up before your brain can reactivate your muscles and this is when Sleep Paralysis happens. (**Ch. 10**)

PARENTS: Unless there is an issue with your parents, they most likely refer to yourself as a parent. Do the way your parent or parents act in the dream relate to how you behave as a parent or how you feel about your parenting right now? (**Ch. 9**)

PARK / PARKING LOT: Something is on hold right now in your life. Is it time to get it started again or do you need the break? A recreation park may suggest there is something you need to get out in the open and speak up about. It can also mean you need to relax, get back in touch with your fun-loving carefree self. (**Ch. 3**)

PARTY: There is a cause for celebration in your life. Time to reward yourself for a job well done. What have you accomplished lately? May even mean it is time to let loose. (**Ch. 7 and Ch. 8**)

PATH: A path or direction you have chosen to take in life. The condition of the path reflects the ease or the difficulty this path in life has been for you. Are you following someone else's path or are you paving your own?

PENIS: Masculine energy. Time to stand up (hee hee) and be assertive. **(Ch. 6)**

PHONE: Symbolizes your ability to communicate, your ability to get your point across as well as your ability to listen. If there is something wrong with the phone in your dream, then you may be having communication issues with someone in your waking life. **(Ch. 9, Ch. 10, and Final Checklist)**

PIANO: Your ability to have harmony in all areas of your life and be "in tune" with those around you. If something is wrong with the piano in your dream, then ask yourself where in your life is there imbalance? What is no longer working harmoniously for you? Where in your life have you "tuned out"?

PICTURES: How you picture yourself or a particular situation. Could be your dream saying, "Get the picture?!" Perhaps time to look at your past. Pictures are also memories. Your dream may be telling you to be aware of the present because whether it becomes a good or a bad memory is often up to you.

PIG: You or someone around you is exhibiting rude and boorish behavior or selfishness. May also be a reflection of your body image.

PILLOW: A need to be comforted or a need to rest and relax. Pillow talk.

PIMPLE: Acne refers to blemishes about your reputation. You are concerned about how you appear to others, not necessarily physically but how your behavior or your reputation precedes you. You should also ask yourself if there is a festering situation you need to "face" and deal with. What is it that you need to "clear up" and straighten out? **(Ch. 8)**

PINK: Colors almost always reflect your emotions. Pink suggests you or someone around you is displaying or needs to display gentleness and or passivity. Also, put your own associations to pink here. Does the color remind you of an old bedroom? A favorite sweater?

PLANET: Most often, planets represent the very high goals you aspire to that often can seem distant and out of reach. They can also refer to a new phase or chapter in your life, something that seems like "a whole new world" to you.

POISON: Most often refers to something negative and harmful in your life such as negative thought patterns, bad behaviors, an unhealthy relationship, etc. What situation or what person in your real life is "poisonous" to you? If you are poisoning someone, this may reflect your desire to get them out of your life or that you wish them ill will. If you have been poisoned, then your dream is warning you that there is something or someone very harmful in your life that you need to rid yourself of. **(Ch. 5)**

POLICE: Your own ability to put a stop to something, and to know what is right and what is wrong. If police are chasing you, you may be feeling guilty about something. **(Ch. 2)**

POOL: Your emotional pool. Are you containing or holding in your emotions? Could even symbolize something you may want to dive into. Sometimes refers to the "dating pool." **(Ch. 6)**

PORCH: *See* Deck.

PREGNANT: You are about to give birth to something new in your life, something that needs lots of care and attention in order to reach its full potential. Also ask yourself if you are going through a "rebirth"? **(Ch. 6)**

PRESIDENT: Your authoritative, decision-making self. The part of your personality that presides over your affairs. Do you need to be more decisive or commanding lately?

PUPPY: Dogs often point to loyalty and companionship and therefore represent your relationship with someone or your loyalty to something. A puppy would then symbolize a fairly new relationship or a newfound loyalty (perhaps a new loyalty to a new fitness regimen, for example). **(Ch. 5)**

QUEEN: Leadership abilities, your ruling feminine qualities.

RAIN: An emotional downpour, tears, sorrow. Rain is a cleansing element so it may be time for a good emotional cleansing. **(Ch. 8)**

RAINBOW: Most often refers to a promise. Has someone promised you something or did you make a promise? Also, a rainbow can mean you are coming out of a depression and things are beginning to look promising and brighter for you. A rainbow is also a symbol for gay pride. **(Ch. 8)**

RAPE: Indicates that you are feeling someone is taking advantage of you, "screwing you" over. Or someone may be forcing their thoughts or opinions on you. Ask yourself where you are feeling powerless in your life.

RAT: *See* Mouse.

RED: Often means stop or beware. A red flag or warning you are sending yourself through the dream. Can also mean anger or passion. (**Ch. 5**)

RESCUE: If there is a rescue attempt in your dream, then it is very likely directly connected to some aspect of your life that needs help. Look at your relationships, your finances, your career, any projects, even your emotional state, and ask yourself where you could really use a helping hand. If you are attempting to recue someone else in your dream, such as a friend or family member, ask yourself how you think you might be able to aid this person in real life.

RESTAURANT: Ask yourself what you are "hungry" for in waking life right now. Do you feel you have enough options available to you that will "feed" your current emotional, creative, or intellectual needs.

RIBS: Has someone been ribbing you lately? Is it starting to annoy you? The ribs are also a cage that holds the heart. Are you feeling the need to cage in your emotions lately?

RIGHT: The right side usually points to the right thing to do. The right hand is the giving side of yourself.

RING: Rings are most often associated with keeping a promise. Any promises or commitments you need to focus on right now? If you are dreaming of your wedding ring, then your dream is probably commenting on your marriage. If there is something wrong with your wedding ring, then there must be an issue within your marriage you need to fix.

RIVER: The flow of your life. Are you going with the flow or resisting it? If you are fighting the current, then you may be resisting the flow your life is meant to go in. If trying to cross the river, it would indicate that you are trying to cross over into a new area of your life. If you are drowning in a river, then life is overwhelming you right now. If you dream of your child drowning in a river or being swept away, then you are experiencing how life and time pulls all our children away from us. Your child is probably becoming less dependent on you. Rivers and streams are also common symbols for a woman during her time of the month.

ROACH: Bugs usually refer to something or someone in your life that is "bugging" you and the dream is telling you it is time to "exterminate" the situation. But roaches can often refer to your ability to survive a difficult emotional or health situation since they are known to be able to survive a nuclear holocaust. Roaches can also sometimes symbolize smoking weed. **(Ch. 3)**

ROAD: The road of life. The path you are on right now. The direction you are headed. The condition of the freeway will reflect the traffic conditions in your life; very busy and congested, slow going, smooth sailing, etc. Going off the freeway suggests you may be sidetracked. **(Ch. 4)**

ROBBED: What do you feel is being taken from you in waking life? What do you feel you are losing? Your credibility? Your identity? Your energy? An opportunity? Are you having financial difficulties? Is someone taking credit you feel you deserve? **(Ch. 4)**

ROCK: May refer to something in your life that is solid such as a relationship, your belief system, an opinion, etc. If the rock is an obstacle in your dream, then it is referring to something seemingly unyielding that is preventing you from reaching a certain goal for yourself. Many rocks could point to a tough or "rocky" situation. **(Ch. 4)**

ROLLER COASTER: Symbolizes life, it's full of ups and downs. Your emotions. Could reflect a particular situation such as your finances. What in your life is not exactly on the straight and narrow or smooth sailing? What is fluctuating? Could also suggest that you are going along for the ride. **(Ch. 3)**

ROOF: Protection. Feeling secure. Can also point to finances and your ability to keep a roof over your head. If something is wrong with the roof, then ask yourself what may be wrong with your finances or your sense of security. **(Ch. 9)**

ROOMS: Each different room reflects a different aspect of the self. What is that particular room used for? Finding new rooms indicates discovery of new elements to your personality or is an indication you have lots more room to grow as a person. **(Ch. 7)**

ROTTEN: Something in your life may be going bad or has been lingering around for too long. Look at your relationships, any current issues or behaviors or attitudes. Like rotten food, something needs to be tossed out of your life before it becomes foul and unbearable.

RUNNING: Do you need to pick up the pace somewhere in your life? Are you trying to keep up? Things may be going too fast. Slow down. If you are running from something, then you are probably avoiding something or someone in your waking life. **(Ch. 2)**

SAW: Is there anything or anyone you need to separate from your life? Or anything you have been trying to divide up or cut in half such as your time spent on something or with someone?

SCHOOL: Time to learn a lesson or educate yourself on certain matters. You may be feeling tested or that you need to pass a particular situation with flying colors. Do you have a fear of failure? If searching for a class you are directionless in some area of your life. If you are late for class you are afraid of missing an opportunity or are feeling unprepared. **(Ch. 3)**

SEED: Represents a brand-new beginning in some area of your life or an idea that needs to be implemented so that it can grow and reach its potential. A sunflower seed is the beginnings of happiness.

SEX: A union of qualities or opinions. Pick three words that describe your dream lover. Apply those words to yourself, to your life. Would you or your life improve if you took on one of those qualities or opinions? Sex in a dream is not always about a physical union you want but rather a psychological union you need. To have sex with someone of the same gender (if you are not gay) means you have probably done something recently that makes you proud of your gender. For example, pregnant women tend to get girl-on-girl dreams because there is nothing more feminine than creating life. Men can get a guy-on-guy dream when they land a hot date or get a promotion. **(Ch. 9)**

SHADOW: A shadow, to the dreaming mind, symbolizes an obscure, unrecognized part of yourself or of someone else. May point to your dark side, the part of you that is moody, depressed, or behaves badly. Is there something shady going on? **(Ch. 7)**

SHIP: *See* Boat.

SHOE: Your ability to stand your ground as well as to stand up for yourself. Can also refer to the direction you need to go and the steps you need to take to get there. If you've lost your shoes, you may be feeling unsure, unstable, or insecure about something. **(Ch. 6)**

SHOOT: Shooting in a dream is usually about "shooting off" at the mouth. If you are doing the shooting ask yourself if you have shot your mouth off recently. Have you said critical or hurtful things to somebody? If you are shot at, has someone said hurtful things to you? Or are *you* being overly critical of yourself? Shooting in a dream can also refer to giving something your best "shot." If the gun doesn't shoot in the dream, then you or someone around you may not be giving their best effort toward something. **(Ch. 10)**

SHOULDER: Your emotional strength. Your ability to shoulder a responsibility. If there is something wrong with the shoulder in the dream, it indicates weakness on your part or someone around you in waking life.

SHOWER: You need to or you are in the process of cleansing yourself of something negative or frustrating. If you are showering in public, then you may be concerned how you will appear to others if you get something off your chest. **(Ch. 7)**

SHRINKING: Something is becoming less important, less powerful, or less of an option in your life. **(Ch. 9)**

SICK: Something in your life is not good for you. There is a person or a situation that is unhealthy. What situation in your life needs to be healed? **(Ch. 10)**

SISTER: If you are dreaming of your own sister, she may not be playing herself in the dream, unless there is a current issue with her that is on your mind daily. Otherwise, your sister is standing in for a part of yourself that is like her. What do you and she have in common? Is that quality—or fault—being helpful to you in life right now? The way your sister is behaving in the dream is a good indication of how this particular quality or fault is helping or hurting you right now. If you do not have a sister but dream that you have one, and you are female, then she represents your sisterhood in the female community. She represents the fact that you are not alone in your current situation in life. If you do not have a sister, but dream that you have one and you are male, then your sister is standing in for your female side, that part of you that can be sensitive, nurturing, a good listener, and creative.

SINKING: Sinking in a dream means something may be going in the wrong direction for you. Do you have a sinking or bad feeling about something? Are you sinking into a depression? Is something in real life slipping away from you? **(Ch. 4)**

SKELETON: May represent "skeletons in your closet," things from your past that you wish to keep secret. Skeletons can also represent issues that you need to realize are over and done with, things, perhaps grudges, that you need to bury and move on from.

SLEEPING: Turning a blind eye to something, or not being fully aware of something that is going on in waking life. If someone else is asleep in your dream, then that person may be unaware of something going on around them. Does this person need to wake up and realize something? Or are they better off not knowing? Sometimes the person who is asleep in your dream can represent a part of your own personality. For example, if your mother is asleep, then she may represent your maternal and nurturing instincts that are lying dormant and not being active right now. **(Ch. 9)**

SLIP: To slip in a dream indicates you feel you've slipped up, made a mistake in waking life. Also ask yourself if you are worried something or someone may be slipping away from you. To be wearing only a slip means you are feeling embarrassed, vulnerable, exposed, or unprepared.

SNAKE: Masculine energy. If you are a woman and are dreaming of snakes, look at the men in your life and ask yourself if there is an issue there with your husband, boyfriend, boss, brother, etc. If you are a man then a snake may refer to your own fertility or masculine power. A snake can also symbolize healing energy. Are you in need of emotional or physical healing? A snakebite means emotional or physical healing is about to begin. The injection of the venom is like the injection of a shot. Snakes can also symbolize wisdom and knowledge (as in the Adam and Eve story). Have you learned something new recently? May also represent a fear or temptation, something that could turn into a poisonous situation. (**Ch. 5**)

SNOW: Usually, anything cold in a dream points to cold emotions. Are you or has anyone around you grown cold emotionally? Has someone been giving you the cold shoulder? Snow may also suggest something in your life is frozen or stuck. (**Ch. 8**)

SOLDIER: *See* Military.

SONG: Pay attention to the title and to the lyrics. Do they say anything about your current situation? Singing indicates there is currently happiness and harmony in your life.

SPIDER: Deceit, a web of lies. Ask yourself who around you may not be trustworthy. Spiders can also mean someone or something is "bugging" you to the point that you are feeling trapped, just as a spider uses its web to trap its prey. (**Ch. 5**)

SPILL: Have you recently said something you shouldn't have? What mistake have you made recently? Or has someone around you made a mistake? (**Ch. 7**)

SPOUSE: Your spouse is usually playing himself or herself. Ask yourself if your spouse was helpful or harmful or benign, in the dream. If they are benign then your dream is telling you they are not able to help you with your current situation in waking life. It is something you need to do on our own. If they are helpful, then ask yourself how in real life the two of you are (or should be) working together to accomplish something. If they are harmful to you, then ask yourself how your spouse is working against you in waking life. Once you figure it out, it may be time to discuss this issue (without pointing fingers). **(Ch. 2)**

STAB: Hurtful remarks. Has someone around you said something mean or critical, something that emotionally wounded you? Can also mean that you need to take a stab at something. **(Ch. 10)**

STAIRS: Progression or regression depending on which way you are going. Stairs are your ability to move on up to the next level in your career, your status, your spiritual journey, etc. They can also mean that you need to take a current situation one step at a time.

STOMACH: Your ability to "digest" information. Is there something going on that is hard for you to "stomach"? Do you need to—or has someone around you—spilled their "guts"? Do you have a "gut" feeling about something? Can also be about your weight or body image. **(Ch. 6)**

STORM: You must be dealing with a stormy situation right now. Or perhaps you or someone around you has had emotional outburst. **(Ch. 8)**

STOVE: *See* Oven.

STRANGER: Part of your personality you are unfamiliar with. Time to become familiar with this aspect of yourself. Pay attention to whether this person was helpful or not to you in the dream. If they were helpful or positive, then they most likely indicate that you are being a positive force in your own life right now. If the stranger was negative or harmful to you, then you need to ask yourself how you may be harming yourself or harming your progress. (Ch. 2)

STREAM: *See* River.

STRING: Is someone stringing you along? Are you stringing someone else along? Can also represents your ability to bond to someone or to hold things together. Can also refer to the saying "no strings attached." Has someone offered you a "no strings attached" opportunity?

STUCK: Anything or anyone that is stuck in your dream suggests that there is a lack of progress somewhere in your life. Look at relationships, finances, creative ideas, etc. Time to find a way to move things along . . . or time for you to move on.

SUICIDE: A forced ending or change in your life or in your behavior. What part of your personality or your life are you trying to end? If someone else in your dream is committing suicide, they may still represent a part of you that is trying to change. But if it is someone you deal with daily, they may be playing themselves in which case you need to ask yourself if they are trying to make changes in their own life. (Ch. 2 and Ch. 10)

SUITCASE: *See* Luggage.

SUN: A sunny day in a dream usually reflects joy and happiness in waking life. The sun often points to truth, honesty, shedding light onto something. (Ch. 8)

SURGERY: You may need to remove something from your life. Something in your life or within you needs reparation. **(Ch. 3 and Ch. 6)**

SWIM: Your ability to handle an emotional situation. If you're struggling to swim, then you are struggling through your emotional issue; you are trying to stay afloat and get through it but it's really tough. If swimming is enjoyable and easy, then your dream is showing you that you are handling a situation in your life "swimmingly"! All is well.

SYNAGOGUE: *See* Church.

TABLE: Hunger for emotional, financial, or intellectual nourishment. Fellowship, family time. Can also point to honesty: laying your cards on the table.

TAIL: Your past. Something you should leave behind you. May also indicate you or someone around you is lying, telling a tale.

TALL: If someone or something is abnormally tall, then it refers to an abundance of something. For example, a very tall person in your dream may mean that you have an enormous amount of respect for them. If it is someone you don't know, then they represent a personality trait of your own that you have an abundance of. A trait that people around you "look up to." **(Ch. 3)**

TEACHER: There is something you need to learn right now in your life. Is it a new skill? Is it a life lesson? Are you learning how to handle a particular issue? If the teacher in your dream is giving you advice or direction, pay attention because this is the way you are telling yourself something you need to know and be wiser from.

TEETH: Most often symbolizes your words. If teeth are falling out then you have been having loose speech, speaking without thinking or gossiping. What have you allowed out of your mouth that should have remained in there permanently, like your teeth? If you are spitting out your teeth or pulling them out then there is something that needs to be said. **(Ch. 6)**

TELEVISION: Time to look at the big picture. What you see on the television most likely is connected to what is currently going on in your waking life that you ought to pay better attention to. Watching TV in a dream can also suggest that you are being too much of a spectator in your life and not taking enough action.

TOILET: Your ability to release and flush away negativity. If the toilet is clogged or filthy, then you are not processing your negativity well, you are holding things in. **(Ch. 7)**

TONGUE: Look at what you have recently said recently or need to say. If there is something wrong with the tongue in your dream, then there has been a communication issue in your life recently.

TORNADO: Tornadoes in a dream almost always point to worry and anxiety. What are you worried about right now? What is causing your emotions to spin out of control? Is there something going on that you are worried you cannot control? If you dream of tornadoes often, it is a good indication you are a proud card-carrying member of the worrywart club! These dreams are a wake-up call to calm down, relax, and "let go and let God . . ." **(Ch. 8)**

TOWEL: Your ability to wipe the slate clean. If you are wrapping something in a towel, then you need to ask yourself what you are trying to keep "under wraps" right now. Could also be a reference to throwing in the towel.

TRAIN: Most often refers to your train of thought or your ability to be on the right track in life. If the train is crashing or derailing, then your thinking may be off or it may have you getting off track from your goals and your purpose in life. May be time to rethink something. Sometimes a train can refer to family. The cars of the train come one after the other just as generations do. **(Ch. 4)**

TRACKS: Are you currently wondering if you are on the right track with a certain decision you have made? A *racetrack* would suggest you are up against a deadline. What are you in a hurry for? Are you being too impatient?

TRAPPED: Lack of movement in your life. Are you stuck in a situation you don't know how to get out of? Might be time to ask yourself how you have contributed to your lack of progress or inability to get out of the situation. **(Ch. 2 and Ch. 10)**

TRUCK: Your vehicle through life or a particular situation. Most often associated with work. Your ability to carry a heavy burden. **(Ch. 4)**

TUB: This is your ability to cleanse yourself of negativity and frustration. What negative issue or energy do you need to wash out of your psyche right now? Can even refer to a need to cleanse your body of toxins. **(Ch. 7)**

UFO: Some situation that is unfamiliar or "alien" to you. Can also symbolize a higher awareness or your ability to reach your high goals. **(Ch. 4)**

UNDERGROUND: Anything underground refers to something (a memory, an emotion, an issue, etc.) that you have pushed below the surface of your conscious thinking. Usually, it is something you hope to forget but that your dreaming mind wants you to delve into and deal with. Can also mean it is time to look deep within yourself for the answer and truth you need right now.

VAGINA: Feminine energy and qualities: passivity, sensitivity, creativity, the ability to nurture, or give birth to something new. **(Ch. 6)**

VOMIT: Something in your life is not good for you. Your dream is telling you that you need to purge yourself of this negative issue, person, or behavior immediately. **(Ch. 4)**

WALL: An emotional obstacle or barrier you have built yourself. An inability to connect or communicate with someone else or an inability to progress in some situation. What walls are you hitting in waking life?

WAR: Usually points to fighting within self. What or who are you fighting right now? Are you in a war of words with somebody? *See* Battle. **(Ch. 3)**

WATCH: *See* Clock.

WATER: Your emotional state. The state of the water will reflect the state of your emotions. Can also symbolize creative juices. A healing energy. *Calm clear water* suggests you are clear about emotional decisions. *Muddy, murky water* is connected to emotional confusion and depression. *Rising flooding water* means you may be getting in over your head, getting in too deep. An increasingly tough situation. Being *underwater* indicates you are in over your head and feeling overwhelmed. **(Ch. 4, Ch. 8, and Ch. 10)**

WAVES: Large waves or tidal waves suggest that you are feeling emotionally overwhelmed. Ask yourself what it is that is threatening to "sweep you away" emotionally or sweep you away from your normal routine. Waves can also refer to a wave of inspiration. What in your life is ebbing and flowing like the ocean? What seems to come in and out of your life again and again? **(Ch. 4)**

WEB: Has someone around you created a web of lies? Are you the one being dishonest? Your dream is showing you that dishonesty will trap you. A web can also refer to networking in business or the World Wide Web.

WEDDING: *See* Marriage.

WEEDS: An unexpected or uninvited element in your life that is unwanted and is growing rapidly. Like a weed, it is something that you need to remove before it seemingly overtakes your usual daily routine or thoughts. If you are pulling weeds

in your dream, then you are actively working to remove this
unwanted element from your life.

WHITE: Time for a new beginning. Wipe the slate clean. Purity, innocence.

WIND: The winds of change are blowing through your life right
now. Could be preparing you for a stormy situation ahead.
(Ch. 8)

WINDOW: Your perception of things. Your ability to see through
a barrier. What is your current point of view? **(Ch. 4)**

WINE: Drinking in knowledge. Celebration. Spirituality. Can
be a play on words for someone who has been whiney lately. If
red, can indicate your menses is on the way. **(Ch. 7)**

WINGS: Your ability to rise above where you are now, as well
as your ability to rise above what is weighing heavy on you. If
there is something wrong with the wings in your dream, then
ask yourself what is weighing you down in waking life? What
is keeping you from progressing and reaching a higher level?
Wings can also mean you are "winging" it, trying to get by on
a wing and a prayer.

WOLF: Aggressive, greedy part of self. Or someone around you
who is aggressive and greedy. In a woman's dream, can often
symbolize a man. **(Ch. 5)**

WOMAN: Feminine aspects of your personality, such as creativity, sensitivity, ability to nurture, passiveness. **(Ch. 2)**

WOUND: Wounds in dreams usually reflect an emotional wound that need to heal in waking life. Also, look at other areas of your life that may be wounded such as relationships or your ego.

ZOMBIE: Something that you thought was "dead," gone, and over is trying to come back to life. Often refers to a grudge you are "keeping alive" over an issue that is dead. Are you or is someone around you unemotional and no longer in touch with feelings or reality? **(Ch. 7 and Ch. 10)**

Index

amusement park dreams,
  58–61
  message of, 60
Anderson, Pamela, 61
animal dreams, 85–105
  bears, 100–102
  birds, 102–104
  bugs and spiders, 104–5
  cats, 89–90
  dogs, 86–88
  horses, 98–100
  predatory cats, 93–95
  snakes, 91–93
  wolves, 95–98
attic dreams, 137–39
  message of, 139

baby dreams, 20–22
  message of, 21–22

basement dreams, 139–41
  message of, 141
bathroom dreams, 144–46
  message of, 146
battlefield dreams, 53–55
  message of, 54–55
bear dreams, 100–102
  message of, 102
bedroom dreams, 143–44
  message of, 144
being chased nightmare,
  193–95
  message of, 194–95
Bible
  and dreams, 3
bicycle dreams, 80–81
  message of, 81
bird dreams, 102–104
  message of, 103–4

blood nightmare, 211–13
   message of, 213
body dreams, 106–27
   butt, 118–20
   chest, 114–15
   eyes, 111–14
   feet, 121–22
   genitals, 122–24
   hair, 110–11
   hands, 116–17
   legs, 120–21
   pregnancy and birth, 125–27
   stomach, 117–18
   teeth, 107–10
boss dreams, 29–31
   message of, 30–31
boss sex dreams, 177–78
   message of, 178
Bowie, David, 61
bug and spider dreams, 104–5
   message of, 105
bus dreams, 75–78
   message of, 78
butt dreams, 118–20
   message of, 120

car dreams, 63–67
   message of, 67
cat dreams, 89–90
   message of, 90
   predatory cats, 93–95
celebrity dreams, 25–29
   message of, 29
Charles, Prince, 61
Chauvet Cave (France), drawings
      in, 3
cheating sex dreams, 170–72
   message of, 172

checklist
   advice and questioning, 224–25
   being about you, 223–24
   connected to the previous day,
      222–23
   end of dream as the moral,
      226–27
   as metaphors, 222
   numbers and amounts, 225–26
   objects representing skills and
      abilities, 225
   puns and figures of speech, 222
   waking life, emotions connected
      to, 224
chest dreams, 114–15
   message of, 115
child dreams, 22–25
   about your own child, 26
   message of, 25
Chinese
   and dreams, 3
classmate dreams, 36–38
   message of, 38
coworker sex dreams, 175–77
   message of, 177

death nightmare, 197–98
   message of, 198
death of a loved one nightmare,
      198–201
   message of, 201
doctor dreams, 31–32
   message of, 32
dog dreams, 86–88
   message of, 88
dream checklist
   advice and questioning, 224–25
   being about you, 223–24

connected to the previous day,
222–23
end of dream as the moral,
226–27
as metaphors, 222
numbers and amounts, 225–26
objects representing skills and
abilities, 225
puns and figures of speech, 222
waking life, emotions connected
to, 224
dream journals, 61
dreaming
about people you are familiar
with, 9
in color, 38
inspired by, 1
REM (Rapid Eye Movement)
dream state, 1, 4–5
and the sexually suppressed
self, 4
dreams
duration of, 1
outside interference, 164
remembering, 2
through lifetime, 3

elephants
sleeping habits, 105
end of the world nightmare, 207–9
message of, 209
ex lover sex dreams, 172–74
message of, 174
eyes dreams, 111–14
message of, 114

falling nightmare, 195–97
message of, 197

father dreams, 13–15
absent fathers, 14
message of, 14–15
feet dreams, 121–22
message of, 122
flood dreams, 155–56
message of, 156
Freud, Sigmund
and dreams, 3–4
friend sex dreams, 179–80
message of, 180

genital dreams, 122–24
message of, 124

hair dreams, 110–11
message of, 111
hand dreams, 116–17
message of, 117
haunted house dreams, 134–35
message of, 135
horse dreams, 98–100
message of, 100
hospital dreams, 50–51
message of, 51
hotel dreams, 51–53
message of, 53
house and home dreams, 128–47
attic, 137–39
basement, 139–41
bathroom, 144–46
bedroom, 143–44
haunted house, 134–35
house in disrepair, 129–31
kitchen, 141–43
mansion or castle, 131–32
moving, 135–37
trailer, 133–34

house in disrepair dreams,
129–31
    message of, 130–31
hurricane dreams, 152–53
    message of, 153

ice and snow dreams, 158–59
    message of, 159
inner ear
    and REM sleep, 127

Jung, Carl Gustav
    dream philosophy, 4, 169

kitchen dreams, 141–43
    message of, 142–43

leg dreams, 120–21
    message of, 121
lightening dreams, 156–58
    message of, 156
location dreams, 39–61
    amusement park, 58–61
    battlefield, 53–55
    hospital, 50–51
    hotel, 51–53
    parking lot, 46–47
    prison, 48–49
    public bathroom, 44–46
    restaurant, 56–58
    school, 40–44
    wedding, 55–56

mansion or castle dreams,
131–32
    message of, 132
masturbation dreams, 188–90
    message of, 190

men and women dreams, unknown,
15–20
    message of, 19–20
mother dreams, 10–13
    as actual mother, 11
    message of, 12–13
motorcycle dreams, 78–80
    message of, 80
moving dreams, 135–37
    message of, 137
murder nightmare, 201–5
    message of, 205
mystery lover sex dreams,
166–70
    message of, 170

nightmares, 192–216
    being chased, 193–95
    blood, 211–13
    death, 197–98
    death of a loved one, 198–201
    end of the world, 207–9
    falling, 195–97
    murder, 201–5
    paralyzed, 213–16
    trapped, 205–7
    zombies, 209–11
nightmares (ending), 217–20
    adding conversation, 218
    changing the ending, 218–19
    journal entry, destroying,
    219–20
    writing down dream, 218
nocturnal erections
    REM sleep and, 191

oral sex dreams, 183–86
    message of, 186

Paltrow, Gwyneth, 147
paralyzed nightmare, 213–16
parents sex dreams, 186–88
    message of, 188
parking lot dreams, 46–47
    message of, 47
people dreams, 8–38
    baby, 20–22
    boss, 29–31
    celebrities, 25–29
    child, 22–25
    classmate, 36–38
    doctor, 31–32
    father, 13–15
    mother, 10–13
    police, 33–35
    unknown men and women, 15–20
plane dreams, 67–69
    message of, 69
Plato
    and dreams, 3
police dreams, 33–35
    message of, 35
predatory cats dreams, 93–95
    message of, 95
pregnancy and birth dreams, 125–26
    message of, 126
prison dreams, 48–49
    message of, 49
public bathroom dreams, 44–46
    message of, 46

rain dreams, 154–55
    message of, 155
rainbow dreams, 162–63
    message of, 163–64
REM (Rapid Eye Movement) dream
    state, 1, 4–5

elephants and, 105
eye movement during, 7
inner ear and, 127
nocturnal erections and, 191
restaurant dreams, 56–58
    message of, 57
    if you work in a restaurant, 58
Romans
    and dreams, 3

same gender sex dreams, 181–83
    message of, 183
school dreams, 40–44
    message of, 44
sex dreams, 165–91
    boss, 177–78
    cheating, 170–72
    coworker, 175–77
    ex lover, 172–74
    friend, 179–80
    masturbation, 188–90
    mystery lover, 166–70
    oral sex, 183–86
    parents, 186–88
    same gender, 181–83
ship and boat dreams, 72–75
    message of, 75
snake dreams, 91–93
    message of, 93
space travel dreams, 82–84
    message of, 83
stomach dreams, 117–18
    message of, 118
sun dreams, 159–62
    message of, 162

teeth dreams, 107–10
    message of, 109–10

Titanic sinking
    dreams and premonitions
        concerning, 84
tornado dreams, 149–52
    message of, 152
trailer dreams, 133–34
    message of, 134
train dreams, 71–72
    message of, 72
trapped nightmare, 205–7
    message of, 207
truck dreams, 69–70
    message of, 70

unknown men and women dreams,
    15–20
    message of, 19–20

vehicle and travel dreams, 62–84
    bicycle, 80–81

bus, 75–78
car, 63–67
motorcycle, 78–80
plane, 67–69
ship and boat, 72–75
space travel, 82–84
train, 71–72
truck, 69–70

wedding dreams, 55–56
    message of, 56
wolf dreams, 95–98
    message of, 98
women and men dreams, unknown,
    15–20
    message of, 19–20

zombies nightmare,
    209–11
    message of, 211